# Negotiating the Glass Ceiling

This book is dedicated to Dr Myra McCulloch our final contributor, who sadly died of cancer at the age of 48, whilst one of the first and youngest women Pro-Vice-Chancellors in Britain.

# Negotiating the Glass Ceiling:
## Careers of Senior Women in the Academic World

*Edited by*

Professor Miriam David and
Professor Diana Woodward

The Falmer Press

(A member of the Taylor & Francis Group)
London · Washington, D.C.

| UK | Falmer Press, 1 Gunpowder Square, London, EC4A 3DE |
|---|---|
| USA | Falmer Press, Taylor & Francis Inc., 1900 Frost Road, Suite 101, Bristol, PA 19007 |

First published in 1998

**A catalogue record for this book is available from the British Library**

ISBN 0 7507 0837 9 cased
ISBN 0 7507 0838 7 paper

**Library of Congress Cataloging-in-Publication Data are available on request**

Jacket design by Caroline Archer

Typeset in 10/12 pt Times by
Graphicraft Typesetters Ltd., Hong Kong.

*Printed in Great Britain by Biddles Ltd., Guildford and King's Lynn on paper which has a specified pH value on final paper manufacture of not less than 7.5 and is therefore 'acid free'.*

# Contents

*Contents*

# Introduction

THROUGH THE GLASS CEILING -
A FEMALE SUPPORT GROUP

Elaine Thomas 1994

# 1    Introduction

*Date of Birth: 9 August 1945*
**Professor Miriam David**
Dean of Research, The London Institute; formerly Director,
Social Sciences Research Centre, South Bank University,
University of London

*Date of Birth: 22 October 1948*
**Professor Diana Woodward**
Dean of the Graduate School, Chelthenham and Gloucester College of
Higher Education


### Context

> If there is anywhere that women professionals should be successful, it is in the
> universities. We think of teaching as a women's forte and universities as meritocratic
> institutions. Yet there is ample evidence that career patterns of women university
> teachers differ from those of men. (Acker, 1994, p. 125)

Sandra Acker, the internationally renowned sociologist of education, writing about
the position of women academics in British universities in 1980, found as others
had before her that women held a minority of academic posts (12 per cent in the
late 1970s), and were disproportionately concentrated in the worst-paid, lowest
status and least secure positions. When she returned to write on this theme in 1993,
Professor Acker found women still to be a small minority of teachers and researchers. The 12 per cent may have increased to 22 per cent by 1991–2, but there
had been little change in the sex composition of senior staff: women still comprised
under 5 per cent of professors, for example, in the 'old' university sector (see below
for an explanation of this distinction) (ibid., pp. 135–6). What the outside world
sees still, she writes, is that:

Nearly all professors in Britain are men; men also hold the vast majority of other senior positions. The impact of the imbalance on British academic life is extreme, especially when combined with tendencies towards hierarchy and elitism still found within many of the universities. Professors in British universities are the people who head departments, represent the university to the government, serve on working parties, act as external examiners, make hiring and promotion decisions. In many universities, the number of women professors can literally be counted on the fingers of one hand, while the men number in the hundreds. When I left my British university post, in December 1990, only two women there were professors. The number has since increased to six. ( . . . ) What needs to be explained is why we find women academics so relatively disadvantaged and men so firmly in control — why we have a man-centred university with some women in it. (ibid., p. 137)

This book is an attempt to look in more depth at some women academics' experiences of being in 'a man-centred university' during the post-war period in Britain, compared and contrasted with some women's experiences in higher education in other countries of Europe and the USA. We chose to edit the book because of our own experiences of working in academia for the last quarter of a century as academics and latterly mainly as managers. We wanted both to document and illustrate some of the changing patterns of women's lives in higher education during this time, which is also a time of massive social change within higher education itself, as in women's lives outside higher education. We also wanted to point out that the changes which may have occurred have been hard won and not without consequences for the women involved. Thus we have carefully selected women whose lives span the generations of women in academia in the post-war period.

However, we also chose to do so as part of the growing developments in both feminist academic work and social science in particular. Moves towards personal reflections and evaluations of work and careers have been a continuing development in the last five to ten years within the social sciences. Indeed, some sociologists have now argued the importance of 'reflexivity' as part of the key changes in social life generally towards the end of the twentieth century (Beck, Lash and Giddens, 1994). Thus our own academic interests and involvements have become part and parcel of broader moves within the social sciences in higher education and more widely in social and professional life. It is difficult to distinguish or to separate out their origins. Although we ourselves are social scientists, we want to map a broader picture of change within academia and women's roles within higher education and its management, situating these within the even wider context of socioeconomic and cultural change. Our aim, moreover, is to provide some critical reflections on senior women's positioning within higher education as we move towards the millenium and to draw future possibilities from that.

As feminist sociologists, we the co-editors (Miriam David and Diana Woodward) have known each other for most of our academic careers. In the 1970s we worked together on various activities for the British Sociological Association, initially and most notably its women's caucus, which was an early attempt to try to improve women's positions within both our professional association and the wider profession in higher education. When we both became heads of departments/

schools in the second half of the 1980s, we took forward our by then usual strategies of feminist and political organizing and set to thinking about new forms of organization of senior women sociologists in higher education. We had both become Heads of Departments of Social Science in what were then polytechnics (later to become the 'new universities' in 1992) and thought that we would find a support group of women in similar positions helpful for our new posts. We knew both from the burgeoning management literature and from our observations of men's strategies that such forms of networking were a vital ingredient of career development. What soon became apparent was that the systems of management in the polytechnics were rather different from those of the 'old' universities, where heads of department rotated on a biennial or triennial basis. Thus few of the women who held such posts in the 'old' universities felt themselves to be in need of the same kinds of support, and our group became largely composed of women in management positions across the binary divide, in the polytechnic sector. However, this group was but one of the 'acorns' out of which grew the oak tree of the Glass Ceiling Group, as we shall see.

Other women in higher education were also organizing similar types of support, perhaps not unexpectedly given our origins and the point we had reached. Clearly our generation of women, the first to be born in the post-war 'baby-boom' and to have the opportunities provided by a modernizing and expanding education system, were the first beneficiaries of the expansion of higher education (see Arnot, David and Weiner, 1996, for a more sustained analysis of this development). For the most part, we entered higher education as undergraduates in the sixties. Those of us who chose to remain within academia after graduating, in the sixties and seventies, found ourselves having to create our careers and our possibilities. New forms of organization sprung up, partly influenced by women's traditional activities and partly through our experiences in the growing and diverse forms of both feminist and socialist activities. By the late 1980s, there were a variety of different groups and organizations of women involved within higher education at various levels, ranging from subject- or discipline-specific groups and associations, to the Women's Studies Network (UK) Association, the Women in Higher Education Network (WHEN), women's groups within the trade unions, and other more explicitly politically based organizations.

### The 'Through the Glass Ceiling' Network

The Through the Glass Ceiling Network of women in higher education management was established in 1990 to provide a forum for peer support and career development for the generation of able women who had risen to middle management posts in universities and colleges, both in academic departments and in so-called 'support' functions such as registry, library and student services. (The gendered politics of the division between academic and support functions in British universities deserves its own book!) Some members aspired to progress higher, and were able to mobilize the informal resources of the Group's members to support them, whereas others were sustained in handling the pressures and tensions of their present posts by this network of congenial peers. Because of the persistent gross imbalance of the sexes at the highest levels in higher education, all of the network's members will have experienced difficulties during their careers in securing promotions and in enduring the cut-and-thrust of life as a manager within their institutions. Not all members, however, would necessarily endorse a feminist analysis of their experiences.

This book has been developed from a Glass Ceiling Network meeting at which certain members presented analytic accounts of their career development, with a view to identifying the factors which had contributed to their success and which currently sustained them. The role of parents and childhood experiences, especially at school and relationships with siblings, were often mentioned, together with reflections on the tensions of managing a career in a male world while maintaining domestic harmony. We will shortly return to discuss the structure of the book, whose contributions broadly follow this pattern, having first sketched the contemporary and historical background of sex inequality in higher education.

Despite our collective successes, many of us are 'refugees' from other institutions, as a colleague has expressed it, carrying with us our battle scars, which fade only slowly. One of the co-editors embarked on an Industrial Tribunal case for sex discrimination against her former institution, at a time when able women were repeatedly failing to be appointed to professorships by a committee chaired by the Vice-Chancellor. Despite trade union backing, she was forced to drop the case on legal advice as one woman had been made a professor at the round of appointments to which the complaint referred, making it unlikely that this case would be won. (Shortly beforehand, media coverage of Alison Halford's case alleging harassment and discrimination within the senior ranks of a police force had provided an alarming account of how an embattled misogynistic employer can intimidate its own staff in an Industrial Tribunal.) Six years on, this latter woman remains one of only two female professors out of fifty-five, and the three unsuccessful women applicants from that period have subsequently been awarded professorships at other institutions. In the process of applying for senior appointments at several institutions in the period following this episode, it was made abundantly clear to the writer that the Vice-Chancellors' old boys' communications network had been effective in ensuring that knowledge of her reputation for allegedly causing trouble preceded her interviews, or kept her off the shortlists of appointable candidates altogether.

The other co-editor, by contrast, was awarded the title of professor in the inaugural round at her institution in which just eight were awarded, some two years after her arrival as a 'refugee' from an 'old' university in search of promotion. She became the first woman professor there (and remains the only professor yet to have delivered an inaugural lecture!). In 1996, the institution was able to boast that it had the highest proportion of women professors in the country, there being ten in post. Nevertheless, discriminatory actions have since taken their toll at her institution, but they took a different turn. First, managerial reorganizations clustered departments and ushered in a smaller number of schools, rendering some Heads of Department 'redundant' in 1991–2. At that point the new Heads of School were made *ex officio* professors, entirely changing the nature of professorial appointments and creating two parallel types of professor. As one created for her research record, she was given the 'small prize' of being made Head of Research in the newly-formed school, and subsequently became Head of Research in the Faculty. This led to a 'new' career in research management within the university, and involvement in research policy issues nationally. With the appointment of a new male Vice-Chancellor, she was given a wider research brief throughout the university and appointed Vice-chair of the newly-formed University Research Committee, the Vice-Chancellor being its chair. In this capacity she was also asked first to develop the university's new research policy and plan, and second to chair the advisory group to the Vice-Chancellor for the UK-wide 1996 Research Assessment Exercise, and to manage the process of preparing the university's submission. However, no new post, title or room was forthcoming; she held these responsibilities as the university's senior professor outside the official management structures of the institution. At the time of writing she had recently been appointed to a new post as Dean of Research at the London Institute.

### The Position of Women in Higher Education in Britain

In recent years the position of women appears to have improved somewhat. However, since the dissolution of 'the binary line' between the 'old' universities and the former polytechnics which became universities after the 1992 Education Act, reliable statistics on university staff are no longer kept to compare with those formerly collated by the defunct Universities Funding Council, which Acker was able to use. At the time of writing there are still only six women among the 103 members of the Committee of Vice-Chancellors and Principals, shortly to be joined by another, but one is soon to retire early through ill-health. The *1994 World Yearbook of Education* (Stiver Lie, Malik and Harris, 1994) provides a valuable series of international comparisons about the position of women in the wider society and in education, including higher education, as students, teaching staff, and professors. In none of the countries surveyed did the proportion of women academics reach one in three, nor over one in five professors. Abstracting data on women academics in the countries represented in this collection, we find the gross underrepresentation of women to be a general phenomenon.

*Table 1.1  The relative position of women in higher education (Adapted from Stiver Lie, Malik and Harris, 1994, table 19.3, p. 208; data for 1988–1992)*

|  | Percentage of faculty who are female | Percentage of full professors who are female |
|---|---|---|
| USA | 26.0 | 14.0 |
| Norway | 24.2 | 9.3 |
| Greece | 20.5 | 6.3 |
| UK | 20.5 | 4.9* |
| Germany | 17.6 | 5.0** |

\* Data for pre-1992 universities only
\*\* Average of data for the former West and East Germany

In recent years gender equity has been achieved in Britain for students at undergraduate level: by the 1995–6 academic year women represent 51 per cent of the total student population, although they are still outnumbered by men at post-graduate level by 55:45 (HESA, 1996). It must be said, however, that wider demographic and cultural change has probably been far more influential in bringing this about than any changes in universities' declarations of their respective missions, their admission policies and their organizational cultures. The more limited changes in the proportion and distribution of women staff in universities and colleges still fall a very long way short of parity in access to positions of power. However, these small gains have been achieved in less than twenty years of progress following centuries of misogyny and discrimination against not only women, but also virtually all other social groups except white men from the upper social strata who were members of the established church. We turn now to a brief review of the early origins of the universities, since the term 'higher education' is of far more recent origin, and as late as the turn of the century was used to refer to what we now know of as secondary education.

## The Early History and Origins of the 'Man-centred' Universities

'The universities were undoubtedly one of the most significant creations of the medieval world' (Green, 1969, p. 7). They originated in the monastic and cathedral schools of the European cultural centres such as Paris, Bologna and Salerno, which by the twelfth century had outgrown both physically and intellectually their ecclesiastical origins. The growth of literacy within both clergy and laity, and their thirst for knowledge for its own sake, stimulated by the cultivated intellectual life of Islamic Spain, all contributed to the establishment of these early universities. They comprised groups of *male* scholars who laid the foundations of intellectual discipline, rational thought and scientific culture, which made it possible to interpret society's law and customs, paving the way for legal education; to administer its governments; and to develop and refine theological arguments, to provide an educated clergy capable of undertaking the church's teaching and supporting its authority with intellectual arguments. Later, the development of scientific thinking supported the establishment of medical education within the early universities (David, 1980).

The rapid growth of the medieval universities spawned an entirely new class of educated men who shaped the character of Western civilization with their habits of logic, rational thought and calculation. By the fifteenth century there were some seventy European universities, sharing a common culture of religion, language and culture (Ashby, 1966), from which ideas were disseminated through travel by students and masters, and the transmission of documents. Although originally institutions subordinate to the formal authority of both church and state, the universities also represented a force for liberalism and progress. The concept of academic freedom therefore has a long and distinguished history.

The first English university was established at Oxford in the early thirteenth century. Cambridge University was established soon after, its growth helped by an influx of students from Oxford following an early episode of town/gown conflict. In Scotland the first university was established at St Andrews also in the thirteenth century. For several centuries the average student was either in holy orders or intending to take them. The dominant intellectual activity took place within theology, and the universities were essentially ecclesiastical institutions until the Protestant Reformation liberated them from the control of the church, but brought them more closely under the control of the crown. However, even after this period and much later, beyond the Industrial Revolution, Oxford and Cambridge still functioned mainly to serve the needs of the upper classes and those intending to enter the Anglican ministry (Halsey and Trow, 1971).

Elsewhere dissatisfaction with the dominance and theology of Oxbridge led to the formation in the eighteenth century of Dissenters' Academies, funded by wealthy industrialists, in such places as Daventry, Warrington, Manchester and Hackney, to educate ministers and laymen intending to enter teaching or commerce whose religion (namely non-conformism) barred them from Oxford and Cambridge. More middle class than upper class in character, their location and ethos reflected the rising prosperity and rapid urbanization taking place in the Midlands and the North of England associated with industrialization. By the second half of the nineteenth century men who had prospered in industry and commerce perceived the need for improved education at all levels of British society, to educate future generations, to provide better health care in a society increasingly concerned with health and hygiene, and above all to provide the scientific and technical knowledge necessary to keep British industry competitive in world markets. The ancient universities were unwilling or unable to meet this challenge.

By the Great Exhibition of 1851 this had become abundantly clear. By then England had four universities, at Oxford, Cambridge, London and Durham, but the combined total of their graduates was about 1000 per year, many of them destined for the Anglican priesthood. The political values of the industrialists and business-men whose endowments helped to establish the institutions which were the precursors of the great civic 'redbrick' universities of England's industrial cities, were as visionary as their philanthropy. Although motivated by issues about industrial and commercial competitiveness, they were also often concerned about matters of liberal theology and political reform, and were even prepared to listen to the radical demand that the full facilities of these new universities be offered to women, more of whom were now being educated to an appropriate level (Green, 1969, p. 102).

In other towns and cities the educational needs of their citizenry were being met by the establishment of Mechanics' Institutes, whose lectures were often open to women, or through Extension Colleges which prepared students for degrees by external study awarded by the universities of London, Oxford or Cambridge. These institutions became university colleges and there were parallel creations of colleges of technology, or polytechnics modelled on French higher education institutions. By the end of the nineteenth century, there was an array of educational institutions providing post-school education. However, it was only the traditional universities that were included in the group to be provided with central government funding after the end of the First World War. In 1919 the Universities Grants Committee

(UGC) was created to provide the financial wherewithal for these institutions to continue to provide higher learning for a wider range of students. The more vocational and technological institutions continued to receive their funding from local authorities.

### The Universities and Higher Education Expansion in the Post-war Period

After the Second World War some of the university colleges created in the nineteenth century became universities in their own right in places like Exeter, Hull, Leicester, Nottingham and Southampton. By 1957 there were twenty-one British universities and all allowed for the entry of women as undergraduates. Since then, there have been at least three significant phases of development and expansion, creating a network of institutions within a sector eight times larger within a forty-year period, and marking a major period of educational and social change, including the significantly increased involvement of women as students, if not staff to the same extent.

In the late 1950s the then Conservative government's fears about national economic growth and educational expansion led it to set up the only Royal Commission yet on higher education, chaired by Lord Robbins. His recommendations in 1963 still resonate today, given his concerns about how a 'graduate tax' might have the effect of being a 'negative dowry for women'. In the years which followed the publication of the Robbins Report, significant phases of university development took place, including the establishment of the greenfield campus universities in the early 1960s at Sussex, East Anglia, York, Essex, Kent, Warwick and Lancaster; and the elevation of the Colleges of Advanced Technology (CATs) such as those at Bradford, Bath, Uxbridge (now Brunel), Battersea (which became the University of Surrey), Salford and Aston to universities, as recommended in the Report. Nevertheless, only a few years later, under a Labour government, a twin track system of higher education was announced. Anthony Crosland, Secretary of State for Education, in a speech at Woolwich in 1966 created the 'binary system' of higher education, whereby thirty of the remaining Colleges of Advanced Technology would be eligible to become polytechnics, but funded by local authorities rather than central government, as were the universities. The first group of polytechnics came into being in 1970 with more to follow and, more recently, were designated universities under legislation passed in 1992. The greenfield universities were seen as innovatory in their curricula (for example, Sussex's interdisciplinary courses) and their structures (several adopted a neo-Oxbridge collegiate system), and tended towards the social sciences and humanities, rather than science and engineering. The former CATs and polytechnics, on the other hand, had their roots in local authority-funded technical and vocational colleges, and many had strong departments of engineering and applied science, with close ties to local industry including undergraduate 'sandwich' courses incorporating six or twelve months' industrial placement. One might expect the post-1992 universities to be less bound by traditional notions about the place of women in academic life than the latter but, as some of the contributions to this book demonstrate, this is not necessarily so.

Higher education has undergone enormous expansion in recent years. There are now 148 higher education institutions in England, with a student population of three-quarters of a million full-time students and one-quarter of a million part-time. Thirty per cent of school leavers now enter higher education, compared with the seven per cent of men and six per cent of women reported to the Robbins Commission in 1962. Women now comprise over half of the student body (HEFCE, 1994; HESA, 1996; Dearing, 1997) double the proportion of 1962 (Robbins, 1963, pp. 16–17). However, huge disparities remain in the proportions of men and women students within subject areas, ranging from engineering and technology, where men comprise 86 per cent of new entrants to undergraduate courses, and computer science, with 79 per cent, to the subjects allied to medicine, where 83 per cent of new entrants are women, and education, where 74 per cent are women (HEFCE, 1994, p. 8). Many of the women students are mature rather than 18-year-olds. There has been remarkably little change in the class composition of entrants to higher education in the post-Robbins period (Blackburn and Jarman, 1993). Data on students' ethnicity defy easy generalizations, with differences by ethnic group between discipline and type of institution, and no easy mode of distinguishing between British-born students and those who come expressly to study in Britain. Data on university entrants' disability status are, as for ethnicity, flawed by many respondents' understandable reluctance to reveal such information at enrolment without knowing what the implications of disclosure might be. Information on students' sexual orientation is, of course, non-existent. Evidence about the socio-demographic profile of the student body can have an important bearing on academic careers: universities which profess a commitment to equal opportunities are coming under increasing pressure to adapt the profile of their staff to match more closely that of their students; and the next generation of academic staff is recruited from today's generation of students.

## Women's Struggle for Access to Higher Education

For centuries women had no access at all to university. In the second half of the nineteenth century, as they began their attempts to secure access to higher education, through the Women's Educational Movement, they suffered the most appalling discrimination (David, 1980). This was justified by recourse to paternalistic Victorian attitudes about women's capabilities, although in practice few women had access to the kind of academic schooling required for study at this level. The story of their struggle, notably to obtain medical training, is now well known. For many women, particularly in provincial cities, access to higher education was restricted to attendance at part-time university extension classes. In London there were two women's colleges by 1849, but neither really provided more than secondary-level education until the University of London permitted women to take its degrees in 1878 (Purvis, 1991). The London Ladies' Educational Association arranged separate women-only lectures, finishing on the half-hour and with the women admitted by a side door to minimize the risk of contact with male students. Women were only awarded degrees at the Victoria University, Manchester, in 1880, at the Scottish universities in 1892 and at the University of Durham in 1895, but their participation was often hedged with restrictions.

In 1869 Emily Davies established a house at Hitchin, twenty-seven miles from Cambridge, for five students to prepare for University of Cambridge examinations, taught by Cambridge lecturers who arrived by train. In 1873 this became Girton College, located then, as now, far enough outside Cambridge to deter casual visitors. Newnham Hall, founded by Henry Sidgwick, began as a house of residence for five female scholars in central Cambridge in 1871. Both eventually became full women's colleges of the university, after a very lengthy struggle. At the University of Oxford and, particularly, at Cambridge, women's full access to lectures, examinations and graduate status was denied and frustrated for decades. Women were finally admitted as full members of the University of Oxford in 1920, but not at Cambridge until 1948 (McWilliams-Tullberg, 1975). There remained only two women's colleges at Cambridge until New Hall was founded in 1954. Around 1970, when one of the co-editors was a postgraduate student at Cambridge, only one student in nine was female. It is a matter of regret to many of us that so many former women's colleges at both Oxford and Cambridge have felt forced to admit men students in recent years in order to maintain their ranking in their universities' final examination results.

For most of this century of struggle to storm the bastions of male power that were the universities, the strategies adopted by the female protagonists were strict conformity to prevailing norms about femininity and respectability, tireless lobbying, and gratitude for the support and sponsorship of influential men. Many young women also faced implacable opposition from their families in seeking to enter higher education. In 1914 the mother of Vera Brittain (later to become a feminist writer and mother of Shirley Williams) faced censure from the ladies of Buxton for permitting her daughter to prepare for entry to the University of Oxford, which must have been all the more galling as she did so reluctantly.

> 'How can you send your daughter to college, Mrs. Brittain!' moaned one lugubrious lady. 'Don't you want her ever to get married?' (Brittain, 1933, p. 88)

Gradually the numbers of women obtaining university degrees grew and, as paid employment for middle class women became a legitimate activity before marriage and a way to earn one's living if one did not marry, more of them entered professional employment. After the First World War, through the Sex Disqualification Removal Act (1919), the Civil Service and teaching became acceptable forms of employment for unmarried women, the latter helping to increase the pool of well-qualified female applicants for university places. Women's range of occupational destinations remained narrow. As late as the 1970s, when one of the co-editors worked on a large study of graduate employment, few women graduates went into careers in industry and commerce except in such traditionally female areas as personnel work, and many of them soon left to become full-time mothers or moved into teaching (Chisholm and Woodward, 1980). There was little conception, by the women themselves, nor by their educators or employers, that any discriminatory attitudes or practices underlay this situation. From the end of the Second World War until the early 1970s, academic analyses of women's employment echoed popular sentiment with its liberal perception of teaching as an ideal career for women, and part-time work as the solution to women's 'conflict' between their domestic responsibilities and the benefits of employment (most notably, Myrdal and Klein, 1956).

## The Position of Women Academics in Higher Education Since the 1970s

The second wave of feminism from the early 1970s slowly permeated academic work in the social sciences, including analyses of the position of women in the workplace and the home. Until recently, however, little attention was paid to women academics; it was professionally and politically more acceptable to conduct research into 'safer', external topics such as women in the manual trades or in other male-dominated professions (such as medicine, science and engineering). This situation has now changed, with a flurry of recent publications addressing this subject in the form of scholarly analysis, autobiographical accounts, commissions and reports. Examples include McAuley (1987), the Hansard Society Report (1990), CVCP (1991), Bagihole (1993), the CUCO Report (1994), Lie and O'Leary (1990), Morley and Walsh (1995) and Griffiths (1996). Even the doubly-ignored groups of black women, lesbians and disabled women staff in higher education have recently had their situation brought to public attention (Kitzinger and Wilkinson, 1993; Wilton, 1993; Matthews, 1994; Rassool, 1995; Safia Mirza, 1995; and Potts and Price, 1995). All of these document, in their various ways, women's enduring disadvantage in the male world of higher education at the close of the twentieth century. They chart minor successes and limited gains, to be set against the larger picture of the enduring marginalization of women (as both staff and students) and their concerns.

A range of theoretical explanations have offered for this situation, derived from the sociology of education, of organizations, labour market theory, management theory, feminist theory, postmodernism, and others (see, for example, Acker, 1994; Walby, 1988; Hearn et al., 1989; and Witz, 1992). This book does not seek to provide an analysis of the reasons for women's subordination in the male world of academe. Rather, it contributes some critical and reflective experiential material which may enable others to progress with that endeavour. The following accounts chart women's achievements and setbacks as they seek to climb the greasy pole (lubricated with Brylcreem?), in the hope that they will inspire and encourage those who follow them, in the interests of shifting the balance of power and the distribution of resources towards women's needs, concerns and interests.

*Miriam David and Diana Woodward*

## The Concept of the Glass Ceiling

Since the 1970s there has been great interest from a range of academic and lay sources in the growing numbers of women entering careers in business, industry and the professions. Equally widely noted, despite the passage of equal opportunities and equal pay legislation in Britain twenty-five years ago, are women's lower incomes and worse promotion prospects than those of their male colleagues, even when factors such as qualifications, experience and measures of productivity are held constant. The notion of a Glass Ceiling, and also now that of the Glass Wall, has become widely used in books, articles and the quality press to describe middle managers' aspirations to senior posts (or, in the case of the Glass Wall, to lateral career moves within an organization or to another organization, undertaken as a springboard to further promotion), but their inability to attain to such posts. The earliest usage of this term, which has mainly been applied to women, can be traced to American management literature in the late 1980s. One influential early example is Breaking the Glass Ceiling: Can women reach the top of America's largest corporations? (Morrison, White, Velsor and the Center for Creative Leadership, 1987 and 1992). The authors undertook this study of senior women executives ('pioneers on the corporate prairie', 1992, p. 9) following an earlier research project into the characteristics of successful executives, which had included virtually no women. They explain the concepts of the glass ceiling and the glass wall in the following terms:

> We began this research prepared to accept the notion that there might be a glass ceiling, a transparent barrier, that kept women from rising above a certain level in corporations. ( . . . ) In conducting the research we began to perceive more than one barrier that keeps women out of powerful executive positions. Women who manage to break through the glass ceiling often find that they are walled out of more senior management.
>
> Many women have paid their dues, even a premium, for a chance at a top position, only to find a glass ceiling between them and their goal. The glass ceiling is not simply a barrier for an individual, based on the person's inability to handle a higher level job. Rather, the glass ceiling applies to women as a group who are kept from advancing higher *because they are women.*
>
> The glass ceiling may exist at different levels in different companies or industries. For the purposes of this book, we have placed it at just short of the general manager position. Even in more progressive companies, it is rare to find women at the general management level. ( . . . ) A position at this level represents a major and difficult transition in responsibility, according to both the female and the male executives we interviewed. ( . . . )
>
> It is difficult to break through the glass ceiling, but an increasing number of women are doing so. ( . . . ) Once women break this first barrier, however, they unexpectedly encounter another barrier — a wall of tradition and stereotype that separates them from the top executive level. This wall keeps women out of the inner sanctum of senior management, the core of business leaders who wield the greatest power. (Morrison et al., 1992, pp. 13–14)

The US Department of Labor uses a more formal definition, defining the Glass Ceiling as 'those artificial barriers based on attitudinal or organizational bias that prevent qualified individuals from advancing upward in their organization' (US Department of Labor, 1991). Following a review which found that many federal contractors effectively discriminated against women and minorities in their promotion practices, a Glass Ceiling Commission has been set up, under the Civil Rights legislation (Dominguez, 1992). In Britain the concept received formal acknowledgment in the Report of the Hansard Society's Commission on *Women At The Top*, which examined the underrepresentation of women in posts of responsibility in parliament, the British civil service, the judiciary, top management, the universities and the media:

> For many women, there is a glass ceiling blocking their aspirations, allowing them to see where they might go, but stopping them from arriving there. In any given occupation, and in any given public office, the higher the rank, prestige or influence, the smaller the proportion of women. (Hansard Society, 1990, p. 2)

The Commission concluded that the barriers to women's equality in Britain are general and pervasive, and include outmoded attitudes about the role of women; direct and indirect discrimination; the absence of proper childcare provision; and inflexible structures for work and careers (see Alimo-Metcalfe and Wedderburn-Tate, in Davidson and Cooper, 1993). Recent government-sponsored initiatives such as Opportunity 2000 have sought to address this issue through positive action with employers (see, for example, National Health Service Women's Unit, 1994).

The book by Morrison et al. (1992), like many of its kind, eschews any theoretical analysis of the absence of women from the most senior posts in business, commerce and industry, failing to move beyond 'explanations' such as the additional pressures faced by women because of their higher visibility than men in managerial posts; or their inability to acquire the same range of experiences as men which are required for promotion; or behaviour by fellow employees displaying prejudice, discrimination and stereotyping. The 'solutions' proposed are the employers' provision of challenge, recognition and support, including an executive development programme to 'keep the momentum going', to promote 'the ascent of women and people of color into top management' (p.164). Much of the other literature on women in management, from both sides of the Atlantic, similarly focuses on individual cases or on readily identifiable barriers to women's progress, leading to recommendations to women themselves and to employers for actions to reduce women's 'problems' and 'stress' (Davidson and Cooper, 1992; Flanders, 1994). One reason for the prevalence of this perspective is that some of the literature is clearly exhortatory, written for an audience of businessmen (sic) and industrialists; and even the academic literature in business and management studies rarely reaches the level of theoretical and analytic rigour which are the norm in other social science disciplines. Where in this literature is the analysis of power within organizational cultures which makes the arguments in books like *The Sexuality of*

*Organization* (Hearn et al., 1989) so compelling, or the theorizing based on careful research of Cynthia Cockburn (see, for example, Cockburn, 1988 and 1991)?

Another stimulating contribution to this debate has been made by Buzzanell (1995), who argues that the way in which language is used to think about and to 'do gender' is a fundamental element of organizational life which must be changed before the social order which underpins the glass ceiling can be successfully challenged. (Interestingly, support for her thesis comes from a government review of the Glass Ceiling in American industry, which found significant gender differences in the language used for performance evaluations. Whilst men typically 'met objectives' and contributed to 'the bottom line', women were 'happy' and 'got along with other people' (Dominguez, 1992). Buzzanell (1995) has produced a stimulating feminist critique of the way in which the concept of the glass ceiling has been used, arguing that:

> By conceptualizing the glass ceiling as a problem that can be managed by providing opportunities to women that men routinely obtain, they preclude discussions and social action that could create transformational change. (p. 327)

Liberal attempts to improve the position of women at senior levels in business, industry and the professions by piecemeal reform have done little to redress the gross imbalances in promotion prospects and salaries which have existed since women first began to enter these male worlds. To return to Acker's incisive work on women academics, where this Introduction began, a socialist-feminist or radical-feminist analysis of our position may well provide an effective blueprint for effecting change.

### The Biography/Life History of the Book

As we noted earlier, this book grew out of a variety of origins but most specifically from a meeting of the Through The Glass Ceiling (TTGC) Network at which a number of members presented their own career life histories, with a particular brief to address questions of family, childhood and educational perspectives. Several of these contributions, adapted for this volume, are included here in the book in parts Two and Three. They are augmented by other members of TTGC and senior women academics from Europe and North America whose contributions complement and contrast with those. In particular we aimed to achieve a balance between contributions from senior women academics and/or managers in both the new and old universities.

Thus in part Three we now have six contributions of which three (Myra McCulloch, Dorothy Severin and Elaine Thomas) have spent a recent part of their careers in old universities, and three (Maggie Deacon, Eileen Green and Dianne Willcocks) have spent most of their recent careers in new universities, with four reaching the position of professor. However, it should be said that of the three who have 'spent time' in the old universities, only one has spent the lion's share of her career there (Dorothy Severin) and she is distinctive in that her formative educational years were spent growing up in the USA. The other two were in instititutions that through amalgamations became 'old' universities (Elaine Thomas and Myra McCulloch) and furthermore Elaine Thomas has recently moved from her relatively unique Northern Irish university to a new university in England. She has taken the post vacated by one of our other contributors and member of TTGC, who recently retired (Mavis Ainsworth) whose contribution is to be found in part Three. Our last contribution from a TTGC member is also to be found in part Two, since Angela Crum-Ewing has also recently retired from her managerial post at an old university. In other words, the majority of the contributions from our TTGC members are from women whose careers have been largely in the new universities. This may have something to do with both our gender/sex and, more specifically, our 'sixties and seventies' generation and the related changes currently taking place in higher education. We will return briefly to this theme in our conclusion.

In order to set these contributions from TTGC members in a wider context, we deliberately sought other contributions from some key senior women both here in Britain and from selected countries abroad. The other four contributions in part Two are from women who are also all now retired but who spent the majority of their careers in the old universities (Dorothy Wedderburn, Meg Stacey, Hilary Rose and Dulcie Groves) and all reached very senior positions in their careers, and mainly as professors, either as heads of an institution (Dorothy Wedderburn), a professional association (Meg Stacey) or as very well-known feminist academics (Hilary Rose and Dulcie Groves) acting as a role model to many of us more 'junior' women in the post-war period. Only one of these four women ventured across the old 'binary divide' (Dulcie Groves), where she spent several years as one of the first senior women managers in a polytechnic. Several have become widely known outside the academic community for their committee work and other research-related activities.

The four contributions that we have included from abroad — three from Europe (Berit Ås, Chryssi Inglessi and Gertrude Pfister) and one from the USA (Karen Doyle Walton) — provide equally intriguing contrasts and complements to our British accounts. The first is also from a retired extremely senior woman and feminist academic and politician from Norway (Berit Ås), where she headed the feminist university. The second is from a woman who has reached a level of seniority in academia in a German university in a discipline dominated by men (Gertrude Pfister) and the fourth has achieved a similar position in a university in Greece (Chryssi Inglessi). The third contribution in this section is from a woman who has attained high office both in academia and in 'management' in a university in the USA (Karen Doyle Walton). All of these four contributors locate their own careers within the context of women in higher education in their country today, providing us with a panoramic view of changing women's lives in the context of changing higher education. Inglessi, in particular, presents us with the voices of women that she herself studied for her PhD who were involved in higher education, focussing on the hopes and possibilities as well as the constraints and difficulties.

### The Organization of the Book

We turn now to these rich and varied accounts of senior women's lives in 'man-centred' higher education. First, in part One, we look at the four women from abroad, starting with Berit Ås, who recently retired from heading a unique institution — the feminist university in Norway — and here visualizes her life reflected through the medium of a tape recorder, which can be wound and rewound; second, Gertrude Pfister who is a professor of sports science in Germany where, perhaps not surprisingly, this subject has achieved high academic status; third, Karen Doyle Walton, who is chief academic officer — a unique blend of academic and administrative roles — at a relatively new university on the East coast of the USA; and fourth, Chryssi Inglessi who plans to use her relatively unique position at the University of Athens to establish a proper academic basis for women's studies in the institution, a task that still confronts many of us in British universities.

In part Two, we move through to the generation of women who forged the way in Britain for their successors, exemplified by six very diverse and yet challenging accounts of doughty role models. Here we start with Professor Dorothy Wedderburn whose record is exemplary as a key figure in the social sciences, ending as the head of a former women's college, turned co-educational, within the University of London. Professor Meg Stacey's account of her career follows. Her trail-blazing achievements in the fields of sociology and health care barely need an introduction. She has reached these senior positions despite enormous odds, and in her own inimitable style, whilst displaying great patience in helping junior women colleagues in the first stages of their careers (including one of the co-authors, whose first conference presentation was chaired by Meg). Next Professor Hilary Rose recounts an equally exemplary record in similar fields, but also including social policy. Then Dr Dulcie Groves describes a model combination of both administrative and academic roles — especially to the forefront of feminist social policy — across the sectors and laced with a good deal of family care. Next Angela Crum-Ewing tells how she turned her hand to academia after the rigours of raising a family to excel at academic administration, and becoming President of the British Association of University Teachers (AUT), no mean feat. Finally, Mavis Ainsworth, awarded an OBE in the 1997 New Year's Honours List, looks back at her career at the point of her retirement from heading a large and enormously successful school of humanities and arts at a new university.

Finally, in part Three, we turn to six women who are all pursuing their careers in universities with a varied mix of humour and resignation at the end of the twentieth century. Here we move straight into Professor Elaine Thomas' story as she moves into Mavis Ainsworth's former post, from such a different background as a Dean of Arts and Humanities in an 'oldish' university; second we turn to Professor Dorothy Severin, a former Pro-Vice-Chancellor who also hails from an 'old' university in a humanities discipline; third we move on to Professor Eileen Green who set up one of the first centres for women's studies in a new university with all the consequent struggles to remain a *bona fide* academic, and who has recently moved institutions to head another research centre; fourth our gaze turns to Professor Dianne Willcocks who, having come late to academia as a mature woman student, has had a meteoric rise through research into management and is currently Assistant Principal at a new university; fifth we move on to Maggie Deacon who has also risen rapidly from a post in a local authority into senior financial management in a university; and so finally to Dr Myra McCulloch who was, at the time Pro-Vice-Chancellor for teaching quality at an 'old' university, where she has also served as Dean and Head of School, having started her career as a school teacher. Sadly she died of breast cancer on September 9, 1997, as this book was in its final stages of preparation for publication. This book is therefore dedicated to her and her courageous struggle against breast cancer.

All these stories bear witness to the wide tapestry of cultural, socioeconomic and educational change and how they have been experienced within the field of university education by this unique blend of challenging women. In the conclusion to this book we will draw together these varied threads and themes to point to future possibilities.

### Acknowledgments

We would like to record our thanks to Fatih Ozbilgin, a doctoral student at Cheltenham and Gloucester College of Higher Education, for his help in locating literature on the early usage of the concept of the Glass Ceiling; and to Arlene Phipps, Secretary to the Social Sciences Research Centre at South Bank University for her secretarial and administrative support during the preparation of this manuscript. We are also indebted to Elaine Thomas, a member of the Glass Ceiling Network, who contributed not only a chapter for the book as she began a new post (taking over from Mavis Ainsworth, another contributor), but also produced the cartoons which illustrate the text. We acknowledge our gratitude to the publishers Phi Delta Kappa Educational Foundation, of Bloomington, Indiana, USA, for permission to reproduce Dorothy Wedderburn's contribution, 'A Lifetime of Learning', which first appeared in Karen Doyle Walton's edited collection *Against The Tide*, published in 1996 and is reprinted here by permission. Karen's own chapter includes sections originally published in the same book.

### References

ACKER, S. (1994) *Gendered Education*, Buckingham: Open University Press.

ALIMO-METCALFE, B. and WEDDERBURN-TATE, C. (1993) 'The United Kingdom', in DAVIDSON, M.J. and COOPER, C.L. (eds) *European Women in Business and Management*, London: Paul Chapman Publishing.

ARNOT, M., DAVID, M.E. and WEINER, G. (1996) *Educational Reforms and Gender Equality in Schools*, Research Discussion Series, Manchester: Equal Opportunities Commission.

ASHBY, E. (1966) *Universities: British, Indian, African*, London: Weidenfeld and Nicolson.

BAGIHOLE, B. (1993) 'How to keep a good woman down: An investigation of the institutional factors in the process of discrimination against women academics', *British Journal of Sociology of Education*, **14**, 3, pp. 262–74.

BECK, U., LASH, S. and GIDDENS, A. (1994) *Reflexive Modernisation: Politics, Tradition and Aesthetics*, Cambridge: Polity Press.

BLACKBURN, R.M. and JARMAN, J. (1993) 'Changing inequalities in access to British universities', *Oxford Review of Education*, **19**, 2, pp. 197–215.

BRITTAIN, V. (1933) *Testament of Youth: An Autobiographical Study of the Years 1900–1925*, London: Gollancz.

BUZZANELL, P. (1995) 'Reframing the Glass Ceiling as a socially constructed process: Implications for understanding change', *Communication Monographs*, **62**, December, pp. 327–54.

CHISHOLM, L. and WOODWARD, D. (1980) 'The experiences of women graduates in the labour market', in DEEM, R. (ed.) *Schooling for Women's Work*, London: Routledge and Kegan Paul.

COCKBURN, C. (1988) 'The gendering of jobs: Workplace relations and the reproduction of sex segregation', in WALBY, S. (ed.) *Gender Segregation At Work*, Milton Keynes: Open University Press.

COCKBURN, C. (1991) *In the Way of Women: Men's Resistance to Sex Equality in Organisations*, Macmillan: London.

COMMISSION ON UNIVERSITY CAREER OPPORTUNITY (CUCO) (1994) *A Report on the Universities' Policies and Practices on Equal Opportunities in Employment*, London: CUCO.

COMMITTEE OF VICE-CHANCELLORS AND PRINCIPALS (CVCP) (1991) *Equal Opportunities in Employment in Universities*, London: CVCP.

DAVID, M.E. (1980) *The State, the Family and Education*, London: Routledge and Kegan Paul.

DAVIDSON, M.J. and COOPER, C.L. (1992) *Shattering the Glass Ceiling: The Woman Manager*, London: Paul Chapman Publishing.

DEARING, R. (1997) *Higher Education in the learning society: Report of the National Committee of Inquiry into Higher Education*, London: HMSO.

DOMINGUEZ, C.M. (1992) 'Executive forum — The Glass Ceiling: Paradox and promises', *Human Resource Management*, winter, **31**, 4, pp. 385–92.

FLANDERS, M.L. (1994) *Breakthrough: The Career Woman's Guide To Shattering The Glass Ceiling*, London: Paul Chapman Publishing.

GREEN, V.H.H. (1969) *The Universities*, Harmondsworth: Penguin.

GRIFFITHS, S. (ed.) (1996) *Beyond the Glass Ceiling*, Manchester: Manchester University Press.

HALSEY, A.H. and TROW, M. (1971) *The British Academics*, London: Faber and Faber.

HANSARD SOCIETY (1990) *Report of the Hansard Society Commission on Women At The Top*, London: The Hansard Society for Parliamentary Government.

HEARN, J., SHEPHARD, D.L., TANCRED-SHERRIFF, P., and BURRELL, G. (eds) (1989) *The Sexuality of Organization*, London: Sage.

HEFCE (1994) *Profiles of Higher Education Institutions*, Bristol: Higher Education Funding Council for England.

HESA (1996) *Data Report: Students in Higher Education Institutions 1995–6*, Cheltenham: Higher Education Statistics Agency.

KITZINGER, C. and WILKINSON, S. (1993) 'The precariousness of heterosexual feminist identities', in KENNEDY, M., LUBELSKA, C. and WALSH, V. (eds) *Making Connections: Women's Studies, Women's Movements, Women's Lives*, London: Taylor and Francis.

LIE, S. and O'LEARY, V. (1990) *Storming the Tower: Women in the Academic World*, London: Kogan Page.

McAuley, J. (1987) 'Women academics: A case study in inequality', in Spencer, A. and Podmore, D. (eds) *In A Man's World: Essays on Women in Male-Dominated Professions*, London: Tavistock.

McWilliams-Tullberg, R. (1975) *Women At Cambridge,* London: Gollancz.

Matthews, J. (1994) 'Empowering disabled women in higher education', in Davies, S., Lubelska, C. and Quinn, J. (eds) *Changing the Subject: Women in Higher Education*, London: Taylor and Francis.

Morley, L. and Walsh, V. (eds) (1995) *Feminist Academics: Creative Agents For Change*, London: Taylor and Francis.

Morrison, A.M., White, R.P., Van Velsor, E. and the Center for Creative Leadership (1987, updated 1992) *Breaking the Glass Ceiling: Can Women Reach The top of America's Largest Corporations?* Reading, MA: Addison-Wesley.

Myrdal, A. and Klein, V. (1956) *Women's Two Roles: Home and Work*, London: Routledge and Kegan Paul.

National Health Service Women's Unit (1994) *Creative Career Paths in the NHS: Reports on Top Managers (No 1); Managers Who Have Left the NHS (No 2); Managers in 15 NHS Organisations (No 3); and Senior Nurses (No 4)*, NHS Executive, London: Department of Health.

Potts, T. and Price, J. (1995) '"Out of the blood and spirit of our lives": The place of the body in academic feminism', in Morley, L. and Walsh, V. (eds) *Feminist Academics: Creative Agents For Change*, London: Taylor and Francis.

Purvis, J. (1991) *A History of Women's Education in England*, Buckingham: Open University Press.

Rassool, N. (1995) 'Black women as the "other" in the academy', in Morley, L. and Walsh, V. (eds) *Feminist Academics: Creative Agents For Change*, London: Taylor and Francis.

Robbins, Lord (Chair) (1963) *Committee on Higher Education Report*, London: HMSO Cmnd. 2145.

Safia Mirza, H. (1995) 'Black women in higher education: Defining a space/finding a place', in Morley, L. and Walsh, V. (eds) *Feminist Academics: Creative Agents For Change*, London: Taylor and Francis.

Spencer, A. and Podmore, D. (1987) *In a Man's World: Essays on Women in Male-Dominated Professions*, London: Tavistock.

Stiver Lie, S., Malik, L. and Harris, D. (eds) (1994) *World Yearbook of Education 1994: The Gender Gap in Higher Education*, London: Kogan Page.

U.S. Department of Labor (1991) *A Report On The Glass Ceiling Initiative*, Washington, D.C.: U.S. Department of Labor.

Walby, S. (ed.) (1988) *Gender Segregation At Work*, Milton Keynes: Open University Press.

Walsh, V. and Morley, L. (eds) (1996) *Breaking Boundaries: Women in Higher Education*, London: Taylor and Francis.

Wilton, T. (1993) 'Queer subjects: Lesbians, heterosexual women and the academy', in Kennedy, M., Lubelska, C. and Walsh, V. (eds) *Making Connections: Women's Studies, Women's Movements, Women's Lives*, London: Taylor and Francis.

Witz, A. (1992) *Professions and Patriarchy*, London: Routledge.

# Part One

# International Perspectives

MALE   NETWORKS   I — "THE TIES THAT BIND"

Elaine Thomas
1993.

# 2   Rewinding the Tape: Starting Anew

*Date of Birth: 10 April 1928*
**Berit Ås**
Professor Emeritus and former President of the Feminist University,
Norway, and former Professor of Psychology, University of Oslo,
Norway

I am leafing through a series of recent profiles of me in some Swedish and Norwegian papers. I am a Norwegian, with all the personality traits generally attributed
to members of my society: confident, competitive, highly moral, empathetic and
kind (Jonassen, 1983). But it is in Sweden that I feel like an internationally known
celebrity, because five years ago a Swedish community of 7000 inhabitants, the
community of Växjö, asked their Committee for Equal Rights Between the Sexes
to produce an educational video about my theory of body language. This is a theory
about how a dominant group can use wordless signals and symbols to suppress,
intimidate and harass members of a subordinate group. (To construct middle range
social theories has, throughout my life, been my greatest challenge!) I was awarded
an honorary degree for this theoretical work at the University of Copenhagen in
1991. The title of the video is *The Five Master Suppression Techniques: A Theory
About the Language of Power* (Växjö, 1992), and it has been written up in different
forms in at least twelve languages, including Chinese, Tibetan and Sami (formerly
Lapp). It is used in many leadership training courses in both Denmark and Sweden,
because it shows how men use their body language to suppress women. It has also
been translated into English. Considering the long time necessary to develop this
'therapeutic theory' that it required more than twenty years to do the observation
and analysis and to write it up, the video producer who clipped and edited my many

hours of lectures into a video of twenty-nine minutes was, indeed, a professional genius. The challenge to write my own biography in just a few pages intrigues me. I feel just like this producer.


### Travelling Forwards; Looking Backwards

Now, today, I am travelling by a fast inter-city train heading for the Feminist University in Norway; a special educational institution which I set up in 1983. I realize as I observe the beauty of the autumn colours in the woods and fields outside my window that I am, indeed, 68-years-old or, to be more exact, 68 and six months. That amounts to about 18,000 days and around 400,000 hours, of which a third has been spent asleep. So tell me: how do I select from among those days and hours the events which give the most accurate picture of my life's exceptionally rich opportunities? And of the ingenious structural and cultural resistance to feminists' attempts to change my patriarchal society for the better? My train travels fast. When I reflect about my experiences, I realize that I should draw on my training in advanced statistics and methodology at the University of Michigan's doctoral program as long ago as 1959–60. As a mother of four, I was told that the Board of the Institute for Psychology had been very doubtful about accepting me. I had won the American University Association of Women's Scholarship. That counted positively. My grades from the University of Oslo were good. But a young mother of four? It would have been different, of course, had I been a father of four! The Institute had a rule which they had been following for a while: to admit three women for every seven male students with degree results of a similar standard. I found this a shocking state of affairs when I first heard about it, especially as the reason given was that the Institute needed scholars who in the future would become famous social scientists, an outcome which could not be expected from female students since they would gradually disappear from their jobs to have babies and take on family responsibilities. This was certainly a pre-Friedan society, implementing the patriarchal rule: 'Keep them barefoot and pregnant to support the US economy by bringing new consumers into the market!' But the quota argument had such an impact on me that I remembered it clearly when I later became an elected party leader in 1973 back in Norway. Then I demanded new rules including a quota system which would guarantee at least 40 per cent representation by women at every level of the party's organization. This was possibly the first set of regulations of this kind in the world of politics (see Ås, 1984).

As a scholar I should be able to do the selection samples, especially since for most of my professional life as a lecturer, as an assistant professor and then as a full professor, I taught research methods in social psychology. From 1968 until 1994 I was employed by the Institute for Psychology at Oslo University, teaching social psychology. It included teaching applied social science, especially consumer behaviour and accident research, areas in which I have developed my professorial competencies. In 1988 the ability to implement research findings won me the international Bernardijn ten Zeldam Prize in the Netherlands. The lecture which I was asked to give in the Nieuwe Kirk in Amsterdam was called 'Managing visions from invisibility to visibility: Women's impact in the nineties' (Ås, 1988). My work has certainly included the technique of selecting samples. So what to choose? How to proceed? What to select? Some years ago I was asked to take stock of my achievements as a politician, feminist and professor for the tenth anniversary edition of our research journal for women's studies. I did. Counting initiatives for which I had invested sometimes years, sometimes months, I found that I could count eight successes and thirty-two failures; a success rate of more than 20 per cent. I should add, however, that at least half the fiascos would not have turned out badly if I had been initiated by a man: a male scholar, a male politician or a male organizer. Somehow I felt quite good about this success rate, especially when I realized that many of my initiatives and suggestions had been picked up, taken further, and accomplished, years after I counted them as failures. My conclusion at the time of writing that piece, which became its title of that paper, was: 'If you are not ahead of your time, your time will never arrive.'

Summing up: as a person of 68, I am now entering my third year of retirement. I left my job as a social scientist and professor of social psychology because the conventional education system in the university did not allow time to teach what I found most important in our old suffering world, namely: recent scholarship in women's studies and a feminist critique of methods and theories in most disciplines (Ås, 1985, reprinted 1989); and also how ecological problems influence our lives, and damage women's and children's lives more than men's, in both the developed and developing countries. Imagine what consequences we would document and foresee if we worked from the assumption that a strong, enduring but invisible female culture existed everywhere! (see Ås, 1975). I wanted to teach peace studies and to direct research on conflict resolution and non-violent actions (Ås, 1982). My strong motivation for this stemmed without doubt from my childhood wartime experiences, from my father's absence when he was in a concentration camp, and later from the influence of my American friends who worked in the peace movement.

Through my twenty-six years of teaching at the University of Oslo, I have been invited to different foreign universities as a visiting professor: to the University of Missouri, Columbia, USA (1965–66), to Mount Saint Vincent University, Halifax, Canada, (autumn 1981) and the University of Uppsala, Sweden (autumn 1989). The frustration I have felt during my career finally provoked, in 1976, the idea of building a feminist university. As time went by, this idea became almost an obsession. The impetus came from not being allowed to teach women's studies, reinforced by my strong belief that the way we have constructed our current knowledge base in our Western white male world is pointless. Strict disciplinary boundaries and the fragmentation of science, the lack of truly relevant knowledge and the exclusion of feminist theorization from mainstream work have brought about the present situation. We need to reorganize our disciplines and to integrate recent important research findings into a new knowledge base. My visits to forty universities around the world strengthened my conviction that the common include inheritance from the Middle Ages on which most universities have been built is now obsolete

(Ås, 1990). In searching for this invisible female culture and a new knowledge base, I also visited groups of indigenous people, as well as religious and feminist groups. The construction of this knowledge base, as well as numerous critiques of patriarchal paradigms in science by feminist scholars, led to a plan for opening the Feminist University in Norway in 1985.

During eight of the twelve years for which the institution has existed, I have functioned as the President of the Board. One of my main motives for continuing this work has been the need for women's education. This was strengthened by the findings of a research project which I directed during the 1970s to map women's needs for adult education in a large county in Norway.

I am a retired university professor. I have just been visiting and teaching at the Feminist University at Loten. In their library I was reminded of all the articles, projects and applications for funds which I have written during recent years to try to secure financial support for teaching about research in women's studies to those women who can use this knowledge in their daily lives. I am back on my express train again heading for home.

### Five Decisions on a Parallel Track

We stop. The train is reversing into a parallel track. The attendant explains that this is necessary to let a faster train pass. It reminds me that I myself have travelled on many parallel tracks! Indeed, some of my experiences in public life between 1960 and 1980 need to be included on the tape. I had better use this quiet stop to mention events from my political life, my participation in the women's peace movement and my community activities. Returning from Ann Arbor, Michigan in 1960, where I had done my postgraduate work and my husband did his research in industrial sociology, I had five important decisions to make. The first concerned my own research. As I wanted to start my research career, I applied to the National Research Council for funding for a study of 'the female society', and received a clear-cut answer that what I wanted to do was 'women's lib' and not proper social science research. If, however, I would consider doing accident research, I was obviously qualified for that, and they were willing to provide me with financial support. I accepted and undertook my first comprehensive study on 'Accidents and sex roles' (Ås, 1962).

This was to have an important influence on my community work, as no traffic safety arrangements existed, in spite of a rapid growth in private car ownership and a frightening increase in the numbers of road accident victims. I decided to work with politicians, parents' organizations, and planning authorities, which brought me into political activism and taught me that I had to become politically active in order to be able to plan and rebuild the road infrastructure in my community. Since three Norwegian political parties sought to recruit me, I accepted an invitation to join the most welfare-oriented of them, Labour, for which I entered the local Community Council in Asker in 1967.

My second decision involved working with other women. The male members of the forty-seven-strong Council wanted to give top priority to building new main roads and to promoting the use of private cars, while the women members, especially those who were mothers, were arguing strongly for better planned traffic safety. We came to see that, without a majority of women on the Community Council, no road safety measures would ever be introduced. In the election of new members in 1971 I took part in a national campaign which brought about a majority of women on our Council, and resulted in a majority of women in two city councils, Oslo and Trondheim. From this experience and from my new position as Deputy Mayor in Asker, I could clearly observe sex-stereotyped interests in political issues. That decided my fate in politics: I became convinced that women must be considered the new proletariat, to whose interests few mainstream politicians are willing to give priority within our conventional party systems. I became a feminist politician.

Thirdly, I returned from the US in 1960 deeply affected by a meeting there with the Norwegian-born Elise Boulding in Ann Arbor. She was a peace research person, a Quaker as well as a leader of the Women's International League for Peace and Freedom in her country. Having had the opportunity to observe how she worked in community activism as well as academically, I became and was for many years involved in the Norwegian Branch of WISP (Women's International Strike for Peace), which I started. Her *World History of Women* fascinated me and inspired my long years as an activist and research worker on women's peace organizations and women's social and economic development (Ås, 1981).

Fourthly, my stipend to go to the US was funded by the International Federation of University Women (IFUW). I had been a student member of that organization. Now I wanted to pay my dues for the opportunity which this organization had given me. I became first the leader of its Oslo Branch, then later I was for many years its national leader. As such, I became well acquainted with women's difficulties in academia, both as young student mothers and as competitors with men for stipends and academic positions. In 1951, when my first child was born, I initiated and was a member of the first student committee to build a nursery and day care institution on the Oslo University campus. Most important, however, was my awakened interest in how women in our society could be given opportunities to educate themselves in adult life. I felt it necessary to initiate a research project, which I have already mentioned, to establish the barriers met by women who want to educate themselves as adults. Three students graduated with research degrees on the basis of this project, writing their theses on different aspects of the data collected.

Finally, as the fifth challenge came the political work. In 1966 I decided to join a political party and chose the Labour Party of Norway. My main reason for doing so was to rebuild the community in which my family lived, so that I could implement the results of my research into accidents and my specialist knowledge of road safety measures. This brought me further into political activity until I ended up as Deputy Mayor in my own local community council. During the heated debate about Norway's possible membership of the European Union in the early 1970s, I took a stand against membership and organized women from all parties into a united protest front. After the referendum, in which then, as now in the latest referendum, women's votes had an important effect and resulted in Norway staying outside the European Union, the Labour Party leadership was very angry with me. To punish me they excluded me from the nomination process to our Parliament, the Storting. They invited me, however, to rejoin the party after the nomination process was over and they had successfully prevented me from being nominated as a parliamentary candidate by my own county. A very interesting and supportive book has been written about my suspension and this party struggle (Winther, 1973).

To cut a long story short: when I was offered the chance to rejoin the party after the nomination process was over, I left Labour to form a new socialist party called the Democratic Socialists (AIK). It was mostly older men from the strong steel union who encouraged me to become Norway's first female party leader and to organize a party somewhat to the left of the Labour Party which has gradually changed, moving to the right as most Social Democratic parties do as they 'mature'. During the spring of 1973 an Election Alliance was formed, in which my party participated. It won sixteen seats of a total of 155 seats in the Norwegian Parliament. I entered the Parliament as a party leader and was later elected leader of the Socialist Left Party in 1975, when the election alliance wanted to become a more coherent group. The quota rule was included in the party's regulations from the beginning.

For some years my position as a politician necessarily led to a less central role as a researcher and university teacher. This period lasted from 1973 to 1981. During these years I worked as a parliamentarian, as a party leader, a UN representative, and a member of the government's Committee for Foreign Affairs and Constitutional Questions, where I finally proposed a change in the Constitution to guarantee a fair representation for both sexes: a 50:50 per cent representation of men and women in our Parliament. I lost, of course, but the issue had been introduced and it has influenced most of the parties in Norway in favour of including a quota rule in their regulations.

Who am I? I am rewinding my tape. The inter-city train starts running again. I am on my way home and I recapitulate my journey: I am 68 and enjoy teaching and organizing as never before. I teach from what I have read and learned during my life as an academic, a feminist and a politician. At 63 and 60 years old I received my honorary degrees in Halifax and Copenhagen and an international prize in Amsterdam. In 1983, when I founded the Feminist University, I was 55-years-old, but I had thought about it a great deal from the end of the UN Women's Year Congress in Mexico City in 1975. In 1973 when I was 45 and a Deputy Mayor in my community, I was suspended from my party and I organized a new party. At that time I directed a study (lasting from 1972 to 1979) on the barriers facing women who want to take up adult education and paid work. When I was 38 I entered party politics to rebuild the roads in my community and to participate in decision-making about road safety, consumer economics and single mothers. I was 33-years-old when I organized the Norwegian Branch of WISP, becoming involved with opposition to the Vietnam war, the protest against atomic weapons and theoretical work on military strategy, peace and conflict. At 32 I first held office in the International Federation of University Women. I have been working continuously from 1953, when I graduated from university. My fourth child was born when I was 29.

How funny! 29 years is the age I always have been. When I was a teenager, I felt so much older than my peers. As a serious young woman opposed to the German occupation of Norway during the Second World War, I felt sorrow and pity for the children of the Nazis. How could they understand what they were doing? In the dying days of the war I suffered as I observed the young boys of 15 and 16 years of age, called up to serve during Germany's last days. I suffered when I learned about the way the Russian and Yugoslavian prisoners were treated in the German concentration camps. The Jewish tragedy made me weep for the dead and tortured. Today, as for the last twenty years, I have been crying for the Palestinians.

We have recently been through a war of the most horrible kind in Bosnia. All over the world so-called civilized countries have manufactured and profited from the sale of land mines. Today a million refugees from Ruanda are on the run. Without food or water, mothers are leaving their dying children behind. I have seen much, but at 29 I feel as helpless as a child. Nations and banks are building dams all over the world, from which we earn our money in Norway: we are the experts on hydroelectric power. In the northern part of Namibia we are damming again to put under water the fields and woods where 20,000 indigenous people live. As a 29-year-old woman I may be responsible and hard-working in my own neighbour-hood, but without the slightest influence on the world events which are planned and implemented by grown-up politicians.

As the most natural thing we maim and sell children to be used by adult men for pleasure. Wives are abused and killed. Boys are taught how to become heroes, but end up as criminals. Give me a thousand years of wisdom. And let me, as a 29-year-old, cling to my hopes for a better world!

### Childhood Experiences

I am rewinding the tape until I can start it from the beginning. My life is like a tape. How come all this happened to me? What factors account for my successes and failures? My upbringing? My sex category? My playmates — only boys, who mostly laughed at me and my ideas — and have, to a certain extent, continued to laugh as mighty grown-ups. My intelligent and supportive spouse? Parents who encouraged me to think for myself, although they sometimes forgot their own advice and tried to push me back towards a more conventional path? A mother who was a teacher and painter, poet and organizer. A father who had wanted to become an inventor, and who successfully invented the most useful and odd gadgets for home use, in addition to inventions which he could not afford to put into produc-tion. For instance, magnetizing steel under low temperature, as early as 1933. That my parents fitted into a sociological theory about upward mobility, and therefore motivated their children to aim for university degrees? And I am starting anew, turning on the tape at the year I first arrived on this planet, 10 April 1928.

When I was born in Frederikstad, a small town south of Oslo, I was expected to be a boy. As a newborn child I should have followed the partiarchal line of males christened Knut, entering that line as 'Knut the Sixth'. However, I never heard either my father or my mother express any frustration about my sex. But a vague feeling of guilt for not having fulfilled my father's expectations may have shaped my mother's welcoming sentence when my firstborn arrived twenty-three years thereafter, and happened to be a boy. 'It is as it should be that the firstborn shall be the prince', she uttered, which coincides with what my mother taught me at an early age: that we live and breathe in a partiarchal world.

My academic career undoubtedly began when I was born into a family where both my mother and father had graduated from teachers' colleges. Norwegian sociologists have shown that most academics are recruited from academic families, and that the majority of university students have parents who are grammar school teachers. They carry with them ambitions inherited from their own parents, who were in most cases small farmers or public servants. In due course my parents' generation implanted their ambitions in their own children. I was one of those children.

My mother's and father's education ended after teachers' college, in spite of my father's attempt to become an engineer so that he could become a famous inventor later on in his life. His son, my baby brother, was born when I was 5-years-old. He usurped many of my privileges. My brother became an inventor at Slack, the technical centre at Stanford University. My twin siblings, a sister and a brother, born when I was 11, became a lawyer and a medical doctor. Among my father's brothers, one became a teacher and two became ministers. Their schooling, as well as their sisters' nursing careers, were paid for by my deeply religious grandfather on condition that they would become missionaries in darkest Africa. My father, who wished to become an inventor, received no financial support from his family of origin. He earned the money for his college fees by working in a grocery, thinking that he would fund his further studies in science and engineering from his teacher's salary. But then he met my mother. Among my mother's ten siblings, seven became teachers and six married teachers. I have listened to discussions about pedagogy and theories of learning and to teachers' stories throughout my childhood holidays.

My background goes a long way to explaining my view of the world. I learned to read by spelling my way through the twelve volumes written by Jules Verne. I believed strongly that almost anything could be achieved if only we put our minds to it. I was teased by my friends in the street and was told that I was crazy when in 1934 I declared loud and clear how flying in the air, travelling under water and walking on the moon would, indeed, be the future of our civilization. Everything my parents said I believed to be absolutely true. I even wondered if I should become a criminal in order to be recruited for the first moon flight, since Columbus had recruited from criminals in the dark prisons of Madrid when he set off to search for his new route to India.

I was a good student. My mother taught me for the first three years, then my father taught our class some of the time for the next four years. I learned English from him. He mastered many languages and told us that Esperanto would be the language that would finally wipe war from the surface of the planet. Mastering Esperanto, we all would be able to understand one another. In addition, technology and new inventions would save us from hunger and disasters.

My mother believed in organized behaviour. She was a member of a number of health and welfare organizations and belonged to a club for business and professional women. She went to international conferences in many different countries. As an artist she worked for art exhibitions in schools. As a feminist she established and led the women's council in our small town. When she was 91 she wrote her autobiography, about how it felt to 'look backwards on her life as an educator' (Skarpaas, 1992). It was her *Goodbye Mr Chips*.

Sometimes I wonder how my life and behaviour has influenced my own children. They have had problems. When I was a government-appointed member of the Committee on Smoking and Health, two of them conspicuously smoked in their school playgrounds. My daughter, who was tiny, fought to be allowed to take lessons in carpet-making and insisted on playing the tuba in the school band, leading her teacher to remark that she could do so, if her mother would push her to band practice in a wheelbarrow! My oldest child is a sinologist. I think he had to run away from me, far away, to find himself. So he studies in China. My daughter is an artist who later became a homeopath and a healer. My grandfather on my mother's side was well known for his healing powers and his gift of being able to see into the future. 'This is not a mystery', he insisted. 'Some time in the future we will find out how some of us have developed these abilities.' My third child, a son, has 'tried everything'. At the age of 40 he finally decided to become an engineer. He has a very inventive mind. My youngest son graduated from agricultural college, but works as a businessman. He loves to organize things and to keep everything in order. All my cupboards and shelves looked nice and neat from when he was 5. He is the only one who has children: two girls, who are healthy and bright. My daughters-in-law are artists and therapists. My husband, who is still doing his research on housing and the environment, insists that he never gets bored with me, and that I am a clown in some ways. He sings. He has recently translated the songs of the Russian poet and actor Vladimir Vysotsky for use by his Asker Socialist Choir. I am obviously a lucky lady. Leafing through some of the articles written about me, I find that the *Christian Daily* has me 'walking on water'. In a trade union newspaper I am seen as someone 'who never gives in'.

Why, then, do I feel so helpless? Why is that, when I cry, I wonder if it is from sadness or from joy?

## References

ALFSEN LIE, M. (ed.) (1988) 'Jeg er en stakar — min far er en helt' ('I am unworthy — my father is a hero'), in *I Min Fars Hus: Fjorten Døtre Forteller (In My Father's House: Fourteen Stories for daughters)* Oslo: Pax.

Ås, B. (1962) 'Ulykkesfugler og trygge barn' (Accident-prone and safe children), *Tidsskrift for Samfunnsforskning (Journal for Social Research)*, **3**, March, pp. 1–16.

Ås, B. (1975) 'On female culture: An attempt to formulate a theory of women's solidarity and action', *Acta Sociologica*, **18**, 2–3, pp. 142–61.

Ås, B. (1981) 'A five dimensional model for change: Contradiction and feminist consciousness', *Women's Studies International Quarterly*, **4**, 1, pp. 101–14.

Ås, B. (1982) 'A materialistic view of men's and women's attitudes towards war', *Women's Studies International Quarterly*, **5**, 3–4, pp. 355–64.

Ås, B. (1984) 'Hr. Noah var den første som kvoterte' ('Noah was the first to use a quota'), in LIKESTLLINGSUTVALGET (The Equal Rights Committee) *Kvinner på Universitetet 100 år (A Century of Women At The University)*, Oslo: Oslo University.

Ås, B. (1985) 'The feminist university', *Women's Studies International Quarterly*, **8**, 4, pp. 391–4, reprinted in (1989) *Radical Voices: A Decade of Feminist Resistance,* The Athene series. Oxford: Pergamon Press.

Ås, B. (1987) 'Hvis en ikke er forut for sin tid så kommer den aldri' ('If you are not ahead of your time, yout time will never arrive') *Nytt Fra Kvinneforskning* (Tenth anniversary issue) Oslo: Sekretariatet for kvinneforskning, Norges Forskningsraåd (The Norwegian Research Council), pp. 48–59.

Ås, B. (1988) 'Managing visions from invisibility to visibility: Women's impact in the nineties', lecture given in the honour of Bernardijn ten Zeldam, September, Amsterdam.

Ås, B. (1990) 'A feminist university in Norway', in STIVER LIE, S. and O'LEARY, V.R. (eds) *Storming the Tower: Women in the Academic World*, London: Kogan Page.

Ås, B. (1995) 'A feminist university in Norway', *Feministische Kontexte: Zeitschrift Fur Hochschuldidaktik*. Österreichisher Studien Verlag. 19. Jahrgang. Heft 2 [book. Place of publication]

JONASSEN, T.C. (1983) *Value Systems and Personality in a Western Civilisation: Norwegians in Europe and America*, Columbus, OH: Ohio State University Press.

SKARPAAS, I. (1992) *En Pedagog Ser Tilbake (An Educator Looks Back)* Oslo: Hovseter.

VÄXJÖ KOMMUNS JÄMSTÄLLDHETSKOMMITTÉ (Växjö community's committtee on equal rights) (1992) *De fem härskarteknikerna — en teori om maktens språk. (The Five Suppression Techniques — a theory about the language of power)* Box 1222,351 12 Växjö, Sweden.

WINTHER, L. (1973) *Da Partipisken Smalt i Asker (The Crack of the Party Whip in Asker)* Oslo: Pax.

# 3    The Struggle for Balance: The Career of a German University Professor

*Date of Birth: 12 December 1945*
**Professor Gertrud Pfister**
Institute for Sport Science, The Free University Campus, Berlin, Germany

## Introduction

Currently I am a professor in the Institute for Sport Science at the Free University Berlin. The University, which is located in the part of the city formerly controlled by the Western powers, as the name 'free' implies, has about 50,000 students. I have leading roles in quite a number of national and international scientific institutions and organizations. Among other 'jobs', I am President of the International Society for Sport History, and Vice President of the German Gymnastic Federation, which has four-and-a-half million members. But I do not feel anything like VIP, but just a normal person with strengths and weaknesses like everybody else. I do not tell everybody about my professional career because the people I meet outside the University, when I am playing tennis, skiing or visiting a concert, get to know me as person and not as a professor. Often I ask myself why I took on all these tasks and duties, which bring power and prestige, but also a lot of work. Especially in the last few years when I have achieved so much in my professional life but when at the same time my workload has been increasing continously, I sometimes think about how I became what I am and why I am doing what I do. Before I share with you a part of my biography and describe the story of my professional career, the conflicts and problems, the successes and the failures, I will sketch in some background information about the university system in Germany, the position of women within this system, and explanations of the gender hierarchy within the scientific community.

## The Situation of Women in Sport Science

In Germany virtually all academic teaching and research within the field of sport science is carried out at institutes of sport sciences which are incorporated into universities, generally as distinct faculties. (Our Institute constitutes a faculty together with education and psychology.) These institutes provide higher education for future physical education and sports teachers, who also study a second subject, as well as for students preparing to enter other professions, who graduate with a diploma or a master's degree. These studies take four to five years. In order to become a teacher you have to spend a further two years in school-based teacher education and you have to pass another examination. In Germany it is not possible to leave university after undergraduate study with just a bachelor's degree. The institutes for sport science are entitled to award doctoral degrees and habilitations, thus also providing access to an academic career in sport science. (The habilitation is a second postgraduate qualification required for an academic career, comparable with a higher doctorate.)

Sport has long been a men's domain, both in theory and in practice; as recently as 1991, in what was then West Germany, this course of study was chosen by more men (56 per cent) than women (44 per cent). Typically, gender differences are also evident in the students' choice of career: more women than men opt for the shorter course of study leading to a teaching career in primary and elementary schools, while the opposite is true for students aiming at secondary-level (including sixth-form) teaching (Dieckelmann, Pfister and Sack, 1992). The decision to seek a career in higher education is taken after completion of the university course, in opting to pursue a doctorate. Comparatively few women do so: in 1989 the proportion of women among the 17,901 students gaining a doctorate in the Federal Republic amounted to 26.5 per cent (Bundesminister für Bildung und Wissenschaft, 1991, p. 211). In the Federal Republic, as well as at the Free University of Berlin, between 1989 and 1991 the number of male graduates gaining doctorates was roughly three times as high as the figure for female graduates. In the Department of Sport Sciences at the Free University of Berlin 2 per cent of female graduates but 6 per cent of male graduates gained doctorates in this period (Report from the Central Ombudswoman's office at the Free University of Berlin for the period March 1991 to January 1993). There are even fewer women at the next stage of qualification: women comprised only 10 per cent of those who were awarded a habilitation in the former Federal Republic of Germany (FRD), which qualified them to teach and examine at university level (cf. Schmude, 1993). Even in the former German Democratic Republic (GDR), women were also in a minority in the academic world, representing 36 per cent of those gaining doctorates and 13 per cent of those with a habilitation. A survey of the higher qualifications awarded in my own disciplinary field (although without any claim to completeness) is given in the journal *Sport Sciences*; here, between 1980 and 1991, 739 doctorates are reported as having been conferred. The proportion of women remained relatively constant during the whole ten-year period at roughly 20 per cent. In the same period the journal reported fifty-one habilitations, only three of which were awarded to women. (In Germany the discipline of sports science is defined very broadly, to include historical and social scientific work, and not just 'hard science'.) From this we can conclude that higher education is today by no means a privilege confined to men, yet on the higher rungs of the qualification ladder women begin to fall back. As in all subjects, the percentage of women in sport sciences falls, the further one climbs the academic ladder.

And what are the ratios of men and women in the university labour market? Although women form a majority of support staff such as secretaries, men represent 82 per cent of all academic staff in universities and colleges of higher education. On the topmost rungs of the university hierarchy women still play a very marginal role. In 1990 in the FRD women represented little more than 6 per cent of university teachers, and a mere 3 per cent of C4 professorships (the highest category of professorship in Germany) (Federal Ministry of Education and Science, 1992, p. 9). At universities in the former GDR women also formed a small minority: only 5 per cent of all professors (Central Office for the Advancement of Women's Studies and Research, Newsletter Summer Team, 1992, p. 60). Women, then, are already at a considerable disadvantage in the middle ranks of university teaching, even in comparison with the numbers of women students and graduates (Wermuth, 1992, p. 38). In sport science departments, just like all the other university departments, women are strongly underrepresented, comprising 21 per cent of all full-time academic staff in 1990 in the FRG. In the same year one single woman occupied a C4 professorship along with seventy-three men; of the 179 professors of all categories, 9 per cent were women (data published by the Federal Ministry of Education and Science, 1992).

After 1989 reunification brought major changes for the universities in Eastern Germany, which had to adapt to the patterns in the West. Universities, institutes, research groups and individuals had to undergo evaluation processes, which often led to a removal of surplus personnel or the replacement of poorly-rated scholars and teachers. One problem was the high staff:student ratio. Therefore the universities had to dismiss staff, which particularly affected the many women who held tenured positions in the middle levels of the hierarchy, but lacked sufficient power to fight effectively to keep their posts. Because of restructuring and the negative evaluations given to many former professors, a considerable number of new professorial posts became available. The nationwide invitations for applications and the principles followed for the selection process, which followed those used in the West, had the effect that most of these positions went to men from the former West Germany. In recent years the financial crisis in Germany has led to a continuous reduction of resources for all universities. Therefore vacant positions cannot be filled, and all the fine promises to support women are not worth the paper they are written upon. It is quite apparent, then, that the higher the post, the lower the proportion of women occupants. Senior posts at institutes of sport sciences, which are invested with power and prestige and provided with financial resources are, now as ever, firmly in the hands of men.

## Women in the Scientific Community

Status and prestige, influence and resources stem only partly from one's professional position. In the scientific community what is important is how much funding one is able to acquire from the various sources, how frequently and in which journals one publishes articles, how frequently one is quoted and by whom, to which committees and organizations one is appointed or elected and, finally, on which subjects one carries out research. On the publishing boards of important sport science journals, on the grants committees of public funding bodies, just as in sport science organizations and their steering committees, women form a minority. Of the six board members heading the German Association of Sport Sciences, until 1995 there was only ever one woman; currently it has four men and two women. The most effective way of gaining prestige and influence within the scientific community is through the publication of articles and books. Surveys show that women publish less than their male colleagues (Kuckartz, 1992) and, since there are fewer female sports scientists than male, women and women's issues receive scant attention in the specialist literature. An analysis of various periodicals of sport psychology, for example, revealed that women were considerably underrepresented as far as authorship was concerned: between 1987 and 1992 only 16 per cent of the articles in the German journal *Sportpsychologie* were written by women (Alfermann, 1993). To interpret this, one has to remember that only 9 per cent of the professors and 21 per cent of the full-time academic staff at German Institutes for Sport Science are female. The articles published in these and other sport science journals report research that is related much more frequently to men than to women. Furthermore, the subjects of research as well as the methods and theories involved are often not only developed by men but are also applied to men, and the findings interpreted from an androcentric point of view. This goes hand in hand with the tendency to regard men as the norm and women as deviations thereof; male experience and male patterns of behaviour are generalized and 'man' is equated with 'human'. Moreover, the power of men in universities and as members of powerful committees outside the universities also has an effect on the allocation of research funding. The German Federal Institute of Sport Sciences, for example, which is responsible for the administration of research grants, has funded only very few projects related to women's issues. The conclusion to be drawn from this is that in the scientific community, as elsewhere, women have so far been able to gain little power and influence.

## Background and Causes

Generally speaking, the outsider status of women at institutes of sport sciences and in the scientific community as a whole is not considered a very serious matter.

There is a widespread belief, firmly anchored in people's minds, that science is neutral in terms of gender and that in the universities equality of the sexes is guaranteed. The small number of female lecturers and professors is interpreted, according to one's view of the world, as a result of their unsuitability, lack of drive, the consequence of mistaken decision, or a relic of historical development. It is only a matter of time, say the optimists, before the ratios of women match those of men in all areas and at all levels. Unfortunately, there is no empirical basis for such confidence: as shown above, the percentage of women lecturers in sport sciences even fell in the 1980s.

With regard to the sexual hierarchy, universities are a faithful reflection of society as a whole, characterized as it is by an imbalance of power and status. Like the universities, the entire labour market is marked by a vertical and horizontal segregation according to gender. An examination of the causes of women's underrepresentation in the scientific community and their absence from the upper echelons of institutionalized sport sciences must take account of both sides of the supply and demand equation. Supply-oriented approaches seek explanations for the situation of women in the labour market in the specific features of the labour supply, namely in qualifications and career orientation, as well as in the life-circumstances of women and their capacity for work as a whole. Capacity for work is dependent both on the balance of power in a society and on its economic structure, with the division of labour according to gender (namely, women's responsibility for housework and bringing up children) playing a pivotal role. Women's labour is characteristically caught up in contradictions, discontinuities and ambivalences, since labour in the context of the family is governed by quite different factors and requires quite different qualifications from labour which is sold as a commodity.

Decisions, qualifications and competences depend on a great number of factors and a person's path through life is already marked out in childhood and youth. Numerous studies have demonstrated that male and female adolescents differ considerably not only in their interests, attitudes and plans for the future but also in their self-confidence and self-evaluation. Thus, in the course of their socialization, a different orientation to work develops between the sexes which also has an effect on the choice of occupation, women for example attaching less importance than men to opportunities for promotion or higher income and more to the atmosphere at the workplace or the content of the work itself (Stiegler, 1982). Moreover, the choice of occupation as well as the motivation to 'pursue a career' is decisively influenced by the anticipation of family duties. This is equally true of the decision whether or not to study for a doctorate and to take up a post in sport sciences (Küspert, 1992; Kootz and Püschel, 1992). Moreover, women's opportunities for work are influenced by their family situation. Studying for a first degree may not take place at a time of life when one is normally building a family and bringing up children; but writing a thesis does, and all scientific work requires a great amount of time, energy and concentration, not to mention flexibility. And since it is women who do the housework and look after the children in the great majority of families (Opaschowski, 1989), time is scarce for women scientists who still have to cater for the well-being of their children or even just their partner. The flexibility of working hours and the scope for being able to work in the evening or at home may appear at first glance to be an advantage, especially for those who have a family; but it is this very flexibility, which demands such a high degree of self-discipline, that frequently leads to delays in completing a doctoral or habilitation thesis, or even to abandoning it entirely (Joas, 1990; Schultz, 1991; Neusel, 1992; Kuckartz, 1992). On the other hand, the family should not be seen solely as a burden or as an obstacle to a career in science. Children provide new experiences, give life new meaning, bring happiness and make one look at the world with different eyes. It is not children that make it so difficult to reconcile family and profession, but rather the prevailing conditions: the conflicting demands made on women's labour power by the family on the one hand, and by employment outside the home on the other (see the German Association of Academic Women, 1988).

Given the fact that promotion at one's own university is rarely possible in the German higher education system, mobility is a prerequisite for every step up the career ladder. However, since many women consider their partner's profession to have priority, moving to another university is, as a rule, a very difficult decision to make. Another problem is the double qualification needed in Germany where a PhD is not enough to get a tenured position (with exception of teaching practical lessons in the different types of sport). After the doctoral examination, individuals aiming at a professorship (the only permanent position at a German university) have to conduct another time- and energy-consuming research project and to write another thesis. It is obvious that this poses special problems for women who want to have a family.

That women publish comparatively little and that they are not really integrated into the scientific community are two further aspects of women scientists' capacity for work which reduces their competitive edge in the sport science labour market. These factors are not wholly attributable, it is true, to the burdens placed on women by their families. It is more likely that women have different priorities from men. Not having the 'right' contacts or choosing the 'wrong' thesis topic might also help to explain why women publish less than men. Finally, the fact that women are more committed to teaching (as revealed in surveys carried out in several institutes at the Free University of Berlin, as elsewhere) may also play a role. Since university careers are still based on the motto 'publish or perish' and teaching still counts for little in the selection of lecturers and professors, women's greater commitment to teaching tends to be a disadvantage in the long term.

While traditional supply-oriented approaches lay the blame for the sexual segregation of the labour market and the underprivileged status of employed women at the door of the women themselves and the 'decisions' they take, demand-oriented concepts examine labour market structures and the strategies pursued by employers (Willms-Herget, 1985; Rabe-Kleberg, 1987). Taking the demand-oriented model of the segmentation of the labour market, then women tend to be employed in marginal segments of firms or institutions because of their stigmat-ization as unreliable workers. Since women might have children or give their family priority over their work, they are neither entrusted with leading positions nor given the opportunity for promotion. Investment in labour is only profitable if it is at the firm's disposal the whole day and uninterruptedly. Even though it is not openly admitted, this stereotyping of women as potentially unreliable employees probably plays a role in the filling of vacant positions at universities, too. After all, maternity leave can cause considerable problems, especially in small departments. Further obstacles in the way of women's careers are ideals and prejudices. Even if women's suitability for scientific work is no longer openly called into question, it is obvious from the findings of many studies that cliches about women and their efficiency are long-lived and still very widespread (Schultz, 1991, p. 1). Such notions and expectations also play their part, whether consciously or not, in appointments to lectureships and professorships, which are carried out according to the principle of cooptation. Here certain rules apply: new members must above all fit in well with the other members of the department, and help to increase the prestige of the group as a whole. Women, as the 'opposite sex', with low status, fulfil neither of these conditions.

Supply-oriented and demand-oriented approaches have been combined to form a theory of acculturation, propounded among others by Schultz (ibid.), who sees the university as a 'homosocial world' in which men have practically everything to themselves and in which male values and standards, male forms of communication and male behaviour are the norm. By contrast, women, especially in university teaching, are expected not only to adapt themselves in the process of acculturation, but also to obey and apply rules which they have never had the opportunity to learn (Clemens et al., 1986). While male scientists, socialized in a male-dominated world, are admitted to old boys' networks and their names enter the lists of quotable authors, women have neither the backing of other women nor role models to motivate them and show them the way forward. Due to socialization-based orientations on the one hand and patterns of exclusion on the other, acculturation is a process which, although it may finally succeed, does not take place without conflict.

The exclusion of women from the upper echelons of the university is not, however, a formal disbarment, since the university is acknowledged to be a merito-cracy, where advancement is supposedly based on ability and academic achieve-ment. Nevertheless, one cannot disregard gender in considering interactions and communication, or definitions and evaluations. The marginalization of women also has a direct bearing on their interests and fields of research. In the debate following a question put to the German government by the Social Democratic parliamentary party in 1989, a woman member declared:

> When women wish either to examine or to apply new research issues and methods, they all too often fail at the hands of the male-dominated steering committees, which have the power to define and which dismiss women's projects as either irrelevant or unscientific. This is especially true when . . . the demand is made for gender to be taken into account as a fundamental category in analysing social structures and processes. (Dürkop, 1990, p. 10)

It is often overlooked that research into women's issues involves asking new ques-tions and seeking new ways of answering them, shifting perspectives away from the androcentric point of view; and that, through all this, science can be enlivened, enriched and transformed. Dürkop urged, with good reason, that the differing life-circumstances of men and women and their resulting different interests and qualifications — the whole 'productive difference between the sexes' — be put to use for the benefit of the universities.

To sum up: gender-based segregation in higher education begins on the day of matriculation, accompanies one through the entire process of passing examinations and obtaining qualifications, and continues onto the university labour market, with the conditions governing labour supply and the demand side complementing and reinforcing each other. Not only the stigmatization of women scientists as (potentially) family-oriented and lacking originality, but also their reluctance or inability to adjust completely to the masculine world of science, lead to the exclusion of women from the top rungs of the university hierarchy. The decisive factor in this regard is women's responsibility for the reproduction of labour power and the economic structure of our society, which can be described as a dual economy in the sense that paid labour in the field of production exists side by side with the unpaid labour of reproduction. Domestic labour (that is, housework and raising children), which women perform without pay and without previous training, is indispensable for our society (Beck, 1986, p. 179). The fact that girls and women are prepared for their roles as housewives and mothers in the course of a complex life-long socialization process is therefore something that cannot easily be changed. The division of labour based on gender is so deeply rooted in our wider social structures that direct appeals to women, or hasty and superficial attempts at reform, are generally doomed to failure from the beginning. However, this should by no means lead to the conclusion that reforms are not worth trying or that changes are not worth striving for. I now want to show how individual women are influenced by these structures and ideologies, using my own biography as an example.

## Biography

I come from a typical middle class family and grew up in a small Bavarian town. My father was a high school teacher and my mother worked in a kindergarten, but left work when I was born in 1945. It must have been a hard time for her after the war to care for the family. She had a strong Catholic background and it was her deep belief that women had to become mothers, and mothers had to stay at home. But anyhow, in the difficult period after the war it would have been impossible for her to find employment in her profession. Although she was thoroughly convinced that the sex-specific division of work and tasks was good and 'natural', she was never very happy with her life and she always felt that her family did not provide adequate compensation for her former career. There was never any question that my sister and I would have an academic education. On my father's side of the family, all the children became academics and humanist values were held in highly esteem; my father and his three brothers all attended the gymnasium (academic high school, with a curriculum based on the classics) and learned Latin and Greek.

As the elder daugher, I was expected to follow the family tradition. In the small town where we lived there were two high schools, one for girls and one for boys. Because only the boys' school offered Latin and Greek, I was sent there. For many years I was the only girl in my class. Later on, there were two, sometimes three, girls among thirty male students. I tried very hard to be accepted and treated like all my fellow pupils. My strategy was, at least in the first few years, to be invisible as a girl. I adopted the values and behaviour of the boys and wanted to be better than them, or even to be like a boy. My classmates accepted me as a 'mate'; in my leisure time I was a tomboy and loved to play cowboys and Indians, to climb trees and to have adventures. I was always good at sport, which became a very important part of my identity. Skiing was a major activity for me, and I worked very hard to pass several examinations to become a qualified ski instructor. Tennis, mountain climbing and canoeing were my favourite sports in summer.

These experiences in school, especially my integration in the male peer group and my engagement in sport, shaped my biography. I learned to be independent, achievement-orientated and ambitious. What I did not learn was how to play the traditional female role and to demonstrate my femininity. After graduation from school it was clear to both me and my parents that I should go to university. Because I had passed the final examination at school with good marks, I could freely choose what I wanted to study. (In Germany the final high school leaving examination qualifies pupils for university entrance. When there are more candidates than places in a certain subject, such as medicine, then students with better marks have priority.) My mother wanted me to become a medical doctor, but I chose instead to study physical education, Latin and history in order to become a high school teacher. But it was my love of sport and the attraction of studying it, rather than the prospect of teaching, which influenced my choice. My mother was not happy about this because of the low status of physical education and sport science. I chose to study at the university in Munich, which was the nearest one to my home town. I had no financial problems, as in Germany university education is free. My parents supported me financially, and I worked in the vacations. Among other jobs, I often worked as skiing instructor, which I loved.

After my final examination the decisive switches had to be thrown. My mother hoped that I would move back to my home town, marry my boyfriend, get a job as a teacher and have at least two children. But this was not a very exciting prospect for me. Working on my thesis had awakened an interest in research, so I decided to continue my studies by working for a PhD in history. I moved to another city, Regensburg, which offered better conditititons for my chosen subject. To finance my studies I first got work as assistant teacher, then later I got a grant. Shortly before finishing my PhD, I applied for a job as assistant at a sport science institute 700 km away from Regensburg, which had not only been my home but was also where my partner lived. When this job was offered to me, I had to make one of the most important decisions in my life. If I turned it down, I would have to become a high school teacher, which promised a well-paid job with a secure future. Also, as a teacher it is possible to work part-time and to have a family. On the other hand, this assistant post offered me the opportunity to continue with my scientific work.

But this would also mean opting for insecurity: in Germany assistants only have five-year contracts, with no scope for extension to stay on at the same university. I decided to accept the job offer and to try for a scientific career. It helped that my partner decided to come with me and to look for a job in the city where I was going to work. As an assistant, I only had two courses to teach, so I had plenty of time to work for my second qualification, the habilitation. I received a great deal of support from one of the professors, who believed in team work and networking. I got the chance to join one of his research projects, and he also encouraged me to write articles, to participate in conferences, and to get involved in the scientific community. After three or four years I started to apply for positions all over Germany, and finally I got a post as professor in Berlin. I represented the compromise candidate: in the committee which had to evaluate the candidates and to construct a shortlist, there were two factions who were fighting over two candidates, and eventually they agreed to nominate me for the position. So in 1981 I was offered a position as a professor at the Institute for Sport Science at the Free University, Berlin.

Berlin was again 600 km from the place where I had worked before and where my partner lived. Once again, I had to decide if I wanted to accept this position. In the beginning of the 1980s, following a period of expansion, the situation at German universities deteriorated, the number of vacancies fell dramatically, and it was especially difficult to find a position in a sport science institute in the area of social sciences, which was what I was seeking. So I did not have much choice. If I did not want to face unemployment and become financially dependent on my partner, I had to take this position in Berlin. In the first year I travelled back at weekends, and in the next year my partner moved to Berlin, but one year later we separated.

In the following years I did quite a lot of administrative work in my Institute and in the University. I was a member of several different boards and committees, including the committee responsible for the disbursement of research money in the University. We had to evaluate a large number of applications for funding, which was very interesting, but very time-consuming, too. For a two-year period I was the elected Head of our Institute. Because of the many conflicts between its members, this work was very complicated, time-consuming and stressful, and so I was glad when my turn was over. My successors have had the same problems, and even now many of these conflicts remain unresolved.

## My Life Today

These days my work encompasses several different areas. My first priority is my job at the University, which involves a combination of teaching, examining and administration. Much of my time is dedicated to research and writing for publication. I have several research projects, which means a lot of organization, advising the research assistants, reflecting about methods and theories, and interpreting the results. My main research area is the history and the present position of girls and women in sport, and it is a constant challenge to publish findings and to try to use them in order to improve women's lives. Another part of my work is my involvement in the scientific community, working on committees and in organizations, being a member of the scientific boards of book series and journals, giving lectures and taking part in conferences, or even organizing them. It is very difficult to achieve a balance between all this work and my personal life. I love to work, to go into the archives, to conduct interviews, to read, to reflect and to discuss theses and results. I find it challenging and exciting. The problem is that there are only twenty-four hours in the day. I manage to go to theatres and museums, to meet friends and to do sports like running, tennis or fitness training. But work seems to eat up almost all my time and energy. However, most of my work is voluntary, it is my own choice to do it, and I feel that I get a lot of satisfaction, benefits and esteem from my peers out of my work.

## Opportunities and Obstacles

What factors have promoted the development my academic careeer? First, my experiences in the boys' school and my identification with the boys. I developed achievement motivation, I learned to fight, I was proud of my academic and sporting achievements. Second, I never defined myself through femininity, but this brought with it the problem that I had difficulty in accepting myself as woman and accepting other women; I thought for a long time that I could get along much better with men as colleagues or friends, than women. Next, my mother provided a negative example: I did not want to become a housewife and I did not want to become like her. Fourth, with my partners we had never the traditional male versus female roles. Each of us was responsible for his/her own life. But this type of 'equality' cannot work if you have children, and also it seems to be difficult for men to accept this way of living. In the end, many men decide to opt for a tradi-tional family with a wife who takes care of both the children and him. These days I live alone, and I enjoy the freedom of being able to live according to my needs. For many people, living alone sounds sad, but that is by no means true. I have many friends, and so my life is not lonely at all. Finally, there is the women's network. In the 1970s I got interested in the women's movement, which changed my life considerably; I learned the benefits of working with women and relying on women's networks. I started to study the history and situation of women, and this research led to many insights which influenced me as person, my interests, and my life as a whole. Some female colleagues and I founded a group called Women's Studies in Sport Science, and with this group and other female colleagues we have now quite a lot of support for our private as well as our professional lives.

## Problems

In Germany, a major barrier for women who want a career in science is the insec-urity of many posts and the periodic need to change universities. For me these decisions to move have not been easy. Each time it meant leaving friends, networks and — at least for a time — my partner. For women with a family, this need for mobility is a major problem. Another big problem is the inextricable connection between life and work; the time required for academic work is potentially endless, you never finish all the tasks you have promised to do, you never have time to read all the books you want to read, and you can never be sure that you have found the best way to interpret the results of your research. So your life gets more and more tangled up with your work. For women many of the rewards are double-edged. Women have to be much better and to invest much more energy in their work than men in order to achieve academic success, but this success often brings yet more tasks and duties. To be involved in many committees and decisions means power on the one hand, but brings more work on the other.

Backlashes: I have applied several times for promotion in the last few years, and have had it put to me that my research is on a marginal topic (namely, women). I found out that the informal relations and networks between men are still very strong; women are very often outsiders. One of the positions I applied for was given to a man who had virtually none of the qualifications which had been asked for in the recruitment advertisement. Despite many protestations of support for women, female scholars, especially when they are involved in women's studies, are still marginalized. A backlash can also be discerned in the general level of interest in feminist research. For example, it has become much more difficult than it was some years ago to interest students in courses about women and sport. There is a tendency these days to stigmatize feminism as old-fashioned and unnecessary.

What do I want and expect for the future? My outlook for the future is ambivalent: I hope to retain my resources for teaching and research, despite the general financial crisis in German universities. But there will be no vacancies for which I could apply, and it will be very difficult to support women, women's networks and feminist research in a situation where resources are being cut. This deterioriation will intensify the struggle for promotions and I hope that this does not lead to a worsening of women's opportunities. At least this situation is a chance to give the women's movement a new impetus; those women who are now utterly convinced that they will encounter no problems in the academic world will discover that universities are still a male domain. In my private life I will aim for a balance between work and leisure. Anyhow, looking back, I do not regret my decisions and I feel very privileged to work in a university. University teaching is something of an ideal job, with the freedom to choose your own priorities for work and research; the chance to meet many different people; plenty of scope for travel, to catch up with old friends and to make new ones; opportunities to keep on learning and constantly to have new experiences; and the conviction that you are working for important aims.

### References

ALFERMANN, D. (1993) 'Wie weiblich ist die Sportpsychologie?', *dvs-Bulletin*, **4**, pp. 27–34.
BECK, U. (1986) *Risikogesellschaft. Auf dem Weg in eine andere Moderne*, Frankfurt-am-Main: Suhrkamp.

BUNDESMINISTER FÜR BILDUNG UND WISSENSCHAFT (ed.) (1991) *Grund- und Strukturdaten*, Bonn: Bundesminister für Bildung und Wissenschaft.

BUNDESMINISTERIUM FÜR BILDUNG UND WISSENSCHAFT (1992) *Personal an Hochschulen 1982 bis 1990*, Bonn: Bundesministerium für Bildung und Wissenschaft.

BUNDESMINISTERIUM FÜR BILDUNG UND WISSENSCHAFT (1993) *Studenten und Studienanfanger an Hochschulen 1975 bis 1991*, Bonn: Bundesminister für Bildung und Wissenschaft.

CLEMENS, B. et al. (1986) *Töchter der Alma Mater: Frauen in der Berufs- und Hochschulforschung*, Frankfurt/New York: Campus.

DIECKELMANN, D., PFISTER, G. and SACK, H.G. (1992) 'Erstes Staatsexamen: was nun?', *Sportunterricht*, **41**, pp. 445–54.

DÜRKOP, M. (1990) 'Frauen an Fachhochschulen: Perspektiven und Stratagien', *ifg Frauenforschung*, **8**, pp. 1–15.

KOOTZ, J. and PÜSCHEL, E. (eds) (1992) *Studentinnen im Blick der Hochschulforschung: Empirie und Studienreform*, Berlin: Freie Universität.

KUCKARTZ, U. (1992) 'Auf dem Weg zur Professorin. Empirische Befunde zum Zusammenhang zwischen Wissenchaftskarriere, Familiengründung und Elternschaft', *Zeitschrift fur Pädagogik*, **38**, pp. 681–700.

KÜSPERT, G. (1992) 'Studieren — und was dann? Zur Situation studierender Frauen an der Universität Tübingen', in KOOTZ, J. and PÜSCHEL, E. (eds) *Studentinnen im Blick der Hochschulforschung: Empirie und Studienreform*, Berlin: Freie Universität.

NEUSEL, A. (1992) 'Wissenschaftlerinnen', *Uni*, **16**, pp. 50–3.

OPASCHOWSKI, H. (1989) *Freizeitalltag von Frauen*, Hamburg: BAT.

RABE-KLEBERG, U. (1987) *Frauenberufe: Zur Segmentierung der Berufswelt*, Bielefeld: Kleine.

SCHMUDE, J. (1993) 'Professorinnen und weibliche Habilitierte an deutschen Hochschulen', *Mitteilungen des Hochschulverbandes*, **3**, pp. 175–9.

SCHULTZ, D. (1991) *Das Geschlect läuft immer mit . . . Die Arbeitswelt von Professorinnen und Professoren*, Pfaffenweiler: Centaurus.

STIEGLER, B. (1982) 'Frauen in untypischen Berufen und Positionen', in MOHR, G., RUMMEL, M. and RUCKERT, D. (eds) *Frauen: Psychologische Beiträge zur Arbeits- und Lebensituation*, Munich/Vienna Baltimore: Urban and Schwarzenberg.

WERMUTH, N. (1993) 'Frauen als Wissenschaftlerinnen an Universität', *Mitteilungen des Hochschulverbandes*, **3**, pp. 183–8.

WILLMS-HERGET, A. (1985) *Frauenarbeit: Zur Integration der Frauen in den Arbeitsmarkt*, Frankfurt-am-Main.

# 4    Against the Tide: The Career Paths of Women Chief Academic Officers of American Colleges and Universities

*Date of Birth: 8 June 1944*
**Karen Doyle Walton**
Vice-President for Academic Affairs, Allentown College of St. Francis de Sales, Pennsylvania, USA

The career paths that have led women to the position of chief academic officer (CAO) of American colleges and universities have, in many cases, been diverted by societal influences. However, there are particular milestones with respect to educational background and academic administrative positions that most of those women CAOs have reached. Before generalizing to a statistical profile of women who have reached the highest academic positions in colleges and universities, perhaps the following case study of an individual female CAO would be instructive.

### One Woman's Swim 'Against the Tide': Preparing for the Swim

I was born during the war year of 1944 to a mother of Swedish heritage and a father who was compelled to leave his pregnant wife when the Second World War called him to lead a surgical unit behind the front lines in Belgium and France. If the immediate bonding that occurred in 1946 between the returning physician and his 2-year old daughter had not been the marvelous, life-determining gift that it was, psychologists would, no doubt, blame the delayed introduction of father to child. His bedtime stories about soldiers he patched together in surgical tents under adverse conditions was my first brush with a strong sense of mission. Although my father devoted the remainder of his life to eighty hour-weeks as a urologist, each day of my childhood included fun time during which we shared whatever youthful whimsy I found fascinating. Each day, too, I observed my father engrossed for a half-hour or so in the current *Journal of the American Medical Association*, while I snuggled up and read my more fascinating (to me) fairy tales. His academic background included being the first Notre Dame University graduate to be accepted by Johns Hopkins Medical School, a fact that brought quiet satisfaction to a man who showed no hint of hubris throughout his life.

My mother provided warmth and nurture like my father, devoting her life to me, my sister, and our aging grandparents. Although she was well-educated (with bachelor's and master's degrees), she lived the happily then-expected, conventional life of homemaker, volunteering as director of church and hospital projects. While serving as State President of the Women's Auxiliary to the Pennsylvania Medical Society, my mother declined a nomination to the national presidency of the Women's Auxiliary to the American Medical Association because of her preferred higher priority of caring for our family. Unlike my father's absorption in medicine, science, and non-fiction, my mother's appreciation of poetry, fine literature, and the well-spoken word buffeted me between the Scylla of the science of earth and man and the Charybdis of the music of the spheres. I remember fondly one evening during high school when I discussed atomic structure with my father, followed by pondering Robert Frost's *Mending Walls* with my mother. Perhaps my schizophrenic academic homelife was responsible for my lifelong professional career in liberal arts colleges!

My parents were born and spent most of their lives in Johnstown, Pennsylvania, but my father's thrill of adventure became evident at the end of his urological fellowship at Washington University in St. Louis before he was married. Those were the Depression years, so his monthly salary ranged from zero to $50. Consequently, he took a position as physician in charge of a government hospital in Tanana, Alaska. The other half of the entire professional staff was a nurse who eschewed surgery because she was squeamish about blood! Hence he performed major surgery under spinal anesthesia with the help of an Inuit. My father's respect for this janitor/surgical assistant was evident when he told my sister and me bedtime stories about their hunting excursions by dog sled and boat along the Yukon River. He shared Mark Twain's opinion that 'Travel is fatal to prejudice, bigotry, and narrow-mindedness — all foes to real understanding. Likewise tolerance of broad, wholesome, charitable views of men and things cannot be acquired by vegetating in our little corner of the world all one's life.'

Not surprisingly then, travel has played an important role in my education. I sought new experiences hither and yon; my first during the summer I turned 16, studying at the University of Vienna and living with an Austrian family. After my sophomore year of college, my sister and I studied at the Sorbonne; and the next summer I counselled at a Girl Scout camp in the forests of Germany. Even while married with two small children, I heeded my father's encouragement and joined an archeological dig on a tel in Israel. I have crossed the Atlantic over thirty times by ship and plane, jet and propeller, compelled by my father's vicarious *Wanderlust*.

## Entering Academic Waters with Female Mathematicians

My characteristic impatience had led me to leave high school a year early and enter Vassar, then one of the highly-selective, women's Seven Sisters Colleges, the female counterparts of the then all-male Ivy League Colleges. Skipping senior year of secondary school remains rare in the United States, but that trail was blazed for me (as were many others) by my two-year-older, best-friend sister. Although I entered Vassar as an English major, I left with a degree in pure mathematics, attributable without question to the strong women role models who comprised the entire Vassar mathematics department faculty. During my subsequent master's degree studies at Harvard University, I noted that, as an undergraduate at Vassar, I was taught mathematics exclusively by women, but at Harvard, all my mathematics professors were men. My classroom experiences, too, were dissimilar at the two institutions. Vassar undergraduate mathematics majors were vociferous, participative women who supported each other in every possible way; on the contrary, Harvard graduate mathematics students were almost exclusively men who unresponsively endured male lecturers and gloated when either the professor or a classmate tripped in his logic while presenting a mathematical proof or problem solution.

After my high school sweetheart (Lehigh University, Bachelor's in Mechanical Engineering; University of Pittsburgh, MBA) and I earned our first master's degrees, we married and I began teaching at a private women's college near his first-choice job preference. During the academic year, I strove to instill in my students the same fascination with mathematics that my female professors exuded at Vassar; and during the summer, I pursued a doctorate in mathematics at the University of Pittsburgh. Although I was enthralled with my work, I intended to teach only until motherhood obliged me to retire to part-time teaching. But when I confidentially informed the President of Seton Hill College, a Roman Catholic priest, of my pregnancy and plan to resign my full-time position, he urged me to instead remain full-time and also chair the Mathematics Department. I mentioned his (at that time) highly unconventional proposal to my parents, and my father's spontaneous response was 'Sounds wonderful! The happiest people are those who love their work,' which certainly described my affection for teaching at Seton Hill.

When our son arrived after my successful completion of three of six doctoral comprehensive written examinations scheduled for six consecutive weeks, I ended my studies with a master's degree in pure mathematics (as opposed to my master's of arts in the teaching of mathematics from Harvard). I recall the awkward but comical situation of being the only female taking doctoral examinations in mathematics that summer, during which my energetic unborn baby made sitting and concentrating for the required three-hour stretches extremely difficult. My doctoral advisor, a male professor who proctored the examinations, whispered to me 'Karen, sometimes two heads are not better than one!' The birth of Joseph Doyle Walton later that week marked the happiest day of my life.

My always-supportive husband and I were very fortunate to find a marvelous babysitter who arrived daily at 8 a.m. and stayed until late afternoon, sharing with me the joys and challenges of caring for a newborn. The love and attention my parents lavished on both our sons (the second born four years later) brought us all immeasurable joy and gratitude. My father died unexpectedly at the age of 83 of a massive heart attack one Saturday after attending a monthly meeting at the University of Pittsburgh Medical School. At the time of his death he was still practicing medicine a few days a week and leading a very active life, both mentally and physically. It is a comfort to me that his first grandchild is called Doyle, since my father's surname was otherwise lost with the marriage of his two female children.

## Uncharted Waters for Dual-role Women in Mathematics Education

My *alma mater* has been known historically as a hotbed for women leaders and social activists (for example, suffragettes). However, my dual roles of full-time college professor and mother were surprising even to Vassar alumnae in the early 1970s. I recall being invited to speak to the Pittsburgh Vassar Alumnae Club about combining my professional and private lives. To that audience of knitting and needlepointing women of whom volunteerism was expected, my life style appeared iconoclastic. Twenty-five years later, such a gathering of Vassar alumnae would be impossible and laughable, not only because the college turned coeducational in the early 1970s, but more significantly, because the combined roles of full-time career woman and homemaker now comprise the American paradigm, rather than the exception.

After seven wonderful years at Seton Hill College, my husband's career opportunities forced us to move from Western Pennsylvania to the Eastern part of the state. Leaving my position of tenured associate professor and chair of the Seton Hill Mathematics Department, and more significantly my parents and sister, was very difficult. Full-time teaching positions for women in the Lehigh Valley, our new home, were rare (if not non-existent). Although six colleges flourished in that geographic area, women mathematicians did not. In fact, Lehigh University was embroiled at that time in a court case, charged with denying tenure to a female mathematics professor because of alleged sex discrimination. Half-time teaching in the all-male Mathematics Department of Muhlenberg College was my only option, until I accepted a simultaneous half-time position as Assistant to the Academic Dean at Allentown College of St. Francis de Sales.

When I entered college in 1961, Vassar was celebrating its 100th anniversary. Three years later, in the middle of a cornfield, the Order of St. Francis de Sales ceremoniously turned over the first spade of soil to found Allentown College. The Reverend Daniel Gambet was the first Academic Dean for a faculty of fourteen professors and 156 male students. When Father Gambet became President, Father Alexander Pocetto was the second Academic Dean, a position he held for fourteen years, until I became the third. Those two founding fathers are responsible for the remarkable growth and success of Allentown College of St. Francis de Sales, now a coeducational institution with 2,200 students enrolled on a beautiful 300-acre main campus and two satellite campuses. The faculty of approximately seventy full-time and 250 part-time members offer undergraduate and graduate degrees that ranked Allentown College in the top 20 percent of *US News and World Report's*

1995 academic quality rankings and No. 1 Best Value among regional liberal arts colleges in the Northern United States.

## The Traditional Course to the Position of Chief Academic Officer

My career path of faculty member, department chair, dean, and chief academic officer has been supported by professional activities appropriate to those roles, namely, publication of thirty-five articles in professional journals; fifty presentations at academic conferences; participation in Harvard University's Institute for Educational Management; reviews of books and software in numerous periodicals; leadership activities in professional and civic organizations; and service on state, regional, and national higher education accrediting and consultant bodies. However, without the encouragement, support, and opportunities that Drs. Gambet and Pocetto have given me, I would not have become the Chief Academic Officer of Allentown College.

## Support for Women Who Swim Against the Tide

I have been blessed with generous counsel and caring throughout my life. It is remarkable even to me that after the role models provided by my female Vassar mathematics professors and the nurturing support provided and sustained by my mother and sister, my significant career mentors have been male, my father being the most noteworthy. Few women in American higher education are so fortunate, and most have experienced gender discrimination, as documented by the large percentage of female students but small percentage of high-ranked teachers and administrators. Although my vocation is academic administration and teaching mathematics, my avocation is encouraging women and minorities to study mathematics and science and to pursue careers in those fields. During the last ten years, I have written successful grant proposals to the US Department of Education, the Pennsylvania Department of Education, the National Science Foundation, the Ben Franklin Advanced Technology Center, the American Chemical Society, the National Council of Teachers of Mathematics, and the Woodrow Wilson Foundation to fund in-service education for mathematics and science teachers, while informing them of strategies to promote equity in their classrooms. These activities, which brought over $1 million to Allentown College, fell outside my job description, but were stimulating and revitalizing for me.

## Women Chief Executive Officers of American and British Colleges and Universities

During the fall 1992 semester, I was a Visiting Scholar at Wolfson College, University of Cambridge, and a United Kingdom Fulbright Administrative Fellow at

La Sainte Union College of Higher Education in Southampton. During that three-month period, I interviewed women CEOs of English institutions of higher education, including the women who were then serving as heads of Oxbridge colleges. Although each visit was preceded by only a letter of introduction from the United Kingdom Fulbright Commission, my *curriculum vitae* and a brief cover letter explaining the purpose of the interview, in each case I was welcomed with warm hospitality. Contrary to American popular opinion concerning British restraint and formality, the interviewees were candid and personal. At the conclusion of each session, I invited the CEO to contribute a chapter to a collection of presidential profiles.

Encouraged by the cordial British reception, I repeated a similar procedure with women presidents of American colleges and universities. The result was a book published in 1996 by Phi Delta Kappa entitled *Against the Tide: The Career Paths of Women Leaders in American and British Higher Education*. Each of the twenty women CEOs' autobiographical essays addresses some or all of the following topics: personal background, educational background, career path, helps (such as mentors) and hindrances she has encountered, recruitment for her present position, scholarly activities, public activities, acquiring and developing her leadership style and skills, personal strengths, conflict management, stress, job satisfaction, and encouraging other women to pursue careers in higher education administration. Each author was given wide latitude in the content and format of her essay to maximize the reflection of her distinct personality and style. In short, she told her story 'in her own voice'.

The twenty distinguished women contributors include the first two female Vice-Chancellors of British universities, the founding President of a Cambridge college, and American presidents who have served concurrently as Chair of the Board of Directors of the most influential higher education organizations (such as the American Association for Higher Education and the American Association of State Colleges and Universities). Polarity between these American and British presidents is diminished by the fact that several of them have built and crossed trans-Atlantic bridges. The epitome is Dr. Paula Brownlee whose American mother and English father sent her to Somerville College, Oxford, for her BA and MA degrees. After earning a DPhil. in organic chemistry at Oxford under the guidance of the famed Nobel Prize winning chemist Dorothy Crowfoot Hodgkin, Dr. Brownlee completed a post-doctoral fellowship at the University of Rochester. She subsequently assumed the posts of tenured faculty member, Dean of the Faculty, and President of American colleges. Having received honorary degrees from fourteen American colleges, British-born Dr. Brownlee draws upon her bicultural background in her current position of President of the Association of American Colleges and Universities.

### Women in Higher Education in the United States as Students, Faculty Members, and Administrators

Before moving from the specific case study of one female American chief academic officer to a research study of all female CAOs of American colleges and universities, a review of the status of women students, faculty members, and administrators seems appropriate. Women are well represented as students in higher education in the United States. In 1993, they earned 59 per cent of all associate degrees, 54 per cent of all bachelor's degrees, 54 per cent of all master's degrees, and 38 per cent of all doctorates. In 1995, they comprised more than one-half (55 per cent) of all college students and almost three fifths (58 per cent) of those over 24 years of age (Knopp, 1995). Noting a steady long-term increase in those figures, one might be tempted to dust off the old cliché from the 1960s 'You've come a long way, baby!' But a more accurate observation might be 'You've got so far to go!'

The full-time faculty members standing in the front of those predominantly female classes in 1992 were primarily male (64 per cent), who comprised the majority of all academic ranks, especially those of highest status: full professors 82 per cent, associate professors 71 per cent, assistant professors 57 per cent, and instructors 53 per cent. And just as women's representation was greater at the lower full-time academic ranks, women comprised 50 per cent of all lecturers, who are usually employed part-time. In fact, of all female faculty employed by American colleges and universities, 41 per cent taught part-time, as compared with only 29 per cent of male faculty members. Women in the professoriate are found most frequently in the departments of nursing (98 per cent) and education (56 per cent), as contrasted with their paucity among engineering (6 per cent) and natural science faculty (23 per cent) (ibid.).

At most American institutions of higher education, faculty members who fail to earn tenure after a seven-year probationary period are removed from the faculty and face unemployment. Although 72 per cent of male faculty members had tenure in 1994–95, less than half (48 per cent) of all female faculty held tenured positions. It is also noteworthy that in 1994–95, the average salary of male faculty members exceeded that of female faculty members at each rank (for example, full professor: men $64,560, female $57,160; down to instructor: men $30,560, female $29,080) (ibid.).

While investigating the reasons why women comprise the majority of the student body but the minority of tenured, high-ranked faculty positions, it is appropriate to observe who is managing American colleges and universities. Although women were more likely to be employed in the administrative areas of external affairs and student services in 1994–95, only 27 per cent of those in executive positions were held by women. The College and University Personnel Association (CUPA) 1995 survey revealed that within each administrative category, women earned lower salaries and were employed at lower ranks than their male counterparts (ibid.).

## Women Presidents of American Colleges and Universities

The climate on American campuses appears to be chilly when measured by the figures stated above; however, the environment for women on campuses in the United States is warmer and more nurturing than in other academic settings around the globe. The progress of women in leadership roles in the US can be attributed to a large extent to the American Council on Education's (ACE) Office of Women in Higher Education (OWHE). OWHE's surveys of women college and university presidents highlight the following substantial gains over a twenty-year period ending in 1995:

- A total of 453 women, representing 16 per cent of all presidents, headed regionally accredited colleges and universities in 1995, compared with 148 (5 per cent) two decades before.
- Slightly less than half (48 per cent) of all women presidents were in public colleges and universities, which represented a dramatic change from 11 per cent in 1975 and 36 per cent in 1984.
- Of all women presidents in 1995, three in five were in four-year colleges and universities, and two in five in two-year institutions.
- Women presidents in 1995 were racially and ethnically diverse. Of the 453 women CEOs, 16 per cent were women of colour: thirty-nine were African American, twenty-four were Hispanic, seven were American Indians, and two were Asian American. These data represent a significant increase since 1985 when only 7 per cent of female presidents were women of colour.
- Women presidents in 1995 served in all sizes of colleges and universities: 71 per cent headed institutions with enrollments under 10,000, 22 per cent with enrollments between 3,000 and 10,000, and 7 per cent with enrollments over 10,000. (Touchton and Ingram, 1995)

The following table from *Women Presidents in US Colleges and Universities, A 1995 Higher Education Update* documents the steady increase in the percentages of women chief executive officers over the twenty-year period, 1975 to 1995.

*Table 4.1   Number of women chief executive officers at institutions for selected years between 1975–1995*

| Institutional Type | 1975 | 1984 | 1992 | 1995 |
|---|---|---|---|---|
| (as of) | (31/12/75) | (31/12/84) | (15/4/92) | (15/4/95) |
| **Private** | 132 | 182 | 184 | 237 |
| 4-Year | 98 | 134 | 154 | 199 |
| 2-Year | 34 | 48 | 30 | 38 |
| **Public** | 16 | 104 | 164 | 216 |
| 4-Year | 5 | 32 | 58 | 78 |
| 2-Year | 11 | 72 | 106 | 138 |
| **Total women CEOs** | 148 | 286 | 348 | 453 |
| **Total numbers of institutions** | 2500 | 2800 | 3000 | 2903 |
| **Percentage of women CEOs** | 6% | 10% | 12% | 16% |

*Source*: Touchton and Ingram, 1995

With respect to personal background, the 1985 ACE survey (Touchton, Shavlik and Davis, 1993) found the ages of the women presidents ranged from 36 to 73, with median age of 51. Graduates of women's colleges represented 40 per cent of the respondents, and 63 per cent of the women presidents of four-year independent institutions were alumnae of women's colleges. The highest degree earned by 1 per cent of the respondents was the bachelor's, 17 per cent master's, 62 per cent PhD, 16 per cent EdD, 3 per cent other professional degrees, and 1 per cent gave no response. Twenty-eight per cent of the respondents had length of service in higher education of sixteen to twenty years. Other professional backgrounds included participation in leadership development activities such as the ACE National Identification Program (37 per cent), ACE's National Forum (28 per cent), and Harvard University's Institute for Educational Management (15 per cent).

The majority of the women-president respondents (57 per cent) were highly satisfied with their jobs, 39 per cent were satisfied, and 3 per cent were only somewhat satisfied. When asked about their career plans for the next three to five years, the majority said they would most likely remain in their current jobs, with the most viable other option being another presidency (39 per cent). When the three ACE researchers compared male and female presidents in 1985, they found the two groups to be of approximately the same age, with similar educational backgrounds and career paths. However, a far higher percentage of lay male presidents (93 per cent) were married than lay female presidents (48 per cent), and women presidents had far higher divorce and separation rates. Although only approximately 25 per cent of married women in the United States worked outside the home in 1950, 44 per cent of the women presidents' mothers were in the labor force before their daughters were graduated from high school during that era. The authors remarked that the mothers of the women presidents 'seem to have served as early role models for career pursuit and achievement' (Touchton, Shavlik and Davis, 1993).

No similar comprehensive, longitudinal studies of women presidents of British universities and colleges exist, perhaps because there is no English counterpart of the ACE Office of Women in Higher Education, but more likely because so few women have held the top posts of President, Vice-Chancellor, Principal, or Mistress in Great Britain.

## Women Chief Academic Officers of American Colleges and Universities

In 1991 the author conducted a similar survey of the women chief academic officers (CAOs) of four-year colleges and universities that are recognized by the six US regional accrediting bodies. Sixteen per cent (235) of the 1,711 CAOs were women, and their response rate to the questionnaire was 85 per cent. The average age of the responding CAOs was 52 years, and 55 per cent were 46 to 55 years of age. Forty-nine per cent were married, 66 per cent received baccalaureate degrees from women's colleges, and the majority of the respondents' mothers (53 per cent) worked outside the home before the respondents were graduated from high school. The percentage holding master's degrees was 59 per cent and doctorates 93 per cent (namely PhDs 161, EdDs 22, DA 1, and DBA 1). Thirty-one per cent had been employed in higher education from sixteen to twenty years and an additional 31 per cent from twenty-one to twenty-five years. The highest percentage of respondents were chief academic officers at private institutions (72 per cent) and from institutions with full-time equivalent enrollments between 500 and 999 (29 per cent) as illustrated on the following graph.:

*Figure 4.1  Size of US institutions with female CAOs (student full-time equivalents)*

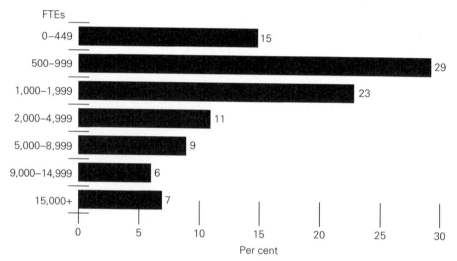

Fifteen per cent of the female CAOs were from doctoral-granting institutions, 33 per cent from comprehensive colleges, 48 per cent from liberal arts colleges, and 4 per cent from professional schools. Twelve per cent of their institutions were women's colleges. The professional development activities of the responding CAOs, like that of the women CEOs, included the American Council on Education's National Identification Program (37 per cent), ACE's Forum (21 per cent), and Harvard University's Institute for Educational Management (14 per cent). The responding female CAOs job satisfaction was very similar to that of the female CEOs, with 53 per cent of the CAOs were highly satisfied, 37 per cent were satisfied, 9 per cent somewhat satisfied, and 1 per cent were not satisfied.

Perhaps the similarity in the profiles of the women CAOs and CEOs can be attributed to the fact that the traditional career path of women presidents of American colleges and universities has been faculty member, department chair, dean, CAO, and finally CEO. Almost three-quarters of the female CEOs had risen to the position of President from other presidencies, vice presidencies, or other positions in academic affairs (Touchton, Shavlik and Davis, 1993). When asked about their plans for the next three to five years, the CAO respondents ordered their preferences to (1) remain in their current positions, (2) assume the presidency at another institution, (3) become the CAO at another institution, and (4) assume the presidency at their current institution.

## The American Council on Education's Office of Women in Higher Education

The ACE Office of Women in Higher Education, under the leadership of Donna Shavlik and Judith Touchton, has been a leading force in increasing the representation of women on the highest levels of college and university administration. The National Identification Program and ACE Fellows Program sponsor conferences at which female role models inform and encourage other women concerning positions of greater authority in higher education administration. On the state level, twelve other women and I comprise the Pennsylvania American Council on Education National Identification Program (NIP) Planning Committee which coordinates biennial conferences and forums for women in higher education. Both the national and state NIP programs provide professional development opportunities and serve as advocates in nominating women for leadership positions in colleges and universities.

In 1990, the first historic Women Presidents' Summit convened approximately 200 delegates, including two-thirds of the United States' women presidents and thirteen of the over 100 women who hold similar positions abroad. The two major purposes of the 1993 Women Presidents' Summit, also held in Washington, DC, were: 'To recognize the past achievements and future roles of women leaders, and to reframe major national and international issues in ways that place women at the center rather than on the periphery.' That important meeting, sponsored by the American Council on Education in cooperation with thirteen other presidential associations, brought together American and foreign women presidents to showcase their achievements and growing influence in the United States and throughout the world. The daunting goal of the 1993 Summit was 'to develop a blueprint for action . . . to guide women presidents worldwide in their efforts to insure that women's voices will be heard on issues of importance to our respective nations and the world', such as war and peace, economics and the environment, and the intersection of public and private life (ACE, 1993).

It is heartening for this author to envision women presidents from around the world joining forces to develop a new global agenda for peace and prosperity. The intelligence, integrity, and goodwill of the American and British presidents I have met give me hope that this mission can be accomplished. As affirmed in the ACE *Overview*, such an image of connectedness 'is conceptually, visually, intellectually, and bodily associated with life-giving force, a power philosophically and historically relegated to the private realm of women'.

### Note

Portions of this chapter were first published in *Against the Tide: Career Paths of Women Leaders in American and British Higher Education*, edited by Karen Doyle Walton (Bloomington, IN, USA: Phi Delta Kappa, 1996).

## References

AMERICAN COUNCIL ON EDUCATION (1993) *Overview of the 1993 Summit*, Washington, DC: ACE.

KNOPP, L. (1995) 'Women in higher education today: A mid-1990s profile', *Research Briefs*, **6**, 5. Washington, DC: American Council on Education.

TOUCHTON, J. and INGRAM, D. (1995) *Women Presidents in US Colleges and Universities: A 1995 Higher Education Update*, Washington, DC: American Council on Education, Office of Women in Higher Education.

TOUCHTON, J., SHAVLIK, D. and DAVIS, L. (1993) *Women in Presidencies: A Descriptive Study of Women College and University Presidents*, Washington, DC: American Council on Education.

# 5  A Malady of Leisure and Travel: The Autobiography of A Scholar

*Date of Birth: 28 July 1937*
**Dr Chryssi Inglessi**
Clinical Psychologist and Lecturer, University of Athens

When people asked my father about the family's plans for the education of their promising daughter he always replied that he considered a professional career detrimental to the femininity of a woman, and that he would not wish to see me in black stockings, wearing thick eyeglasses, on my way to spinsterhood. I was very young when this took place, perhaps 7 or 8-years-old, and the picture of the ugly, blackclad woman he was describing is still vivid in my mind. My father was an educated man, with a good knowledge of languages. An officer in the Greek army, he had been forced to resign after participating in an abortive, pro-Royalist military coup. This event, which marked his life and ours, took place long before his marriage to my mother, a woman twelve years younger than him, with modest education and a substantial dowry. The drama of their life together is intertwined with the history of our country. In the course of one decade Greece fought in a World War, suffered and came through a savage German Occupation (1940–44) and was rent apart by the tragic Civil War which followed. My father's civil career in publishing had declined drastically, as much from the collapse of all socioeconomic life, as from his repeated absences at the front to fight the wars, paradoxically, as an ex-officer of the Greek army. During those dark years an important part of my mother's dowry had to be sold for the survival of the family. These were the years of my childhood and early adolescence.

I have conflicting images of my father: as a valiant officer in uniform and riding boots, on his horse, leading his men to fight the enemy; as a dignified jobless man, in carefully polished shoes and pre-war suit; or, later on, as a man retreating from reality by immersing himself in his maps and dictionaries. My mother, a bright child/student, was brought up in a conservative family which did not believe in advanced schooling for girls. Disappointed to the core of her being, she accepted my father as the embodiment of her ideals on education, and became a serious, pragmatic wife and mother, responsible for the needs of those under her care. In the dismal and difficult years of the war and its aftermath my mother, despite these most unfavourable circumstances, made it her life's project to offer the best possible education to her only daughter.

But it was my father who initiated me into the magic of books. As a political exile in Italy and Paris in his youth, he had enjoyed the intellectual climate of the period between the wars. Nevertheless, his ideas on education for women remained traditional and patriarchal, as were all his values. With an intelligent female child on his hands, he short-circuited the apparent contradiction by imagining an 'encyclopaedic', that is unfocused, education for me. The emotional impact of his aphorism on the fatality of higher education and career to a woman's attractiveness has been with me ever since.

I spent my school years as an excellent student. Encouraged by my mother who participated actively in my education, I quickly arrived at the head of the class and stayed there until the last year of the lycée, a private school for girls only. My mother managed to find the money for the fees by sacrificing other important needs of the family. In the same manner, a professional teacher was hired to teach me English, a decision she took as a tribute to modernity, French having been a pre-war choice. Later, I won a scholarship which waived the fees, alleviating the stress on the family' s uncertain income. These distinctions were never viewed by my mother as my contribution to the family's strained finances but as a moral duty to myself and my parents. My 'job' was to make them proud or, at least, that was how I experienced it. As I write, I realize that at no time did my parents see my education as a means to an end, a qualification, a skill. It was a closed affair dedicated to acquiring knowledge, preferably never to be applied to any practical purpose. 'Knowledge' and my excelling in it were valued as an achievement that would bring me intellectual pleasure and secure a measure of prestige to a family whose status had suffered severely. As the popular saying goes, education for me would be the 'golden bracelet' to adorn my womanhood.

School ended with a jerk. Just before embarking on the last year, I suddenly fell in love, an event that took precedence over everything else. My grades plunged and only the inertia of my diligent years carried me through with a respectable B+. This outcome did not seem particularly important. However, it meant that my chances to pass university entrance examinations were reduced. Just a fleeting thought, as I was never really expected to try. I stood by, watching fellow-students who were less qualified go to university, feeling a numbness which I could not understand.

Anyway, I was in love. I stayed at home doing nothing, waiting for my boyfriend to finish his training abroad with an international company. Getting just any job was not proper for a middle class woman; furthermore, my parents argued, the family's economic recovery rendered it superfluous. I decided to enter the American College in Athens, sitting for the entrance examination which I passed successfully. I finished the junior year with excellent grades, getting a Fulbright Scholarship for the following year. For reasons I could not explain very well to myself, I refused it. Instead, I stayed home, did some baby sitting and waited. Shortly afterwards, I married my loved one and followed him to the Belgian Congo, to the despair of my parents.

Young, inexperienced and politically innocent, I arrived at Stanleyville to start my new life. I was cut off from everything I knew. I felt isolated, did not know how to cook, did not know how to live. Marriage was not fun and I was unhappy in the middle of nowhere. There were no books, no news, no telephone, scarce correspondence. To the great disappointment of my family back home, who had always fantasized an elegant existence for me, I got a job as a ground hostess at the Sabena airport. The news of my father's sudden death reached me ten days after the funeral. All that time, great things were happening just beyond my doorstep of which I was unaware. King Baudoin visited the capital, but we in the hinterland of the colony heard only the echo and the unrest. This visit was to sound the end of Belgian oppression in future Zaire. It was in front of my eyes that Patrice Lumumba arrived at Stanleyville airport, a proud young man in suit and tie, to speak to the black people; it was in front of me, a few days later that the whites carried him, in torn undershirt and trousers, hands and feet tied together, to throw him with a bump on the floor of the military plane which took him to Elisabethville, and his death. I still see his face, clenched jaws and yellow colour, and feel the trembling of my body at this violence. I was petrified but still not conscious of the immense political significance of the event. Next day in the Sabena van to the airport, driven by a friendly Congolese man, we were stopped in the middle of the jungle by hundreds of angry men and women who seemed to pour in from everywhere; I had never seen so many before. They stopped the van, beating at it with big palm branches, shouting 'Dependa', while we sat inside at the mercy of the crowd. I was very scared, but I trusted the driver. After a while the angry people made way for the van to pass. I resigned the next day, and soon afterwards I was evacuated together with other European women and children. My husband soon followed. Stanleyville, a tiny cluster of European houses, roofed in corrugated iron, formed the residential area where, with the exception of nightwatches and cooks working for a few European families, blacks were not allowed after 8pm. The main street, the only one paved with asphalt and lined with shops, started and ended abruptly at the edge of the buildings. Then, the dense tropical forest began. Our apartment was in one of those two storey buildings. During my husband's long absences in the interior, the only comforting sound was the clink-clink of the long sword worn by the nightwatchman making his rounds, in the deserted street. He slept on his prayer carpet, on my threshold. I loved this elderly man, though I never exchanged a word with him: neither of us knew the other's language.

Emotionally and culturally deprived of the things I had learned to value, I attended a few screenings organized by the club 'for whites only'. In 1958–60, the years of our stay in Stanleyville, la Nouvelle Vague in France created films, which, for reasons which are hard to explain, suddenly reached this far-off corner of the world. *Hiroshima, mon amour* was one; *Les Amants* was another. For me they were a revelation, for most viewers they were unintelligible. I remember the drone of the projector, the small screen, and the 'piloulou' insects flying in the light path. If one can say anything about the moment that triggers the process of consciousness-raising, I can say that it started just then, in that makeshift 'showgarden'. Today, it does not seem possible, that so much negation of black culture and denial of colonial oppression could have taken place, that we managed to go through it all and still maintain that criminal 'innocence'. Both my husband and I were products of a conformist, right-wing milieu, brought up in a country under heavy censorship, and encouraged to adhere to the officially propagated Americanization. While in Africa, we considered ourselves 'apolitical', a term I realized later, which carries an implicit allegiance to the status quo. I am ashamed of those years, where a humanistic alibi allowed us to feel so righteous, so superior to the cruel racism of other Whites. Doris Lessing confesses a similar distress about her keen interest, during her adolescence, in the names of flowers in Rhodesia.

My husband's next assignment was in Accra, Ghana. I followed. Nkrumah was in power and African-Americans were visiting the place in search of their roots and identity, as Maya Angelou taught me, decades later. But at the time, I knew nothing about that. What I did experience then was the sense of newly-won freedom of the Ghanaians, so different from the conditions of subjection in ex-Belgian Congo. Here, people acted with confidence and openness that most citizens have in their own country. We saw ourselves as visitors of an African state, not of a Belgian one which happened to be in Africa. I was pregnant. I felt sick all the time; the sweet smell of charcoal-grilled bananas at every street corner made me nauseous. Unlike in the Belgian Congo where Whites never mixed with Blacks, there was no special treatment for expatriates. I waited at the local hospital together with other Ghanaian women to be examined by the run-down British doctor, general physician-obstetrician, all in one. I did not share my fears or speak to the women, in spite of my utter solitude. I could not tell them that I was haemorrhaging and that I was afraid of losing the baby. There was still a gulf between us.

My husband and I used to take walks. My favourite spot was the university grounds, where the smell of the mowed lawns reminded me of Greece. I walked on the turf, but did not allow myself to think of the institution. At a coffee party with other white women, strangers, I spoke for the first time with nostalgia of how promising a young woman I had been ... After the birth of my daughter, I soon became pregnant again. I wanted to have children, I was happy with them. At the children's hospital, I met a strong Ghanaian woman doctor who diagnosed that my child had malaria. The disease had escaped her German colleague's attention; he thought I should force feed the waning child who had lost her appetite, to prove I was a good mother.

Then the family moved to Lagos, Nigeria. My husband was now director for West Africa. I was frustrated, but this time I made a lasting friend, a Greek woman my age, who was equally frustrated. The two of us decided to make something of all those empty hours. We ended up by exploring the possibility of going to the university! Today, thinking back on this decision, I have the feeling that if we dared to think of this transgression at all, it was because it was so alien to us, so unreal; for the same reason I think we stopped short in our efforts to have our documents sent from Greece, and deposited with the admissions office. Both our husbands were furious at the idea and used every argument to dissuade us. Bloody incidents were taking place, forerunners of the Biafra War, roadblocks with the Nigerian soldiers pointing machine-guns as they searched for arms were on every street corner, the situation was unstable. We knew the arguments and were used to the enforced immobility of white wives. My English neighbour took her daily exercise, walking round and round the garden, like a tiger in a cage. The hustle and bustle of the market, the mammy-lorries loaded with big colourfully dressed women, circulating freely, babies tied to their backs, were as distant from us as the inhabitants of another planet. They intimidated us by their sheer dynamism.

However, it was a deeper feeling of non-entitlement that made my friend and me let go of our barely formulated dream, and choose instead to organize our study at home. In the humid heat of the lagoon, we charted out chronologies: History, History of Art, Literature. We read and discussed within our walls, absorbing 'encyclopaedic' knowledge. For two or three years, whenever we were in Europe on leave, we bought the books and had them sent; back in Lagos, we planned our work schedule and studied. Modern odalisques in a hothouse. Until one day a corpse went floating down the lagoon in front of our garden, and a few nights later we woke in terror to see the yard full of men with torches, beating the servant next door, an alleged Biafran. Next morning there was blood everywhere, and I decided I did not want any more of this. Soon after, on my insistence, we left for the United States. I seized on my husband's dormant desire to 'one day get his Master's' and urged him to take a leave of absence from his company. I was growing up and wanted to take my life in my own hands.

In 1966, in Philadelphia, I finally got my chance to enter university, after sitting for the entrance examinations of the American Testing Service. Though I had a high score, I chose to take courses at the Master's level, again in history of art, an eminently impractical move. I knew we could only stay in the US for one academic year, too short for a degree. Still, I had challenged the prohibition and broken the doors. It was an enriching year for all of us; we all left home in the morning, dropping the children at school and nursery, and picking them up in the late afternoon. I was alive. Artists were challenging the status quo, universities were in an uproar, Black Power was on the rise, women's voices were being heard, I was transported. I had been in Lagos when J.F. Kennedy's assassination was announced on the radio, a bad thing, but without a context. I was with American friends to hear Bobby Kennedy's speech when, instead, his assassination was shown on television. The same painful realization took place when Martin Luther King was assassinated in Memphis; I was informed, I knew the tragic significance of these criminal acts. I was even relearning the history of my own country: the campus was full of posters urging students not to visit Greece, not to support the colonels' dictatorship.

In May 1968 my husband was sent to Paris and I went with him. After nearly ten years of confusion and numbness, I would live in the centre of a European metropolis. This time I could be a regular student and try for a degree. Now that my cherished dream had become possible, I vacillated. September came and my husband left for the United States for his final term; I was to accompany him. My mother was to come to Paris to stay with my daughters who had started school. This was not the first time that my mother replaced me. When it came to choosing between my children and a wife's duty, my husband always won. I was morose, talking to a new friend, explaining to her why my plans would have to be postponed till I came back from the States, when she said the magic word: Why? Why do you have to accompany him? Then there was light. I suddenly realized that I had never allowed myself to question my husband's priorities, never acted according to my own needs and wishes. In fact, for a long time, I did not even know I had needs and wishes. When I had persuaded my husband, back in Lagos, to take a leave of absence from his company, I was not even aware that I had encouraged and supported his plans for a degree as a means to obtaining the secondary goal of attending university myself. Such an endeavour would have come to nothing, had I allowed myself to conceive it as mine.

After the illuminating discussion with my friend in Paris, I entered into a feverish activity: I had my papers sent to Paris, I had them translated at the consulate, I sat for the examination in the French language, passed it and called my husband in the States to announce my decision: I would enrol at the Sorbonne to study psychology. He was flabbergasted. An hour later my mother called from Greece to find out why my husband had phoned to say that our marriage was crumbling. I told her I had decided to get a proper education and that no-one could make me change my decision. She said I was mad to think of studies at my age. I was 33 and adamant. The next day my mother arrived in Paris. My husband had implored her to do so, as he was certain that a lover was the real reason for my refusal to follow him. I was very angry at this interference. Still, I was a Greek daughter and I had to put up with it. It is clear now that I did not fight this battle since my priorities lay elsewhere. My mother stayed to chaperone me, and even offered help while I attended courses. To her, sexuality not study posed the threat.

It had taken so long, but I was finally at university. I had tried all the byroads, I had almost succeeded in remaining a housewife. But change was in the air and I was privileged to be part of it. The symbolic permission to transgress the boundaries set for a Greek daughter, wife and mother, had been given by my friend, a woman, and in the years to come, at moments of doubt, it would always be a woman who served this important function urging me on. Back in those days in Paris, I was exhilarated by my acts of daring, but also fearful since I had disobeyed the Word of the Father, who would not have let me enter the male domain. The immensity of this fear, I was to grasp much later, by helping other women find their way. At the time, repeated self-sabotage became the symptom of an internal turmoil, the significance of which lay hidden from me. The day I was to deposit my application form at the admissions office, I 'forgot' the file with all the painstakingly assembled documents, on a bench at the bus-stop. When I went running back for it, it was gone. I will never forget the numbness, the despair. I returned home like a sleepwalker. The miracle happened two days later when a man called to say he had found my file in the gutter, in another part of town. The gutter, was this not what my mother most feared, if I took a lover?

Those years in Paris were productive and exciting. I got my Licence but I still had a year for the Maitrise. My plans were suddenly interrupted with a promotion for my husband and a new appointment: we were sent to Beirut, Lebanon. Punishment, I thought, as I was desperately considering alternatives. I consented when I learned that the University of Lyon had an annexe there. I transferred papers and grades, moved the household, fixed an apartment for the nth time in my life, and prepared myself for the new existence. Conditions were satisfactory, the curriculum, professors, and examinations were closely controlled by the mother-institution, according to the French national standards.

Lebanon was a new territory with a new bloody confrontation for us to negotiate, psychologically and politically, as well as in the tasks of everyday life. The situation was very complex, but one thing was clear: nobody wanted the Palestinians. Their haunting presence in the camps, tin-cardboard ghettos in the middle of cosmopolitan Beirut, warned of bloodier days to come as desperation rose. An excruciating odour hovered over the camps owing to the total lack of sanitation and sewer, not to be avoided by anyone heading past them towards glittering international hotels with their swimming pools. It was a rite of passage, a price that had to be paid to the God of the pariahs. This time, we wanted to know, to understand the drama that was unfolding. The hospitable people of Beirut, Christians, Moslems and Palestinians, not the ones in the camps, but the few others who were participating in business and politics, became our friends. Ours was a split life, and a split consciousness. One moment we were enjoying the privileges of the expatriates, the next we were mourning the victims of explosions and worrying about the fate of friends who were disobeying the rules of the community to which they belonged. Our consciousness, like the city that hosted us, cleared the debris and went on. The remembrance of those friends is very sad, some are dead now, and in my nightmares catastrophe is cloaked in the shape of the Beirut landscape.

But this came later; at the beginning of our stay, things were not, as yet, too bad. My daughters were growing and adapting to the change, the new school and the new friends. Unlike me at their age, they were encouraged to be aware of the oppression and injustice that were around us. In the meantime, I did my Maitrise, and started training at the Psychiatric Hospital. I now dreamt of a PhD, impossible to get in Beirut. It was a difficult enterprise, which a few years earlier I would not have even entertained. Once more, I felt deceived by this fate which for years had made me run, breathless, after the vision of a higher education, and which forced me, because I was a woman, to choose between guilt and desire, between children and husband, between losing him to another woman and a degree. But now that I had started, there was no going back. For sixteen years my husband had announced each of his decisions, promotions and plans as a fait accompli, heedless of their repercussions on our lives and our relationship. It had been an affair of men, between the company and himself. Every time I was expected to be ready for the road, to play hostess, to entertain the wives of visiting executives.

The opposite was true regarding my own plan. I had to fight on all fronts. Not only did I have to fight a long and strenuous battle before he gave in, but I also had the additional burden of attending to the pressures of the family in Greece, who functioned as a reserve force to be summoned, in the name of marriage. It was exhausting, as at the same time I was trying to come to terms with myself on the issue of leaving my children behind. My guilt had to be silenced as well as my fears for the increasing risks my daughters ran in the embattled city. This tremendous shifting of priorities was shaking the very foundations of my being. Until now, conflicts had always been resolved, in reality papered over, within the framework of the Greek patriarchal family; now they had become impossible to negotiate. The heart of the matter was that I was fleeing the marriage which was suffocating me, though I was not conscious of it yet.

I left for Paris, by myself, in October 1974; I was 37-years-old. I had been accepted as a PhD student at the prestigious Ecole des Hautes Etudes. I felt elated, though I was very guilty, and worried. I worked hard. Life in Paris was exciting, the Quartier Latin was swarming with refugees, students from Chile and Argentina; Foucault, Lacan, Barthes were worshipped in their packed seminars. I went to meetings and participated actively in a women's collective. As the academic year was nearing its close, I passed the exams, and handed in my proposal for the thesis. I had to defend it in front of a jury. Among its members was a well known professor, whose book *On Death* had recently been published. When my turn came he was impolite and very negative; he wanted to know how I intended to fill the pages of a thesis on women's issues alone. His position was absurd, misogynistic, unfounded, but it paralyzed me. I could not hear anything else. Not the colleagues who said that his behaviour was directed at my professor; not the rest of the jury who ruled that the subject was good; not even my tutor who assured me of his confidence. I felt his words sounded the death knell for my project; the long dreaded punishment for defying all the prohibitions affecting my gender. Unconsciously, I abandoned my project there and then.

Twenty-two years later, teaching a postgraduate course in Athens University, I read the paper of a student on her mother's life, seen from the perspective of education for women in Greece. The paper contained the answer to my once-upon-a-time examiner/exterminator: it was a moving story of how the 1953 earthquake on a Greek island, though destructive, had at the same time marked the beginning of a new era in the emancipation of women. In her paper, my student showed very concretely how the opening of roads, electricity and telecommunications created the conditions which favoured the claim of her mother to higher education. Before the earthquake, this would have been impossible in a backward, isolated village. This had been the problematic of my failed thesis project: my hypothesis was that the earthquake of 1953, by destroying the physical, social and economic environment, had precipitated the modernization process on this same Greek island. My research would have traced what happened to the women of the small village X, after the collapse of the centuries-old structures. At the time, I had ethnographic material from the village, I had access to the archives, and had located the families who had left for Athens.

My daughters, who had stayed in Beirut with their father, had suffered during my absence. I had spent the major holidays with them, but this absence had been different, even though they had since early childhood accepted my studies as an integral part of our family life and had learned to value them for my sake. I met them in Athens. An important period was starting, so charged with events that it is not easy to see clearly their succession. The situation in Lebanon had deteriorated severely, making staying there a dangerous enterprise. Furthermore, I had had my share of trotting the globe, and like Odysseus, I was ready for the return home; my trip had lasted seventeen years. My husband accepted this decision, and made arrangements that would enable him to follow later; we knew that the relationship was disintegrating.

In Athens I found a job and, a few months later, I moved out of our house, taking my daughters with me. These changes did not happen immediately, nor without psychological stress. I had to fight with the great family, create a new social space for myself, and I had to build up a career from scratch. Having been away for so long, I had lost contact with people of my generation, my one-time friends and acquaintances. This was the first time I had to work for a living. The process of becoming independent was painful, but invigorating. Great changes were underway in Greece after the fall of the military dictatorship. There was an air of freedom, of opening-up, of hope. The second wave of feminism reached the country forcefully, though with a delay. Women were more confident, consciousness-raising groups were forming, periodicals published, important feminist texts translated. The conditions were favourable. In Paris, I had seen an analyst in order to work out my personal impasses, as well as the problems of the relationship. Now, the wish to end the marriage had matured and it seems that it had become possible only on my return to my country.

I fought hard for my divorce. The family was agitated, the children were very unhappy, my husband morally and psychologically violent. My mother came down with an ulcer; her worst fears had come true and I would now be exposed to the temptation of taking a lover. I stood my ground in those troubled times, feeling very guilty for the sorrow I was causing to the persons I loved so much. Family law was not to be reformed for a decade to come. We separated under the Napoleonic legislation bequeathed to Greece in the early nineteenth century, and for this reason, I was relieved to get the custody of my daughters; a monthly allocation was to meet all their expenses, although, after so many years of marriage, nothing was recognized as my due. I had finally come of age; I was 39-years-old. The strain had been immense, but I had got what I wanted. I did not realize then that I had sacrificed my PhD in the process. For years after, I still talked of the research, corresponded with my tutor, even visited Paris, in an effort to exorcise the spell that had befallen my thesis. I did not experience the whole affair in the terms I use today, but only as a difficulty to get down to it, to concentrate, to find time etc.

It took me ten more years before I braved the prohibition which my father as the embodiment of patriarchal law had set for me, and which, renewed by a man whom I had perceived as a punitive and malicious agent of the same law, had paralyzed all my efforts to enter male territory. I did my new PhD in Greece. But before that, many things had happened in my professional life.

My first job in Athens, at the Children's Hospital, owed much to my acquaintance with a well-known psychologist who introduced me to the Director, and asked me to assist with consultations. At the end of the six months, she entrusted me with her own senior position at the hospital, as well as with her private practice. I was to replace her for the whole period of a long leave of absence. My career was launched. This great opportunity, though temporary, gave me access to people and places which in the years to come proved important to my professional development. I worked hard in those years as a clinical psychologist, both privately and in collaboration with institutions. I became involved in adult education programmes for women, organized by the YWCA in the Greater Athens area. My classes became topics of consciousness-raising for an avid audience of women who were bursting the oppressive boundaries of their existence in the euphoric atmosphere of the late 1970s. Their lives were in the grips of family and church, though the villages in question were only a few miles away from the capital. This job ran parallel to voluntary service at a counselling centre, put in place by a group of feminists who belonged politically to the left. In both cases, my exposure to different groups of women, from every walk of life, in the city and the villages, was an experience of learning and empowerment for me. I have reasons to think that it has also been important to the women.

By now, my daughters had left for their studies abroad and I was ready to embark upon my thesis. This time things went smoothly, even pleasurably. The committee who approved my proposal was composed of three women professors, the only feminists in the academy in 1985. I did the research in Athens though I spent several semesters at Harvard University in the US owing to a happy coincidence: my companion, a Harvard graduate, was to pursue his research there, while I worked in the library and attended seminars. It was as if the patriarchal gods were slumbering, their negligence allowing the daughter to trespass. At the Centre for Research on Women, in Wellesley College, I had the privilege of meeting with a woman director who accepted my application to join as a visiting research scholar: a title and an environment which I still value, and which gave me entrance to many an elitist institution in Cambridge, Massachusetts.

Armed with these attributes and with my thesis completed and submitted in Greece, I gave my career a new orientation: academic teaching. Now I am a member of the faculty of Athens University, striving for the legitimization of women's studies in a male-dominated institution. I am responsible for European Union (EU) joint university networks on gender and race discrimination. As a senior researcher I work on issues of discrimination of minorities in our education system. And as Director of a seminar on gender research, I study, together with other women scholars, our women's lives in Greece. I should add that I am also on the Editorial Board of the only scientific journal on gender in the country, founded by our collective ten years ago. Ultimately, it would seem that my professional and political engagements have come full circle, in the sense that they have met with all my past experiences, painful or otherwise.

In reality, the very content of my thesis was a reflection of my personal experience as well as that of the women I met as a psychologist in my practice: it was about the impasses, the confusions, and the inhibitions which run through our life stories, marring our successes, blunting our initiatives. My subjects were twenty-five feminist women with a university education. Their biographies, narrated to me, served as material for the analysis. Different as each story was, when juxtaposed to the others, they tended to reveal certain constant patterns which belied the romantic idea of an uninterrupted progression of life-plans, as expected of this talented, politically-aware population. The women had all been brilliant in their school-years; as young students their future looked promising, and their aspirations were high. Educationally, as well as professionally, however, the women did not advance in a straight line. A closer reading of the biographies showed that strange coincidences seemed to put an abrupt end to plans which were heavily invested in effort; it seemed that every time a new decision was taken it was because a different kind of priority had replaced the older one: an 'irresistible' love affair, a 'sudden' decision to marry, an 'unwanted' pregnancy, a change of orientation. Every time, it was as if the women had been caught unaware. At the time of our meeting, when the women told me their stories, years had passed after the actual events, but a strong sense of frustration still coloured their words of thwarted ambitions.

My reading brought into relief how the fabric of our individual lives is woven from the imperatives and prohibitions that determine our very femininity in the Greek patriarchal society. It is a double bind which inhibits our entering the territories of sexuality openly and with ease, and attenuates our commitment to higher education and a career, traditionally defined as male. Despite the process of modernization, at a symbolic level these areas still remain forbidden to women. Our inner conflicts arise from a 'false permissiveness', the same as that which determines our strategies of survival. The unaccounted for retreats and confusions that fill the pages of the women's stories are in fact psychosocial manoeuvres aimed at appeasing the fear of punishment for transgression. Caught between the permitted and the forbidden, women have had recourse to trade-off strategies in order to counterbalance their advance into forbidden territory. They may be seen as pledges of allegiance to the female destiny. The stories should be told the other way round: we do not stop our studies because we fall in love, because we get married, or have a baby: we do it in order to stifle a symbolically forbidden desire, a desire which is too threatening.

\* \* \* \* \*

A male Odysseus, I returned to Greece. In truth, however, like Penelope weaving the threads to her veil by day, by ruse, unweaving it by night, I still experience the prohibitions that have befallen my gender, and I simulate things 'feminine'. I often feel inhibited, confused and embittered, and I berate myself for it. Only rarely do

I recognize the symptoms of fear, which signal that I am defying boundaries. What I have accomplished, I never take for granted, never consider it absolutely mine, more a matter of chance than a lifelong struggle; I fight for my rights anew, by day, but mostly by night. Last night I dreamt a dream: *Penelope invited me to her country house. When I arrived, I saw with surprise that this was the place where I, too, had a country house. I told her so. 'Wait till I tell you the coincidence', she replied, 'Chryssi is also moving to a house here!' On the table lay a big bunch of keys, each hanging from a cotton thread, and all of them tied together with a cotton thread tightly wound/woven around them. The keys were small, suitcase keys and letterbox keys, like the one I use for my mail at the office in the University of Athens.*

Penelope is a colleague; she was forced to leave her birthplace, Istanbul, after the incidents of 1955 against Greeks. She fled with her family to a Northern European country and went through many an adventure before she could finish her studies. Three years ago she had an hysterectomy; last year she finally got her PhD. I see now, as I write the dream and explore the 'coincidence', that our respective biographies have more in common than I had ever conceived before: that furtive year in Paris, I suffered serious haemorrhages; after my aborted PhD, on my return to Greece, I had an hysterectomy. A bloody proof of femininity. (The abhorrent odour of the pariahs.) I suddenly realize that Istanbul in Greek is Constantinopolis, the city of Constantine; My father's name was Constantine.

# Part Two

# Reflections on Past Careers

GRADUATING IS A PAINFUL PROCESS

1994

# 6    A Lifetime of Learning

*Date of Birth: 18 September 1925*
**Professor Dorothy Wedderburn**
formerly Principal, Royal Holloway and Bedford New College,
University of London

Four years ago I attended a reunion of those of us who had gone up to Girton College, Cambridge, in October 1943 as 'freshers'. As we exchanged news about ourselves I was struck by how much the experiences of women graduates have changed. Very few of my generation had followed 'careers'. Most had entered the teaching profession for a few years; most had married quite soon, had children and had then given up regular work until their middle age. Yet those women were clever; they were highly selected. There were only 50,000 university undergraduates in the country just before the Second World War, the number of women among them was minuscule; and access to Oxford and Cambridge very competitive. But it is clear that even clever young women graduates did not expect to have careers in the forties and fifties. I was no exception. The story of how I came to follow the career I did, first as a university professor, and then, for ten years before my retirement at 65, as the first woman head of a mixed-sex higher education institution (to all intents and purposes, a university although part of a federal system) is at one level the story of the broadening of educational access to include both more people of working and lower middle class origin and also, of women. At another level it is a story of my personal response to these changing opportunities.

I was myself of working class origin. My father was a craftsman, a joiner and cabinet maker. My mother was born in rural Norfolk, left school at 13 and entered domestic service first locally, and then in London in the household of a Church of

England clergyman. She married my father at the age of 28 just before the First World War. I was the last of three children, born as a substitute for the oldest girl who died of rheumatic fever aged 13. The second child, my brother, was 10 when I was born. He became an important influence in my life. He was very clever and won a scholarship to Cambridge to read mathematics. In 1937 he went to Princeton to do research until the outbreak of the Second World War forced his return. After a significant contribution to the war effort as a statistician, he became an academic and gained an international reputation. It was he who supported me when I showed signs of wanting to go to university. He became my yardstick of intellectual achievement.

In our family it was my father, not my mother, who was the parent who valued education, not least because he never forgot that the poverty of his own family had denied him an opportunity to go to grammar school. I well remember that when I was sitting entrance examinations for Oxford or Cambridge, my mother asked, 'What is the use of her going to college — she will only get married?'. My father's response was terse, 'Her brother had the opportunity — so should she', and this was despite the fact that it would delay the possibility of me making a much needed financial contribution to the household income.

Before the Second World War, access to grammar school education was selective. Having passed the examination, I entered an all girls' school in East London. After three happy years, war broke out and we were all evacuated to the Midlands. Looking back now, I am astounded at how we managed to acquire a decent education. We were sent to live with families of diverse origins. I lived with a Dutch family. They owned a local leather factory, and employed a German maid. It would be difficult to imagine a greater contrast with my own family circumstances. The school shared the buildings and sports ground with the local high school. Lessons in the morning were delivered in the run-down home of the local YMCA. School buildings with laboratories and library were only available in the afternoon. Our teachers (all unmarried) became very close to us, although I cannot say that any one of them became a role model for me. We returned to London just as we embarked on our entrance examinations for university. Two of us from my year were successful (our names are still there on the honours board in the London school) and a number of others went to teacher training college. I had been offered places at both Oxford and Cambridge, but chose the latter largely because that was my brother's university and his wife had actually been a student at Girton which was to become my college.

Cambridge was a confusing experience. From the point of view of women it was hostile. We were clearly segregated as far as the colleges were concerned. In 1943 there were only two colleges which admitted women and all the fellowship of those two was female. I was reading economics. Lectures were provided on a university-wide basis. In other subjects there were a few women lecturers but there was only one woman in the economics faculty (although the fact that she was Joan Robinson made up for a lot). On the other hand from 1943 to 1945 male undergraduates were thin on the ground because so many were doing war service. It was thus easier for women to attain position of prominence in university societies.

However, on reflection, I do not think it was my femaleness that made me feel an outsider. Rather, it was my class background. There was only a handful of other working class (or even lower middle class) girls at Girton and we found the articulateness and apparent self-assurance of our fellows, from Roedean and Cheltenham Ladies College, quite overwhelming. Another factor, however, which contributed to the sense of not 'belonging' (although less in 1943 than a few years later) was my membership of the Communist Party. I joined as soon as I arrived in Cambridge, probably in part, once again, the result of sibling influence. In retrospect I see that the Party provided a remarkable training for women.

Among intellectuals, and in the atmosphere of war time, I was not aware of any gender discrimination. It was important to be a good student, and in order to win support for Party policy members were encouraged to be active in other student bodies, to participate in political debates and discussions and to provide efficient organizational skills. Thus I soon became 'noticeable' among my contemporaries. At the same time Communists were always a minority group and were always regarded with some suspicion, which of course grew after 1945 when the 'cold war' developed. At the end of three years when I graduated, these conflicting influences and experiences left me with much self doubt. On the one hand I knew I had done well to get to Cambridge and to win the scholarships I needed to pay my way. Yet I had 'only' got an Upper Second Class Degree and I retained a sneaking feeling that it was all a mistake and at some point I would be 'found out'.

Graduation in 1946 also found me with no clear idea of what I wanted to do. An academic career never crossed my mind. I cared deeply about finding a socially useful niche, and a Labour Government had just been elected in an almost euphoric atmosphere. There was a widespread desire never to return to the pre-war evils of poverty and unemployment, but to lay the foundation of a more socially just society. I decided, therefore, that it would be good to become part of government and to join the Civil Service in that division of the Board of Trade concerned with developing policy for the redistribution of industry which, in turn, was part of a strategy for achieving full employment. At this time I married a contemporary from Cambridge, still serving in the Royal Air Force. Two years later he was demobilized and naturally returned to Cambridge to finish his degree. Just as naturally I assumed I would go with him, and eventually found that I could transfer to the Board of Trade Regional Office in Cambridge, but in a research, rather than an administrative, role. I enjoyed this work. I also renewed contacts with Cambridge economists and was soon approached about taking a job in a newly-established Applied Economics Research Institute in the Economics Faculty. I jumped at the chance. At the same time I began to teach undergraduates, part-time, on the one-to-one system of supervision for which Oxbridge has become famous. Although I was scarcely aware of it, my career as an academic had started.

Over the next two or three years my aspirations crystallized. I decided I wished to become a full university lecturer but it never occurred to me to apply for posts that would take me away from my husband. Apart from any other considerations I assumed I would have children and, when I did, I would give up working, at least for a time. So I remained as a research officer, although I was slowly promoted through the research hierarchy and it was here that I encountered my first and only overt example of discrimination. A senior slot in the department was to be filled. There were two strong candidates of whom I was one. We both had good publication records and were both initiating research programmes. But the appointments committee was swayed by the argument that I was married to a Cambridge don and would therefore be most unlikely to move away to take another job. When I heard this, my indignation was great and my protests made the committee reconsider their decision in my favour and so I became a senior research officer. But those who had argued that I would be tied to my husband were right in their judgment. For in 1965 when he had accepted a chair at the University of London, I moved to a full lectureship at Imperial College of Science and Technology.

Throughout this period, even after leaving the Communist Party, I remained politically engaged with the 'left'. Disillusionment with the Soviet Union had not (and still has not) weakened my belief that it is possible to combine greater democracy with greater social justice and harmony. I joined the Labour Party. In the sixties most of my energies were devoted to the peace movement, and in particular to the Campaign for Nuclear Disarmament, then at the peak of its influence. The need to engage with the scientific arguments around nuclear weaponry revived my interest in the way in which science policy was structured and developed in the cold war world. Moreover, the gulf between the 'two cultures' as described by C P Snow had always fascinated me. So the offer of a post at Imperial College, an institution almost exclusively concerned with teaching and research in the engineering and science disciplines, was intriguing. A few influential members among the senior academic staff had formed the view that Imperial students would benefit from a better understanding of the economic and social context at both macro and micro level, in which they would be applying their knowledge. They had succeeded in persuading the College that a lectureship in economics and industrial sociology should be created (initially to service the engineering departments) and it was to this lectureship that I was appointed.

In addition there were other attractions for me at Imperial. My research interests at Cambridge had initially focused on the economics of social policy generally and particularly on problems of ageing, poverty and inequality. But studies of unemployment and the process of redundancy had encouraged an interest in industrial organization. A year at the London School of Economics to study sociology, then not a subject recognized at Cambridge, had convinced me that the subject of economics, increasingly dominated by mathematical approaches, was moving further and further away from the 'real world'. I came to regard myself as an industrial sociologist. I embarked upon a major study of the way in which the technology of production systems influenced both management structures and workers' attitudes and behaviour. I had discovered that Joan Woodward, then a Reader in Industrial Sociology in the Management Science Group at Imperial, was herself working in this area and the idea of collaborating with her excited me.

In retrospect I understand how once again I had positioned myself as something of an outsider on two counts. The first was sex. When Joan Woodward was appointed to a chair of industrial sociology in 1970 at Imperial College she was only the second woman professor in the history of the institution. As for women undergraduates, there were only a handful. (The toilets were labelled 'staff', 'students' and 'women'.) The second count was in respect of my academic discipline. Although there were visionaries among the scientists and engineers who supported the activities of what became the Industrial Sociology Unit, there was also much hostility. So in addition to our teaching and research we were forced to assume the role of missionaries within the College, constantly fighting for a position, building a public presence and seeking opportunities to explain what we were about.

About this time my external public commitments began to multiply and my national and, indeed, international reputation was growing. Many visits were made to the United States to lecture and present papers on various aspects of social policy. I became a consultant to the Manpower and Social Affairs Directorate of the Office of European Cooperation and Development, and the work I was doing on technology and management organization led to involvement with major industrial companies including ICI and International Harvester, both as sites for my research but also as a consultant. These varied experiences were immensely valuable in introducing me to relationships in the non-academic world and to providing an understanding of the processes involved in the negotiation of consensus between groups with differing backgrounds and objectives.

But in 1971 Joan Woodward sadly died of cancer at the early age of 55. The period between her death and my own appointment to a chair in 1975 was not an easy one. Those in Imperial College who had always doubted the wisdom of supporting alien activities in the social sciences seized the opportunity to insist on a review of the Industrial Sociology Unit. Against this background of uncertainty the chair of industrial sociology was advertised and the two of us who emerged as front runners were both existing members of the Unit. In the end no appointment was made and to avoid, so it was said, making an invidious choice a senior lecturer was appointed as Head of Department, not a strong position when it came to matters like bids for resources, when all the other departments in the college were headed by professors whose powers were such that they were known as 'barons'. In the absence of clear leadership, conflict also emerged within the Unit of both a personal and intellectual kind. Moreover the spirit of '68 was still around with its emphasis upon democratic decision-making, carried to the point where it was thought possible to develop a research policy by voting. I was not good at handling this situation. Despite the fact that 1969–70 had been spent as a visiting professor at MIT where I had first encountered the concept of organization development, and where I had struck up a friendship (which has lasted) with Dick Beckhard, the idea that we, in Imperial College, were facing a change situation which required 'managing' did not occur to me. I made a number of mistakes which troubled me, although fortunately they did not prove fatal to the standing of the discipline and the activity at Imperial.

Indeed the climate was changing outside the College in such a way that the relevance of social science activities to science and technology became more apparent. Increasingly poor economic performance was linked to the shortcomings of British engineering education, and the handicap of the low status associated with the engineering profession. Proposals were developed to extend the length of engineering 'formation' and to broaden its scope to include elements of management. The Industrial Sociology Unit emerged as a key contributor to these changes in Imperial College. By this time I was the Head of the Unit, and as we expanded and embraced more activities we became a full-scale department, resulting in an increase in my administrative responsibilities. External appointments also continued to multiply rapidly. A key one was being appointed as a member of the council of the main government body controlling the distribution of research funds to the social sciences, where I served for six years. Two other major commitments emerged when I was appointed to membership of a government Royal Commission on the Distribution of Income and Wealth for four years and the Council of the Arbitration and Conciliation Service (from 1976–82), the national body concerned with the resolution of industrial conflict. I think a number of factors contributed to my selection for these appointments. The subject matter of both was central to my own research interests. But the fact that I was a woman was also influential. By this time it was very largely assumed that key public bodies should include at least one woman — the 'statutory woman'. Whatever the reasons, membership provided a fascinating experience of operating in a political arena.

By the end of the seventies I felt the need to take stock. It was clear that I was not going to have children. My second marriage had ended. Because of the demands of being Head of Department I was spending less and less time on my own research. I therefore jumped at an offer to spend a year on a sabbatical at the University of Oxford. I had no clear project other than the recharging of my intellectual batteries through access to good libraries and stimulating discussions with distinguished academics in my field. I was aware, however, that I was at a watershed. I was 55. If I was to change direction I needed to do so soon because I reckoned that it would take eight years or so in a new activity to achieve results. In 1979 and 1980 I had been approached about becoming the head of one or two single-sex women's Oxbridge colleges. But I was not attracted. The canvas appeared too restrictive. There was one other approach which initially I did not consider a starter but appeared more interesting as discussions continued. It was to become the head of a rather specialist institution, one of the colleges of the University of London, spanning the range of university disciplines in its teaching and research. I let my name go forward and to my great surprise was included in a final shortlist of two. But there I failed, for the selection committee felt that I would not be tough enough (and I think being a woman was a large part of the consideration here) to deal with the major financial problems which were beginning to confront the higher education system. In the light of subsequent developments there was a certain irony in this. It is possible to argue that in June 1981, when I was again approached, this time about becoming the Principal of Bedford College, University of London, the time was ripe for me to respond positively, which I did despite the fact that the Thatcher government had just announced a major cut in the grant for higher education, which was clearly going to create major problems. But I saw this as a challenge, and so 1 October 1981 saw me take up the new post.

Bedford College was undoubtedly an institution worth defending. It had been founded in 1849, the first institution to provide university education for women in the country, and had become part of the federal University of London, created in 1900. Although the teaching staff had always included men, the undergraduate body was single-sex until 1963. Many distinguished academics, men and women, had brought honour to the college over the years and its graduates were highly regarded. But it was ill-positioned to face the rigours of the 1980s. It was small (only 1800 students), it had a large number of departments which in many cases lacked a critical mass; its buildings had not been properly maintained and the lease on its buildings in a beautiful location in the middle of Regent's Park in London, had only twenty years to run.

As I walked up the stairs to my room on my first day at Bedford I remember thinking 'you have got to be prepared for a lot of unpopularity; the buck will stop with you in a way it has never done before'. How right I was. For when I learned the scale of the financial problems the College faced, I saw that survival as an independent institution was no longer possible. Fortunately a group of senior academics within the college had already contemplated this possibility and so we immediately became absorbed in exploring an institutional merger within the University of London. The questions were 'with whom should we merge and where?', 'how could we minimize the human cost to staff and students?', 'how could we maximize the benefits to create a new forward looking institution?'. Many of the colleges of London were also facing crises, but Bedford's difficulties were probably the most pressing. Speed was of the essence. After a number of false starts, by June 1982 we had agreed to merge with Royal Holloway College. It, too, had formerly been a women-only college. Its academic profile was complementary to that of Bedford and it was located on a beautiful freehold campus just outside of London with room to expand. But it was clear that a complete transfer of Bedford activities was necessary, so that to the task of merging academic departments was added the problems of selling the Regent's Park site and of financing and managing a major building programme.

The story of the merger process is a fascinating one. It presented a wide range of management tasks and called for diverse leadership skills. There were complex negotiations with government and the national authorities of higher education to be conducted. There was the need to win the support of the University of London. There was the academic challenge of developing a vision of what the new combined College could and should be aiming to become in the context of a rapidly changing society. There was the need, initially, to win over vociferous opponents who saw the decision to merge almost as vandalism; and there was the need to provide a sense of security and purpose to staff and students who experienced traumatic disruption. Communication became a major preoccupation. I initiated full staff and student meetings. I visited each department to discuss their problems and I made myself as available as I could to individuals themselves. There was always a tension between the need for speedy decisions and the need to provide a mutual understanding of the issues involved.

By the summer of 1985 the legal hurdles had been overcome. Royal Holloway and Bedford New College was born and I became Principal. But difficulties did not disappear overnight. Change was now endemic in the higher education system as a result of government policy and shortage of resources remained a perennial problem. Up to that point I had had little time to reflect upon my management style. I simply drew upon my relatively diverse previous experience, which certainly stood me in good stead. But now it seemed to me important to pay more attention to process, and to build more formally upon the teams which had emerged, whilst at the same time examining my own behaviour which often displayed impatience and, some might say, arrogance. I sought the help of an organization development consultant, a quite unusual innovation in British universities at that time. She proved immensely helpful. Our first task was to strengthen relationships and to clarify roles within the senior management ream. The second was to work with departmental heads to facilitate the formation and commitment to a medium-term academic strategy for the College. The third was to provide me with a sounding board, if only to make my job less lonely. I wish that I had initiated something along those lines earlier.

I retired in October 1990 at the age of 65. When I am asked whether I miss the job my answer is 'no'. It was very stressful, not least because I felt responsibility not only for the survival and success of the institution but also for the individuals, both staff and students who were involved. But if I am asked whether I enjoyed the nine years in which I did the job my answer is an emphatic 'yes'. I experienced the pleasure and exhilaration of working with a group of people who were not only generously supportive, but shared my ideals. The College which has emerged is a success. It now has over 5,000 students, having been able to expand as a result of changes in government policy towards participation in higher education. It is not free of financial worries because that is impossible in the current climate, but it has a wonderful campus, fine new buildings and, most important of all, its reputation for both teaching and research is growing, and the students love it.

Any career has to be understood in context. I lived through a period of immense change both in the higher education system itself, but also in attitudes to women, thanks to the achievements of the women's movement. To say that we still have far to go should not be to deny how far we, as women, have come.

# 7    A Flying Start

*Date of Birth: 22 March 1922*
**Professor Meg Stacey**
Professor Emeritus, University of Warwick

So here I am, a retired university professor. Would I write about how I negotiated the glass ceiling to become a manager in higher education, the editors asked me. Well, I think I know what they meant, but is that what I did? I have two problems: first, I don't recognize the glass ceiling. Second, I didn't set out to become a 'manager in higher education'. There were professors of various kinds in my youth and heads of departments, but managers were in industry and commerce. And anyway, I didn't set out to become a professor, although professors from afar seemed quite admirable. The image of the glass ceiling ('a barrier to personal advancement, especially of a woman or members of ethnic minorities', *Shorter Oxford Dictionary*, 1993) — which somewhere along the way and relatively recently in terms of my life time slipped into women's discussions — has never been evocative for me and still isn't (see Introduction to this volume for further discussion of the term). I don't know how to interpret it.

The image of a glass wall I used to use with beginning sociology students when trying to help them to understand that they had not chosen a soft option but a rigorous discipline. This sought to illustrate the teasing quality of sociology, namely that each of us has to be our own sociologist in order to live in the world at all, but that the discipline of sociology goes beyond common sense and requires the analysis of carefully collected data, of concepts and of theories. The image was of thinking one could see the way forward, walking along easily so long as one's homespun sociology applied, but bumping into an unnoticed glass wall through which there is a way but one that requires hard work and diligence to find. This is different from the idea of a glass ceiling. Ceilings are above the head. One does not bump into them (unless levitating). Ceilings are got above by going up stairs or elevators, often from outside the ceiling's room.

My vision was not of a world I could see going on above me but could not reach. My path through the world, which had no definite overall goal in material terms but some short term ones, seemed to be strewn with obstacles, some of them unreasonable and deliberately obstructive; some of them I had been insufficiently attentive to notice and get around; others I had simply not worked hard enough to overcome. Nor was it a question of being in a hierarchical organization and being unable to ascend the hierarchies. It was more about being admitted at all. With hindsight I would say yes, it was a man's world, 'a world I never made', to quote Barbara Wootton. Men may have put the unreasonable obstacles there in the first place (unconsciously or consciously) but all too often (which confused the issue), they were presented by women. This I later came to understand as being to do with the nature of oppression and how we pass it on to our daughters — and to women in general.

This man's world was going on all around me; the obstacles were all around me too. (But there were also helpers, women and men, around, as the following narrative will show.) The things that were going on in the part of the man's world which I could not see — and therefore found hard to deal with — were by definition not visible. No glass about it: opaqueness. When the obstacles are in legislation, in contracts, in rules, they can be known and seen, but the obstacles I'm talking about were often invisible, many of the 'not dones', for example, only discovered when one tried to do them. Nor can a woman see the work place in which she is not being promoted as a free-standing hierarchical organization. For it is not. The male bosses at the top also have mothers and wives and daughters and think about work women as they do about house women. And this they make plain. Obstacles on the domestic front are linked in innumerable ways with obstacles on the work front. There's no one 'glass ceiling'.


### Career? What Career?

Someone not seen or spoken to for twenty or thirty or more years whom I had telephoned for advice, with temerity since he was older than me and an acknowledged authority, said 'yes, of course I remember you; you've had a distinguished career'. Well, yes, I suppose one can talk about a career looking backwards, but looking forwards is another matter. I do not see myself as having deliberately built a career, or even having mapped out a life path I would like to follow. There were glimpses of things I might like to do if I got a chance. Some of these came about, but not from any real planning on my part. There were things I wanted to do and other things I felt women, including me, should be able to do if we wanted to but were prevented from doing because they were reserved for men. The shake-up of the war, when once again women were doing 'men's jobs' as they had in my parents' war, led me to a false sense that we women had arrived, that the barriers were down, the doors open. All we needed was the courage and determination to walk through. But still I did not plan a career. I just assumed I would have a family and have a job too. I had ideas at the back of my head about things I might like to do, so if/when an occasion arose I was able to seize it 'by the forelock'. The earlier training 'not for people like us' (discussed below) was thus far overcome, but not so far that deliberate career plotting took place. My life might look now like having had a career, but it has been much more a series of happenings built out of solving (or not solving) the immediate problems, overcoming the immediately presenting obstacles (or not overcoming them) as well as one might; built also from hanging on to what one had that seemed valuable and not to be sacrificed.

In what follows I shall set all this out in more detail covering influences from home, school, war, the London School of Economics, paid work in factories, shops and at Oxford; a decade of unpaid work; the sociology explosion which opened the doors to paid academic work; the links between private concerns and academic research; and finally being elected to a chair.

### Marriage or Career?

The need to make a choice between getting married and having a career, or a regular sort of responsible job outside the home, was a concept and a practicality I grew up with, exemplified by the teachers in my independent girls' school, all of whom were spinsters. Many of them, us girls believed — possibly correctly — had lost their fianceés or boy friends in the massacre that was the First World War (confirmed in Carden et al., 1996, p. 67). My father had come back from the trenches and married my mother, who then ceased to be a teacher and became a full-time wife and mother. She did not take up her profession again until the Second World War, and then only under strong encouragement from her local education authority desperate for replacements for the men who had gone to war as their fathers before them had.

There were other influences on my young life besides the war-time suspension of norms which can be called upon to account for a life path which has left me now as an emeritus professor. My parents were caught up in various ways in the restiveness and the social transformations of the early years of the twentieth century. Among the new (for them) ideas which they espoused were feminism and Christian Science, the latter being the foundation of a nineteenth century American mystic and feminist, Mary Baker Eddy. As a practising adherent of that sect I learned something of what it is to be a member of a despised minority. But I learned also some ways in which feminism could be practised. To start with I was not troubled by the image of God the Father, although that was purveyed in my school. We learned of an imageless Father-Mother God. This was reflected in church services. These were taken, not by a priest or minister, but by two 'readers', always a woman and a man equally sharing the activities. This equal sharing, however, did not extend to my parents: my mother's diffidence held her back from ever (to my knowledge) moving into office.

My daily family model was that of a father who went out to earn the money and a mother who stayed home and looked after the house and my sister and me. When things got difficult in our upbringing (when we rebelled or misbehaved, for example) the absent father was invoked as the authority figure. For an inter-war father ours played an active domestic role not confined to traditional 'men's jobs' such as bringing in the coal. He certainly did nothing approaching half the house-work, but was found in the kitchen and helping in other ways. He did not expect to be waited on. He also taught me overtly that women were now learning and able to do all the things that in the past only men had done. He furthermore believed that the men should 'look out' because the women would overtake them if men did not change their ways. (As I write government concern is being expressed about the better performance of girls than boys in secondary schools.)

Both active feminists before the First World War, my father was a suffragette and my mother a suffragist. He took direct action: I particularly cherish the story of how he cut the telegraph wires on Hampstead Heath one night, subsequently burying the shears he had used in my (very proper) maternal grandmother's garden, without her knowledge of course. (She totally disapproved of him as a suitor for my mother's hand.) My mother supported him but did not herself feel it right to undertake law-breaking activity. She did, however, wait outside meetings to receive him when he was thrown (physically) out of the halls where he with others had been systematically disrupting the meeting. Furthermore she, who had a good voice, joined with other women outside Holloway prison singing as loudly as possible that their support might reach the ears of the imprisoned women as well as swelling the demand for the vote.

Given this background of home, church and school, a conviction grew that an important next step for women was to liberate ourselves from the forced choice between marriage and family on the one hand and a career on the other. This was a collective view among my school mates, although I have only recently realized this (ibid.). Now we had the vote this was a freedom to be claimed. During my school days in many occupations a woman had to resign on marriage: the choice between career and marriage was not only customary but enforced by law or contract in the civil service and elsewhere. I wanted to have children — it seemed part of what being a woman was about — but I did not want to be confined to the house as my mother had been. It was having an outside occupation rather than a career as such which was a goal.

During my last year at school, the first year of the war when I was 17–18, I was living with my sister in a billet in Ashtead, Surrey where our London school had been evacuated. Around that time I remember thinking about the disadvantages of what I later learned to call the 'nuclear family'. My sense (from experience) was that a small family was somewhat suffocating for the children and, I reflected, for the mother too. This led me to think of alternative child-rearing arrangements, but also that in the 'nuclear family' more than two children would be better — more room for give and take, a wider range of people to interact with. There seemed an intensity about a small family which was constraining — larger numbers might somehow 'take the heat off'. A school friend's family of five, which I loved to visit, played a significant part in this vision. I concluded for similar reasons that nursery schools were a good idea; not, as in those days sometimes painted, a way for mothers to abrogate their responsibilities, but a way of enriching the life of children and their mothers (house-husband or -father did not form part of my speculations).

Let me not cast the impression that mine was an unhappy childhood or home life. What in adolescence, and earlier but less articulately, I felt as oppression was the flip side of a loving security. My parents could be relied on to be supportive and helpful as far as they could. Their feminism led them to seek out for us two girls an education 'as good as a boy's'. They found the City of London School for Girls, a late nineteenth century foundation. The school song affirmed that we were:

> Women of England, the half of the nation
> Here the full share of our birthright we claim
> Learning to conquer by willing oblation
> Half of the burden and half of the fame.
> Here to the service of England we bind us
> Vow to live loyal and gallant and free
> True to the line of the ages behind us
> Daughters and mothers of England to be! (quoted in ibid. facing p. 49)

Confused, triumphalist, imperialist, even jingoistic it may have been (and, as I recently discovered, written by a man), but it left no doubt about a mission to claim our rights — and the need to do so. For most women celibacy or motherhood were still the choices, except for a few of the well-to-do. Others may have heard the song differently; for me it reinforced the feminist messages from home.

From my mother came the drive to do well at school — also to do all tasks methodically and thoroughly and always to have regard for others. Her teaching in care and thoroughness I remain grateful for. However I was glad when I began to take school subjects she had never taken so that her insistent detailed supervision of my homework was inevitably restricted. My father's encouragement was to a wider vision, to being adventurous and claiming space, but also to recognizing suffering and doing what one could to alleviate it. He tried to establish his small printing works as a profit-sharing cooperative enterprise and was sad that the workers were not keen to go along with his plans: the not-surprising stumbling block was the risk-sharing. Security in loving parents there was, but not financial security. The 1930s were hard times: the great depression threw many into poverty. We were no exception, although we started from a better base than most workers. Those were the days of the hunger marchers and the means test. My father's business ran into trouble; my mother was recruited to help which she did loyally. We came home from school to an empty house and were left tasks to perform, starting the supper or washing the kitchen floor.

My parents' backgrounds were quite different and partly derived from this I felt (rather than heard) contradictory messages. My father (the fifth of seven children) came from a once wealthy northern industrialist family which fell into poverty during his childhood. His mother was an émigreé from a minor aristocratic central European family. He went to state school and was of that generation which was privileged to be able to leave school at 12 instead of 13 if they passed the relevant examination. He passed and went out to work. Such further education as he had he got by attending evening classes at Owen's College (now the University of Manchester). In contrast, my mother was brought up in a modest but respectable late Victorian house in a suburban development in North London. My grandfather, so far as I knew (he died three months before I was born), was a small business-man. All four of the children were diligent at school and upwardly mobile. The elder son became a free church minister in Eastern Canada; the second an inspector of taxes; my mother, their third child, went to Southfields Methodist College to train as a teacher; her younger sister trained similarly. This sister never married, lived with my grandmother until she died in her nineties; as well as primary school teaching, she ran the Methodist Sunday School.

A boast of my mother's family was that they never went through a meal but someone got up to consult the dictionary or the encyclopaedia. It all seemed very solidly English lower middle class: its underlying perils were that my grandmother was born German (something she hid well including from us) and could barely read or write. In this background my mother learned the importance of the 'proper' and that 'people like us don't do things like that' — all those messages associated with status maintenance and status striving — a tendency too to believe in the printed word, in authority. These messages she passed to us. Somehow I acquired a sense that 'people like us', literate though we were, readers and careful of our grammar, don't write books. And yet, there on the bottom shelf of the book case were books written by my great uncle (my father's uncle) Frederick (or Fritz as we knew him) of the emigreé generation, who had been a professor at Harvard, they said. The messages about 'getting on' and 'staying in line' were contradictory.

After a year or two at the City I had won an internal scholarship without which our parents would not have been able to keep us there. My maintenance grant covered my sister's fees and our parents pinched for the maintenance. There were real shortages: I know that my father often brought home from the printing works less than he paid the workers. As the war approached things got worse: nor, unlike the experiences of some, did they improve during the war. While I was away during the war my parents moved house — from financial necessity I guess — first moving in with my maternal grandmother and then into a (probably rented) house not far away. This just seemed part of the whole unstable world that was the war — not bombed out as many were — but uprooted just the same.

## War: Transition to the LSE

In 1939 the school was evacuated; the headmistress (whom I admired greatly) seemed to rely heavily on me as headgirl to help with the general welfare of the girls; some of the teachers, one in particular, seemed demoralized. Quite often other tasks seemed more important than home work. Apart from one distinction I failed my higher school certificate. Meanwhile, my sister did well in her general school certificate. She recalls she experienced insufficient rejoicing because of general concern about her older sister's disaster. Nevertheless I was admitted to the London School of Economics (LSE), I suppose on past performance and the strong support of my teachers. I had matriculated, the technically crucial thing. The greatest good fortune I had was being interviewed by Norah Anstey as admitting dean; she was one of the few women on the LSE staff then. She asked me what I wanted to read. I replied that I intended to take the Social Science Certificate to become a social worker. She told me in effect and to my astonishment that I was too good for that and I should read for a degree. That was the beginning of my becoming a sociologist.

Why social work? I had been active in the school's missionary work (no, not in 'darkest Africa' but with the poor of London through the Union of Girls' Schools and the Settlement Movement). Around about 1938, helping at a Christmas party for poor children in South-east London, I had been appalled by the poverty. It was a bitterly cold day; the little children were wearing only worn cotton frocks — in layers. In the holidays in 1939 I worked for the Invalid Children's Aid Association visiting people's homes to arrange for holidays for children who were disabled or had been ill. I stayed and worked a bit too in the Peckham Settlement (not to be confused with the Peckham experiment, which I also visited). My father's little works was in Hackney and helping him there I saw quite a bit of Hackney life but had not seen poverty of the kind the 'mission work' revealed. That's why I wanted to do social work: it seemed the only job on offer that might help alleviate the suffering. The choices available seemed to be to go to Oxford if one was good on the arts side — that was not me; to go to Cambridge if one excelled in the sciences; to go to a secretarial college if one was not academically outstanding, or to become a nurse. For a City girl to want to go to LSE was breaking new ground, no girl seemed to have been before. There were no really appropriate sixth-form subjects to take. Many City girls have trodden the path to LSE since.

### Secret Goals

While genuine, the motivation to relieve the suffering of poverty in others was only part of what drove my life course. From an early stage I had a barely recognized ambition to be 'the one up front'. I was frightened of acting and did not volunteer for parts in school plays. However, I do remember thinking, possibly in the first form, the first time I attended one of the rather grand annual prize givings (held in the City Boys' school hall, because ours was not big enough, and attended by the lord mayor and other dignitaries in full regalia) that it would be rather good to be the head girl and lead the three cheers (what/who were they for? I forget). So a little voice said 'I'd rather like to do that job'. Later when I learned about committees and commissions of enquiry and their famous chairmen (always men it seemed) which it was believed had improved the lot of the working class or corrected some injustice, the little voice said 'that's the sort of contribution I'd like to be able to make'.

Going to university was also something that, as a schoolgirl, I couldn't imagine doing. There were girls in school who knew that was what they were going to do. How did they know? Later I realized that many of them had professional fathers or mothers who knew the ropes, for whose families going to university was normal, even if formerly only for the men. When we were asked in class, probably in the fifth form, which of us wanted to go to university, I marvelled at those who put their hands up. My memory of my class at around that stage in school was of a block where most of the girls appeared very self-assured and came, I assumed, from more well-to-do families; a block where the London County Council scholars sat — they joined later than the fee-payers and had started their education in ordinary state schools. Not in either group, I felt at sea. Probably cross-cutting these groups were the girls who were good at sports and gym. That was not me. The only physical activity I really enjoyed was English folk dancing (Cecil Sharp model) which was taught after school by Miss Phipps, the chemistry mistress. Swimming was OK but I had no special prowess. Badminton in the school hall was just tolerable, but as for cricket and tennis . . .

Sometimes coming near or at the top of the class for academic work and sometimes falling flat on my face (there were days when I could do maths and got it nearly all right and days when the logic just wouldn't click — nothing in-between), I lacked self-assurance in that arena too, although almost every year I got a prize for 'general proficiency'. Where I stood in the crowd I had no idea. I often felt lonely. Maybe that's why I was happy to be mission monitor. When in 1939 at the end of the summer term one of the girls, with more 'savvy' than I, said I would be head girl next term, I was bewildered. Apparently none of those who seemed to me more likely candidates were staying on and I was judged obvious among those who were. It was a job I had once thought I'd like to do but never imagined myself doing. She was right however. Head girl I became as war broke out. That end-of-term party, when the leavers hung their school knickers out as flags from 'heaven' at the top of the school, was the last time I was ever to be in the old school again — we were then evacuated to Surrey.

I was staying on because I had decided to do 'Highers' (the certificate which preceded Advanced Levels) and perhaps go to university. A tourist visit to Girton College, led one summer holiday by my father, had made me feel that university was a reality. I recall the possibility entering my head as I slipped and sat down hard and sudden on a missed step in a well-polished corridor — the aroma of that pre-war institutional polish stays with me. I said nothing at the time to anyone. The whole drive of the school was to academic excellence and university was the goal. No doubt teachers had whispered to me that I might be 'university material', although I don't remember that. Sometime, around the end of my school career I guess, or during my LSE days — I don't really remember — my father said to me something like 'People will always call you out to be a leader'. I was astonished; I didn't believe him. Was it prophecy or encouraging a particular goal orientation?

### Going to LSE

LSE, when I went up, was evacuated to Cambridge, along with parts of (the late lamented) Bedford College (see Dorothy Wedderburn's chapter on its history). My memory of arriving in Cambridge is foggy. Maybe my father took me up in his little 1933 Austin 7. I don't remember. In a daze I (we) found Peterhouse where the administration was housed; found Grove House where the students' lending library and the students' union were — I joined some student societies at some point. Somehow I got allocated and into a billet, an absent doctor's house run by his wife and an Austrian or German refugee. The first night there the sirens sounded and we passed it in the empty ground floor surgery. The bombers seemed to go over for ever, no bombs on Cambridge then. Later we came to believe that that was when Coventry burned.

At LSE I found myself for the first time in a world not only where men were in dominant positions, but where one was in everyday contact with them — a stark contrast with life before LSE, at a girls' school with all women staff and a feminist home where three quarters of us were female and our closest contacts were with grandmother and aunt — no man there. All along I had been living in a man's world, but it was not very visible to me. Of course I knew there were certain things only a man might be found doing, like reading the news on the BBC or serving in a bank. And that in some places women were grossly under-represented compared with their talents and training, in orchestras, for example. The detailed control the City fathers retained over the highly-qualified and experienced women staff of the school has only been revealed to me recently in the school history (ibid.).

Students sharing the billet were all women. The contrast was also less stark than it might have been because so many of the men were away, both staff and students. As the pop song of the day warned us that they're either too young or too old, either too gray or too grassy green, the best are in the army — the rest will never harm me . . . A myth that last line. However.

Men students had their call-up deferred for a limited period, but unless unfit for active service were not able to complete their degrees. Women's conscription was deferred until they had completed. Some doubling up was done. For example, I took part of the Social Science Certificate along with my degree, not enough to actually get a certificate, but enough to be accepted by the relevant professional bodies. The deficit of British men students was a little bit made up by refugees who were not deemed safe for National Service; they were from time to time removed to the Isle of Man: Claus Moser was the outstanding example in my year.

Teaching was shared with the University of Cambridge. Lecturers were mostly men, although the social science teachers I had were three-quarters women. Joan Robinson, the economist, was an important example of the possible, stalking along Kings Parade in her distinctive black cloak. Suffrage notions had been written into the LSE Student Union constitution, so that there were to be two secretaries, one a woman and one a man. President and Vice-president were to be of opposite sex too. Elections were in February. I had hardly been at LSE, or so it seemed to me, when someone asked me, to my surprise, to stand for secretary. I agreed and was elected. Then I began to learn. It gradually dawned on my naive consciousness that somehow I was always staying at home doing the minutes and suchlike chores, while my male counterpart was the one who took the trips to interesting places. The notion began to develop from then on that power always lies behind another door than the one you've just got through. Later I learned what an infinite regress of doors that is. Nevertheless the formal egalitarian rule gave me opportunity, knowledge and experiences which I almost certainly would not otherwise have had; experiences like being dressed down on behalf of the Union by the Director on account of a march through the town; trying to lobby a totally unreceptive Conservative Member of Parliament about students interned in the Isle of Man.

In the event I think it was only on account of the war that I was able to go to LSE at all, for how it could have been afforded otherwise I'm unclear. The crucial difference was made by the £1 a week billeting allowance which we were paid because the School was evacuated to Cambridge and we could not live at home in London. On top of this I had a small award from the Middlesex County Council and various small scholarships which with the billeting allowance were enough to live on sparsely. Rationing was a help too — nobody was very well dressed (with a few exceptions). Because of the 'war effort' it was easy to get jobs in the vacation. This necessity I turned into a sort of field-work experience by insisting on registering as a manual worker (the Labour Exchange staff always tried to get me to join the clerical queue, but I refused, not without difficulty). I learned a lot. In British Oxygen the management had set up a special room for students who were to work from 8 to 5. My insistence that I wanted to do the hours of and work with the regular workers led to me working from 6am to 6pm or more, in a room full of women, all of us doing mechanical repetitive jobs like testing whether screw fitments actually fitted. It was just after Dunkirk.

A black-out blind factory of the fly-by-night kind taught me about exploitation and about the suspicion of those with education held by those without. The working conditions were poor; we pasted rough slats onto sheets of poor quality thick paper. There was no protective clothing; gum-dampened fingers handling rough wood soon split at the tips. I got on much better with the other women after some misadventure caused me to swear wholeheartedly. My accent and vocabulary had hitherto been quite offputting to them. In Marks and Spencer's I had difficulty in learning how to take long enough time when sent on an errand — to the store rooms for example — to avoid the censure of other assistants. In Woolworths I learned about the lip service paid to the Shops Act. Sitting on the legally compulsory seat (a tip-up hinged affair behind the counter) was enough to ensure that a supervisor turned up to point out that your counter needed tidying, albeit you had just done that. My maternal grandmother was horrified in her proper lower-middle-class way to think that I was working in Woolworths — of all places! She circled my counter one day leaning on the arm of my aunt; neither acknowledged me. Working in reception centres where the bombed-out were put up were experiences of a different kind, as was working in the air raid shelters in the East End for Father Grocer. It all put flesh and bones on the dry dust of lectures about class and status. I never had any money for books — they all had to come from or be read in the library. I did once win a prize which made it possible to buy two or three books. One year my father raised for me a grant for 'distressed gentlewomen' (!) of £20. Riches indeed!

Although not without its trials, and moving billets several times, being in Cambridge was wonderful: no daily tube travel and we had the best of both worlds — the freedom of LSE, being treated as adults (not 'gated', for example) and the more-or-less equality it offered to women and men — women then were still not full members of the University of Cambridge and not allowed in the Union.

### After LSE

In June of the third year I went back to London to my parents' house; no more billeting allowance. I was exhausted; since February when the Union officers changed so that I was no longer Vice-president, I had spent long hours catching up on all I hadn't read because of Union work. My most astonishing memory of that summer is of a friend ringing up to say I had a first: I had not gone back to Cambridge to find out for myself — no money. There was no question in my mind that now it was war work. I volunteered, when asked, for work in ROF 52 on the Firth of Clyde, west of Glasgow. Here I was a Labour Officer Grade III, working three shifts along with the workers who were making cordite and nitro-glycerine. This post derived from my original thoughts of becoming a social worker.

My intention in training for social work had been to help people overcome poverty. Three years of history, economics, sociology and politics had convinced me that the solutions lay elsewhere; they needed tackling systematically rather than piecemeal. As a personnel officer in ROF 52, the job was not to help people but to police the work force — or so it seemed to me. The problems the shop steward saw, which I could also see, were not the ones the Queen Bee (as we called the chief labour officer) saw. A grade III labour officer was in an intercalary position that I found very uncomfortable. It brought out all the conflicts that were inherent in my being and which I had derived from upbringing and schooling: authoritarian v. rebel; conformist v. unorthodox. In the ROF I felt greater commonality with the communist shop steward on my section than with the Queen Bee.

As 1943 turned into 1944 my thoughts turned to adult education. An LSE contemporary was working for Oxford University's Extramural Delegacy (as it was then called) with the WEA (Workers' Educational Association). So I went to talk to her and later 'applied for my release' from the war factory. Being of conscribable age I was not free to move. The Ministry of Education wanted me released; the Ministry of Labour did not. Neither did the Institute of Personnel Managers. I told the last two if I was made to stay until the end of the war I would not work as a personnel manager afterwards; I resigned from the Institute forthwith. Then suddenly the Ministry of Education won and I was free to move. Later I learned that it was a small network of friendly women who had effected that victory. My friend's mother was working in the Ministry of Labour at the time — she was a founder of the adult education movement — and had put a note on the relevant person's desk. That time a supportive woman turned out to be behind the closed door.

So I went to work for the University of Oxford in Banbury in the Bucks, Berks and Oxon district of the WEA. I took classes in Oxfordshire and North Bucks. The price of being released to a civilian job was that also one had to do forces education — the most daunting was to lecture to several hundred paraded soldiers who had their tin NAAFI cups in hand under their seats ready to rattle in unison when fed up. Lecturing on the British constitution was hardly a comedy show . . . What you didn't learn then, you never would, I reckon. Somehow I also taught social anthropology in Sussex — a long and tedious journey punctuated by enjoyable time spent on the way in the British Museum filling in the many gaps in my anthropological knowledge: Ginsberg had insisted we read some anthropology as part of sociology. In the almost complete absence of sociology in Oxford (total until John Mogey came) I went to social anthropology seminars.

In Banbury I was taking a class on a two-shift basis for the three-shift aluminium factory workers linked with the National Union of Municipal and General Workers. Part of what we were doing was to learn about Banbury. Meyer Fortes had at one time warned me that he might come to Banbury to do an anthropological study. He was at that time going through a phase of believing that it was possible to do anthropology in complex societies which were also one's own, an idea he went off later. I heard no more, but one day went to him and asked him whether he would mind if I did a study of Banbury. There, with the help of the WEA class, began the work which finally — years later — was published as *Tradition and Change* (Stacey, 1960).

In between those two events were two others crucial in the glass-ceiling-penetrating exercise. The first was getting a grant from the Nuffield Foundation for the Banbury study. Meyer had linked me up with Charles Kimber who had read for the Social Anthropology Diploma at Oxford. He was able to work on the survey without wages for he had some independent means. However, we needed more help. Applications for a grant came to nothing until one day I was informed that if I reapplied in my own name, linked with no-one else, there would be a much better chance of success. That I did and received a £2,000 grant — an extraordinary sum for those days. Shedding a man and applying as a young woman on your own may be unremarkable in these days, but was not so then. Charles continued to work with me — and did very valuable work. Everyone assumed he was the boss person; I had to work hard at a later stage to establish my undisputed directorial role.

The second event to note was how I rewrote *Tradition and Change*. There had appeared to be no one at Oxford to supervise the study, so the University of Birmingham took it on. When the writing-up was finally finished and submitted for vetting, the verdict was that the whole thing was no good. When I recovered enough, I asked whether this apparently total failure lay in the design or the execution of the research. 'In the design', came the reply. This astonished me; why in that case had they said nothing all those years? Why indeed had they accepted academic responsibility for a design they thought so utterly flawed? True, the supervisory personnel had changed over time. I became angry as I thought about it, and also convinced the work had value. No one had done such a study in England before. The criticisms had revealed to me faults in exposition and organization. I went home determined to rewrite and show 'em. *Tradition and Change* was accepted by Oxford University Press — thanks I'm sure to a favourable review from John Mogey; was reviewed in *The Times* — thanks to John Morgan, a journalist neighbour in Swansea; and was reviewed critically but at length by Ed Shils in the *British Journal of Sociology,* thus attracting the attention of the post-war generation of British sociologists. Through the constructive use of anger the glass ceiling was negotiated or, in an image I find more meaningful, I managed to get a door opened which had been slammed shut. And that's why *Tradition and Change* has no acknowledgment to Birmingham, nor a preface by a senior academic. But it became a classic in its day and was on most first-year sociology reading lists. That rejected and resurrected study played a major part in my being where I am now.

### Going to Swansea

After seven years at Oxford, first in the Extramural Delegacy and then divided between that and the Social Training Delegacy (training social workers) I was thinking it was high time I persuaded the University to accept my degree so that I could be a member and not just an employee of the University. At that point I left. Frank, my husband (we married in 1945), having returned from the war, and completed his MA and a BPhil, got a job in Swansea as an assistant lecturer. The war and its aftermath had been long enough so I went to Wales with him. According to Frank's report to me John Fulton, the Principal, had told the committee on his appointment something like 'Not only do we have a good man here, but his wife is an excellent academic in her own right'. Fulton had been on my employing body at Oxford. That heralded a decade without gainful employment, not even part-time.

It wasn't that I was without work; I was completing the Banbury study and beginning to acquire a family as well as running a home on an assistant lecturer's salary. But I felt isolated; the position of being a college wife who was also an academic (albeit unemployed) was a strange one. The Workers' Education Association didn't seem to want me, nor the extramural department; my experience counted for nothing. It was not so much that I was a woman, but a married woman and very shortly also a mother. Furthermore of course I was English and this was Wales and on the edge of Welsh Wales. The uncompleted Banbury work was given as a reason for keeping me out (of the Social Work Department when it got started up), but when the Banbury work was completed and acclaimed I was still kept out. The long arm of John Bowlby and his insistence that mothers stay with their small children at all times reached into South Wales (Bowlby, 1953). But this was also a place where a woman was stared at for wearing slacks and goggled at for driving a car. I believe that my children suffered because 'Mam' was not always 'in the kitchen cutting bread and butter' as Dylan Thomas had it. Nor did she wait on the boys hand and foot or pack her husband's bag for him when he went away.

Not so much up as out, was what I wanted. In Swansea the sense of being surrounded by obstacles (as opposed to a glass ceiling image) was clear. People who had the key to letting me out, letting me use my talents/training/education in a paid occupation were all around me. They were colleagues of my husband, husbands of my friends. There was nothing 'see through' about the obstacles. The faces were friendly but no keys to closed doors were offered. One time I was asked whether I'd like to do a bit of hospital social work by the Superintendent of the psychiatric hospital, but declined. I was, after all, a refugee from social work. Another time there was a survey I applied to direct and was turned down. My memory is that the interview had been more about what I would do with my family than it had been about my views on the proposed project. 'You couldn't have done it' said my potential boss's wife the next day, referring tacitly to my, by now, four children. I was employed to do some part-time interviewing for that survey. Then along came the Lower Swansea Valley Project and, Bowlby notwithstanding, I was called from a hitherto most hostile quarter to work on it. Enjoyable and interesting work it was too. In the absence of a sociologist I was supervised by the Principal, a historian, who was supportive when necessary but mostly left me to get on with it. Because I had children it was assumed appropriate to employ me part-time. Hard were the arguments to persuade my employers that because I had four children I needed a full-time job, without which I didn't have the money to replace enough of me in the home.

Finally came the sociology explosion of the sixties. With a male professor appointed to the new Sociology Department (no, I didn't apply), the intention seemed to be to leave those of us who were in research jobs to do just that and to draft in men from elsewhere. When that didn't work a younger man with no more qualifications than I was appointed. After several failed attempts to fill the second post I was offered the job. Other than having promptly applied for a lectureship, the only overt negotiation I did around that breakthrough was to keep the professor waiting for an answer as to whether I would take the post when finally it was offered. OK, so maybe I didn't push myself; maybe I didn't 'market my skills' aggressively. But that was not the way things were done then. Nor was there a network of supportive women (even two or three) to help. The only employed ones were fairly well exploited and powerless themselves. Furthermore, I didn't want to put strain on the marriage or the family by applying to universities further away.

So finally I had a full-time tenured post and was involved in developing a new department. It was hard work and tiring having four, then five, children as well. Love may be infinite, but there are only twenty-four hours in the day. What I did may not have been *kosher* in feminist terms; I treated my academic work, whether research or teaching, as my recreation. When finally I no longer had a houseful to manage I had to learn again how to read novels.

## Moving into Medical Sociology

My early concerns about suffering resurfaced and incidentally led to the next break-through. My children were young when the Bowlby Report came out about children in hospital needing their mothers. The exclusion of mothers (and fathers) was upsetting to parents and children quite apart from theories of bonding and the like.

I was one of the founder members of the Association for the Welfare of Children in Hospital in Wales — at a time when in England the sister association was called Mother Care for Children in Hospital. In Swansea we thought there was a good deal more to it than mothers being allowed in, important though we thought that was. This led to my application to the Ministry of Health to do research on the topic, focused on the resistance of staff to the admission of mothers. The Ministry insisted the project should include stuff about the mental health effects on the children to satisfy the major Bowlby interest. The negotiations around this research were not about my career, but about two wishes: one to see what could be done to reduce the suffering of children in hospital (which was real) and the other a sociological fascination with the question: why the resistance to the humane proposal to admit mothers? That research turned out to have career implications nevertheless. It ultimately led to my secondment as Director of the Medical Sociology Research Centre in Swansea: I had already been promoted to senior lecturer. Once he had me on board, the professor was quite fair in his treatment of me.

During all those years in the wilderness nobody had seemed to want to use my talents for anything. Once I got a full-time job the demands seemed to be ceaseless. I had an image of a piece of dry toast with no butter representing those 'not gainfully occupied' years and then it all suddenly heaped on one corner. I would have been more comfortable if it had been spread more evenly over all the years. As well as requests for talks and the like locally, in the mid-1960s Joe Banks, a champion of feminism and women and a leading member of the British Sociological Association (BSA), rang up one day to ask me whether I would stand for the post of BSA Secretary. Again I was astonished, and flattered to be asked, agreed and was elected. There began a connection with the BSA hierarchy which saw me through to becoming the chair and later (in 1983) President.

### Public Service

I began also to get involved in various public service activities. Eirene White, then a Welsh Office Minister in the Labour government, heard of my activities. She asked me to become a JP. I did not feel able to do that. I knew that all was not well on the Swansea bench and that I would be unhappy to sit on it without trying to improve it. With children and an academic job the sort of reforming work that would be needed seemed too much for me. Anyway, I hate judgmental work. This refusal got me into bad odour. Apparently being informally asked to be a JP was a great honour which one should not refuse. I thought it was a job of work. Eirene also asked me to go on the committee then responsible for primary health care in Swansea. I refused because Frank was on it already and I felt that would make too much overlap in the kitchen and bed — there was enough already with working in the same University College. Eirene was not to be put off: finally she rang personally to say would I accept, if nominated, a seat on the local Hospital Management Committee. This I agreed to. That path led me to the Welsh Hospital Board and later, after I was at Warwick, to the General Medical Council.

By the 1970s I was reconciled to staying in Swansea (apart from the educational system which I was not sure was really doing the best for the children). At Frank's suggestion we moved down one contour and 100 yards east to a bigger and better house than the one we had occupied for nearly twenty years. Someone had asked me to apply for a Chair in Social Administration (or similar) when it came up in Swansea. I had not done that — I was still a refugee from social work and anyway did not feel properly qualified. There was another reason: again I did not want to strain the marriage. I sensed my man would find it hard to take if I had a chair on a campus where he did not. I never even discussed it with him. Again, not very *kosher*, was it? Then suddenly Frank started applying for chairs in England. I announced that I would stay in Swansea unless and until I had a job to go to: not another decade in the wilderness for me. His (Welsh) boss took this as a sign that our marriage was breaking up. Not so. Thus did I arrive in Warwick in 1974 as a Professor in the Sociology Department.

## On Being the First Woman Professor

Warwick University was founded in the mid-sixties, yet it did not have a woman professor until 1974 when I was appointed by open competition. John Rex, the first sociology professor, was involved in my appointment. One day soon after I arrived, having received a summons to my first Professorial Board meeting, I was about to set off when John said 'Wait, I'll take you'. I waited and we arrived late. John opened the door. The Board was already in session. All heads turned when John walked in saying 'I've brought a lady'; for a long moment deathly hush prevailed. I do not remember receiving so clear a sense that I was in the wrong place than one time when, as a student, I was helping in the air raid shelters in London. In the blackout I walked into a gent's lavatory in mistake for the shelter I was looking for. (The smell from the urinals was not so different from that of some shelters.) This was before the days of unisex anything. The same sense of 'I'm in the wrong place' assailed me then as at that first Board meeting.

Now I really was in a man's world. For most men in this world women existed to serve them, either as secretaries, assistants, wives, floozies. Some of the hardest times came from women in circumstances when one might have expected, and certainly hoped for, sisterly support. Totally understandable how it came about, but uncomfortable just the same. Take the case of the creche. Creche provision was deadlocked when I reached Warwick and, they told me, no one was prepared to chair the committee. I said I would, not because it was 'woman's business' and therefore appropriate for me, but because I believed strongly that there should be a creche accessible to staff and students. Radical demands from the Students' Union and especially the women could not be met by a policy which said that a creche should be provided for women students who had got into trouble (that is, single mothers towards whom charity should be extend) but at the same time said that the creche must pay for itself. It was a hard struggle, never resolved satisfactorily to my mind. Along the line the Vice-Chancellor's wife invited me to meet members of the women's society. Membership was mostly University wives; those she invited were mainly senior professors' wives. (I think she was hoping I might gain their support to put pro-creche pressure on their husbands.) They gave me the hardest time: I could see why. They were mostly women who had good academic or similar qualifications and had given up all to serve husband and children. Their jealousy and anger was palpable. They did soften a bit when I finally was driven to reveal that I had not eschewed the marriage-and-children path and had reared five children. Some men expressed personal hostility towards me. When the Professorial Board was making the first set of arrangements for emeritus professors, my neighbour turned to me saying 'Will you be the next?' There were many older than I. He also called out 'Still smiling?' every time he passed me on the campus. Clearly I was a sacrilegious anomaly. There was, of course, sexual harassment: one man referred to me as 'Warwick's top woman', emphasizing the second word in reference to my figure.

That job, being a professor I mean, radicalized me possibly more than anything had before in my whole life. Already while I was in Swansea I had been embarrassed at being called an 'exceptional woman': my reply was that 'no, I had just been lucky — plenty of others could do the same'. This came back to me strongly soon after I reached Warwick when I reread Juliet Mitchell's analysis of this phenomenon, whereupon I concluded that part of refusing to be an honorary male was refusing to be an exceptional woman. This meant taking care to retain solidarity with my sisters and especially younger sisters. I guess this stance did not make my reception any the warmer in the male hierarchy — nor did my overt socialism. In addition to its maleness, the hierarchy itself increasingly seemed antithetical to feminism. Severe doubts arose in my mind, heightened by the work for *Women, Power and Politics*, about whether accepting hierarchical advancement was at all appropriate. As I wrote in the conclusion: 'Sooner or later [in a power position] she will find herself behaving "like a man" or "like a boss"' (Stacey and Price, 1981, p. 183). However, there I was and I determined to use my position to help the cause of women and feminism as much as I could. For example, when Terry Lovell asked for help in getting a women's studies MA off the ground I immediately agreed to help. Another hard struggle. But by then there were increasing numbers of organized and supportive women about in academe.

I had passed through another door; gone up another escalator; had I negotiated a glass ceiling? Fortunate external circumstances (like the sociology explosion), friendly and supportive women (and men too), and taking stands on things I believed in together accounted for this ascent more than any career negotiations. The scene I arrived in was all just as before, only more so; more and harder negotiations; still surrounded by closed doors. Up may be a way to opportunity, it's certainly not a way to freedom.

Would I do it all again? Who can say?

### Acknowledgment

My thanks to Jennifer, my partner of 15 years, for her continuing love and support and for reading and commenting on the first draft.

## Note

This account has been written without reference to external sources, except for *Daughters of the City* which, because it was given to me as a Christmas present, I happened to read after I had written the first part of this chapter but before I had finished it. The account is thus of my memory and my perception of events, not as others might have seen or remembered them or 'as they really were', supposing such a thing to exist.

## References

BOWLBY, J. (1953) *Child Care and the Growth of Love*, London: Pelican.

CARDEN, J., CARDY, J., HAMILTON, R., BAWDEN, P. and SAVAGE, A. (1996) *Daughters of the City: A History of the City of London School for Girls founded by William Ward*, London: James and James.

STACEY, M. (1960) *Tradition and Change: A Study of Banbury*, London: Oxford University Press.

STACEY, M. and PRICE, M. (1981) *Women, Power and Politics*, London: Tavistock.

# 8   An Accidental Academic

*Date of Birth: 14 January 1935*
**Professor Hilary Rose**
Emerita Professor of Social Policy, University of Bradford

With a strong sense of both the political pleasures and difficulties inherent in writing biographical narrative, it is scarcely surprising that for me one of the pleasures of post-modern theory is that it constructs the self as narrative and as both multiple and fractured. It is nothing other than a theoretical and practical relief to abandon that old taken-for-granted construction of the self as some fixed clear entity, which carried with it the always impossible, the methodological and theoretical commitment that to do autobiography, particularly by an academic woman, is to tell not merely 'a' but the 'true' account. It is not, of course, that the events didn't happen, but that the self that I construct here tucked up in bed with flu, is the story I can tell now.

Of course that narrative is crucially shaped by our childhoods, our parents, but also by the stories they told us about their own lives. Mine were school teachers reared as deferential conservatives in deepest Suffolk. But both came from families where the gender norms were disturbed. My mother was one of four children: the two boys went to the village school and were apprenticed as saddlers at 12. By contrast the two girls were encouraged by their mother to get scholarships to the girls' grammar school. Both sisters went on to teacher training college so receiving eight years more full-time education than their brothers. My father's family farmed, not very effectively, as his mother was an invalid, so all three sons learnt all the domestic skills.

What changed my parents for life was getting teaching jobs in the twenties in London, then the doyenne of educational authorities. The condition of the children shocked them. There were no school dinners, and the children fell asleep through hunger. They were dirty and had no boots. The teachers did what they could out of their modest salaries like buying stale cakes and asking the hungriest if they would like to help them out. The worst time was when my father caught diphtheria from his class, and my mother was pregnant with a second child (me). Gradually as he began to recover, their doctor, who had become very close to the young couple, told my mother about the death of a child. The mother had not called him out because she owed him money and still could not pay. The doctor, a good man who would have gone anyway, wept in his frustration that inability to pay denied the child his life-saving skills.

This story was part of why they became socialist, and when we returned to conservative Suffolk during the war, it was one of the stories they would tell us so that their children would also grow up to be socialists and defend the National Health Service. I was also proud that my mother taught at the senior school for only married women teachers were mobilized in the depths of the country. But even then I knew that it was not much fun for some children, above all the evacuees. I had gone with my mother and aunt to the Methodist chapel where accommodation was to be arranged. There I saw the farming families come and choose the biggest boys, refusing to take any smaller siblings on grounds of space. Not everyone was so mercenary. I remember my aunt, though only 25 and with two small children, took in three sisters; their refusal to be separated touched her. Even to my eyes, the way the oldest of the three did her hair, a lock rolled over a piece of rag pinned above her forehead, told me she was into boys. Oh yes I knew about sexuality, but these girls were much older than me, and their sexuality was nothing to do with my pre-pubescent identity. What I was concerned with was how to persuade my mother to take in an evacuee as a longed-for sister. Eventually at the end of the slave-choosing there was a waif-like girl of just my size whom nobody wanted. It was only when we got home that the small urban girl turned out to be almost four years older than the tall country child. It was tough for everyone but I did manage to teach her to ride a bike, which was great till she fell off and broke her arm. Though in its own way that helped as, with the hospital twenty miles away, her suffering made her the centre of attention.

Because the village junior school was so inadequate and so violent, my parents took us away as soon as possible. At 6 my class teacher was the cruel Miss Sparrow. She would pick on the same little boy with closed cropped hair, 'You come from London, Patrick, spell it.' He never could, so next she would make me (the teacher's child) spell London. I did so, embarrassed because it was so easy and hating myself because of what I knew followed. She would shout each letter at the child simultaneously slapping his head. Patrick cried. Because I knew he couldn't help being not able to spell it was somehow my fault that I couldn't stop the cruelty. My next school, the girls' grammar school, had just 100 girl pupils from 7 to 18. I was taught in a group of twelve little girls, by Miss Peachey, the same unqualified teacher who had taught my mother. I loved her and only wanted to please her. As doing well was not about fear or competition but being approved of by someone I loved, I did indeed do well. Sometimes I wonder if my sense of being in an educational elysium during those war years was because I had sampled not only the village school, but another six or seven schools as we tracked around as evacuees.

The war was always there, and so was political discussion. Listening to the talk, and remember mine was a socialist household, I learnt about the Nazis and the concentration camps. I heard about the good society that we were going to build when the war was over; I was less than clear about what this might mean but I hoped that teachers would not be allowed to hit children any more. As a patriot and a Christian my first moment of religious doubt came when I held a German soldier's belt in my hands. The metal of the buckle spelt out 'Gott mit uns'. 'How' I blurted out 'can He be on their side when He is on ours ?' I have a feeling that the answer that I was given, and which I found entirely satisfying, was that the entire German army had false consciousness.

The war was both when and why I saw my first black person. I had looked at pictures of black people in our elderly and grossly imperialist *Children's Encyclopaedia* but seeing real black skin was different. I liked the shiny sort best but felt that, like a lot of other things that I thought about, that this was not a matter for discussion with the adults. I knew from listening to the English adults that white Yanks often treated the coloured Yanks badly; they thought this was wrong and stupid as 'we were all in it together'. This became one of my original stories of anti-racism, as I took solidarity against Nazis as a binding and self-evident truth, although it took learning about Apartheid when I was 15 to really start disentangling my self from an imperialist culture. I was 10 when the war ended and my family returned to London. I cried as the local steam train took us to the junction to meet the London train, over the level crossing where we put halfpennies on the rails hoping for the day when the train squashed the coins in exactly the right place so that they would become pennies, past the field where we, some five little girls, had lit a fire to bake potatoes then when the rain fell, took off our clothes and danced round the fire. I was right to cry, my wonderful magical childhood was over.

As London housing was difficult, we had to split up and stay with family friends. My brother was sent to the boys' grammar school and my parents approached the girls' grammar school. The school explained that although I had already passed the 11+, I would have to resit the examination as I was still 10. There was no appeal mechanism and I was sent to the local junior school of some 300 children. I found it huge and noisy and I was back in the world of children being beaten. On the first day the teacher in charge at dinner time said that anyone who spoke would be caned. A little girl with white face and a great cloud of dark hair, sitting diagonally opposite to me, was caught speaking and was sent out. I don't remember anything else about that school except that I was determined not to go there. Because I shared a room with my mother I made myself cry all night so that they would have to take me away. It worked, and I spent an extremely happy year in what my parents would have otherwise described as a tin pot preparatory school. Miss Peachey's good teaching meant that I was much further ahead than children of my own age so I worked with the 12-year-old boys preparing for their public school exams. There were no games organized for girls, but because I did all my lessons with the boys I was allowed to play football and cricket with them. As a physically self-confident girl this seemed just fine, I gave as good as I got. And anyway these suburban boys seemed positive softies compared with my brother and my village friends.

I have not spoken much about my brother. He was older, stronger and had dark curly hair; mine was straight. Despite my parents' carefully imposed equity, which led to us being brought up on the 'one cuts, the other chooses' principle (and to this day I can cut cake with a microtone accuracy) I both admired my brother and was jealous. We argued about everything and although I tried never to let him see it, I felt he was just so much cleverer and, worst of all, more beautiful than me. In Suffolk this rivalry did not really matter but back in the constraints of suburban life, we irritated each other. The mere presence of the little sister led him to tease me ruthlessly especially in front of his friends. Funnily it was one of his friends who changed how I felt about myself. I was at the local swimming pool and walked across to where he and a group of friends were sunbathing. One said 'Is that your sister, but she is pretty?' Suddenly I knew that having straight hair did not mean I was a total write-off.

When I repeated the 11+, I was selected to go to the local elite girls' school. Initially I was seen as something of a mathematical wunderkind and was given special classes in trigonometry. This special attention made me feel uncomfortable, but what was much worse was a sudden confrontation around my voice. I was entirely unaware of it, but of course I spoke like any other Suffolk child, slowly and with a soft sing-song accent. The teachers, especially my new form teacher Miss Cam, would constantly demand that I spoke 'properly'. I knew that my parents could only about afford the school uniform, including the gym and the game kits, and was very conscious that the 'extra' elocution lessons so many of the other 'scholarship girls' were being persuaded/bullied into, were out of the question. I changed from being a happy child excelling in everything she did, to a thoroughly miserable teenager. My parents were so impressed by the status of the school that they pretty much shared the school's view that I should be grateful to be there. Reading remained my chief refuge. I lost my beloved nature study for that was 'science' and taught by the dreaded Miss Cam. My biggest debts were to the English teachers as my love of language was nourished. By the time I was 13 Katherine Mansfield's short stories had given me a longing to write well.

Outside school, politics saved me. I would attend United Nations Association meetings; there I learnt from young left wingers that the Korean War was not quite the way the media told it. In the fifties, despite the huge Tory majorities, there was a vibrant left culture in the suburbs, particularly among young people. I decided to join the Young Communist League. I was doing fine learning about Communism until I spent an evening at a friend's house. His father, who was what I would recognize later as a rabid Stalinist, spoke, gradually working himself into a rage, so that little flecks of white saliva gathered in the corners of his mouth, of how 'we' would kill the capitalists and exploiters of the working classes when the revolution came. I wanted socialism but with a pacifism that has always been a bit of a problem, I knew I desperately didn't want to kill anyone. It was at that moment that I psychically stopped wanting to be part of that 'we'.

Even then I think knew that refusing to join the Communists just because one member had a pathological desire for violent revenge was pretty silly, but there were other bits and pieces which troubled me. Not least, now that I was getting serious about politics, I needed to understand why my father was a socialist who did not like Communism. I knew that having unpopular views did not trouble him; for him politics were about thinking straight and being loyal to basic values of justice and peace. It was only later when I read the early Orwell that I understood how thirties socialists like my father had been immensely attracted to Marxist revolutionary theory, but had none the less drawn back from the Communist Party because they learnt even as early as the Spanish Civil War that the pigs had gained control. For him the problem was how to secure the communist project without the Communist Party terror.

Much later in the sixties when the decision to join a revolutionary party turned (or at least I thought it turned) on theoretical analysis, my by then deep hostility to the theory of the party stood in the way. I saw insufficient difference between the party of Trotsky and that of Stalin. And as for Althusser, whatever the insights about ideology, his complicated scientist project managed to do without his tiresome and my loved human subjects entirely, I was with consciousness and the making of history from below. But that is a whole other dimension of biography in which only those soaked in the political culture of the sixties and seventies can trade descriptions which make sense at least to one another. To them then, well I was an anarchist Maoist, and to those outside such a culture, it will suffice that members of the left tendency I belonged to were few and far between.

But I am letting the chronological events escape. In brief, after a miserable time at school culminating in a discussion about my future where the headmistress suggested that I became a secretary and I blazed back 'I am not going to be any man's brains' (I tell this as the earliest mark of unequivocal feminism I can recall). She rather icily asked me what I was going to do. 'Politics' I replied, meaning that I wanted to become a Labour MP as a way to make a good society. But first I had to have an occupation, so I entered teacher training. I had also fallen in love with a young man who cared about poetry and politics, and grew roses for a living. We married while I was still 19, I had a baby, was active in CND and the Labour Party, and stood for the local council at 21, only losing by a handful of votes. I taught and we even managed to start buying a house.

Suddenly this small busy happy universe stopped. It was 1958, the last summer of the polio epidemics. John and I and our 2-year-old, Simon, had come back from our first ever foreign holiday in Brittany. Within a few weeks John was dead and I was a widowed mother aged 23 with no very visible means of support. First, however, I had had to learn to be helpless, to watch this young man I loved trapped in fever, then to find, when this eased, that he was paralyzed in both legs and one arm. His suffering and courage and my feeling of uselessness were like a glass wall between us. Feeling I needed to confront the future I had insisted the specialist tell me the prognosis. I was told there was no chance of recovery, and I was left to wonder whether I was a good enough person to devote myself for ever to someone now physically crippled. But even as while I was trying to push myself towards being a heroine, there was a sudden relapse and John was dying.

The very young nurse caring for him in a side ward was so distressed that she begged me to leave. As I stood in the dark night air outside, I felt only relief for John that he was out of the suffering. I did not then know how much succumbing to the pressure to leave his death room before he was actually dead would cost. In those brutally psychologically illiterate days the only support that was offered me by my GP were some pills — purple hearts — a mix of amphetamine and barbiturate. Although sometimes these were the only way that I could bring myself to move, I disliked the feeling of being stoned so I did not become hooked as well as being crazy with grief. It is almost forty years ago but September, especially when it is soft and golden like it was that September, is always the cruellest month.

My parents could not get near my inconsolable angry guilty pain but they offered endless love to my son. They — above all my mother — gave him love when I could not, and, as I slowly mended gave him back to me again. I knew that I was in their debt forever. I also was to learn about being a young widow. The National Assistance Board officer (precursor to Social Security) whom I went to see with my father to get help with the mortgage, at least as an interim measure, looked me up and down. Then he refused any help, saying 'She's pretty, she will get married again'. My father quietly explained that this was not a decent thing for anyone to say, but the feeling of humiliation lingered even through the comfort of my father's solidarity.

If my parents saved my son, it was a woman, Annie, who remains one of my dearest friends, whom I think quite literally saved my life. We had met in CND, then I had noticed her at John's funeral standing alone in a shabby mac at the back and I had felt grateful for her presence. She drew me into her marriage and her friends, fed me on books and music, took me to the newly-formed Universities and Left Review Club which met in an Oxford Street night club and gave me the kind of loving support that I did not know was possible. I needed desperately to do something so found a job at the same school Annie was teaching at. It was an authoritarian girls' secondary modern, but we both had classes in huts well away from the main building and there fought to create pedagogic havens for bottom stream girls who described themselves as 'useless' and as '11+ failures'. I loved the teaching but I was constantly exhausted, as I had nightmares seeing John endlessly dying and lay sleepless afraid to sleep. I was also horrified by my incapacity to control my grief and help my small son. There seemed no way to survive let alone reinvent myself.

The way out appeared by chance. Sharing vicariously in this circle of young well educated socialist intellectuals I learnt to read the current hit books. That winter everyone was reading Richard Titmuss' *Essays on the Welfare State* (Titmuss, 1958). I learnt about the bizarre anomalies of the social security system and found that it was possible to receive a student grant and to keep the unearned income of the widowed mother's allowance. The idea that I went to university began to take on substance, for combining these benefits would give me a better income than if

I taught, where I automatically lost the allowance. Being a student would also give me more time with Simon. I did not feel too much of a welfare manipulator as the National Assistance had already cost me our home.

And at the same time the problem of where Simon and I could live (until then I had gone home to my parents) suddenly took form. Annie, her husband, and a small group of friends decided to find a large house or flat and share it. We were all interested in cooperative forms of living and this seemed a brilliant first step. The idea of a three-year degree seemed impossibly demanding but I had found out about the two-year non-graduate Diploma in Social Science at the London School of Economics which might open a way of doing social work connected to education. The course was in the Titmuss Department. All I had to do was to apply, take an examination and, if I got that far, be interviewed. That was the worst part, the penetrating questions asked by the two entirely kindly academic women were so traumatic that I was unable to recognize them when I was enrolled in the following October.

Meanwhile the huge house we found in Regents Park Road looking across to Primrose Hill was better than our wildest hopes. As new people joined, our cooperative dream faded more or less into sharing, but our neighbours included three Communist families running a cooperative nursery in what had been the ballroom in their equally large house. This nursery was to become a lifeline for Simon and so me. I had already secured a place in the nearby London County Council nursery where only necessitous cases (like Simon) were admitted. The children were cared for like little animals: they were fed, watered and cleaned and all intellectual, emotional and aesthetic development ignored. Simon was bitterly unhappy and suddenly it looked as if the whole reinvention project was going to fail. In my desperation I turned to the cooperative nursery and found it as rich emotionally and intellectually as the state nursery was impoverished. Some of those kids and their parents still come to our Winter Solstice parties.

Meanwhile becoming a student at LSE was like being let into heaven. I had never met people who had actually written books; here I could see them, listen to them and even ask questions. I know that in the height of the students' movement I came to see Titmuss as always compassionate but elitist and deeply undemocratic, but to be taught by someone whom you think can probably walk on water is a special experience. Told that lectures were not compulsory but that classes and tutorials were, I became highly selective. I could read faster in the library, and I had so much reading to do, and had the whole of the cultural and political wealth of London to explore.

The best part were the tutorials. Every two weeks I would meet with my tutor Janet Kydd. Shrewd as they come, she would begin by asking me how Simon was? She never said, but she and I knew that if he was happy then she had a student and if not, not. I would sit with this woman in her good tweed suit, her Scottish brooch, her well ironed blouse, her sensible shoes and became drunk with intellectual pleasure. She would suggest the names of books, the details were unimportant, it was this hunger to find them, read them and be able to discuss them at our next meeting. As the first term progressed I was invited to put in for a Charles Loch

Scholarship, and for the first time experienced that peculiar irony so intrinsic to academic life in which we win honours or prizes named for people we are, to say the least, ambivalent about. Before the end of this first term Janet also asked me if I would like to read a sociology degree, as at that time the Social Administration Department had only the non-graduate diploma and a large postgraduate diploma programme. By then, as against my former caution about spending as much as two years at university, I now never wanted to stop learning. I was given an appointment to see Professor David Glass, a man who had the reputation of mixing kindness and coldness in unpredictable proportions. He asked me what I would do about statistics (women students' notorious weakness), I explained that I viewed them like washing up, as disagreeable but essential. Glass permitted himself a thin smile and admitted me. Actually it was a good deal worse than washing up, and I had to persuade all sorts of graduate students to coach me.

The Sociology Department was theoretically more exciting but lacked the sense of social purpose of the Titmuss Department. Keeping hold of both was like my politics, for I divided my energies between New Left and the Young Fabians. In terms of class politics this double involvement was absurd, but in terms of gender politics (even though the concept was not available) it was entirely sensible. The Fabians had a history of taking women seriously, and though I did not know it then, a strong feminist social research tradition. What I could feel was that here I was treated like a person, whereas the left did not. If I had not been a mother I might have missed the contempt with which women and children were held by the left. It was the time when I asked a man friend, who was driving a carload to a New Left weekend school and the route took them past my parents' house, whether he would drop Simon off. Those self-absorbed men of the New Left leadership ignored the small voice saying 'that's my granny's house'. Eventually the friend noticed the tear stained face and turned the car back.

At that time the Fabians were the think tank for the Labour Party so that when Labour was out of office, as it was by 1959, the Fabian Executive was more or less the Labour government in exile. As Chairman (sorry!) of the Young Fabians I was also a member of the Executive so suddenly given ringside seat to see the Labour elite at work. This was a fluid relatively open grouping of politicians and intelligentsia, some politicians like Shirley Williams, Tony Crosland and Dick Crossman were formidable intellectuals in their own right. The sharp divide between the professional politicians of New Labour and the intelligentsia had yet to emerge. But despite this fluid milieu, I sometimes wonder how I coped. In part it was because I was taught by a series of women social scientists who took their own and their women students' right to think independently for granted. I was immensely proud to be taught, after Janet, by Rosalind Chambers, as she had taken her degree at 40 and got a first. With such women who could think freely and well and who also told me I could, what was so difficult? The second source of my self-confidence was because I did not care. The sheer dreadfulness of John's death was empowering. Existentially I was free, the only inescapable responsible love was Simon.

Gradually the feeling that I had died inside began to ease. Partly I suppose pain just goes away but partly the sixties were tremendously optimistic. We thought we could bring about a wonderful new society if not today then surely by tomorrow. My generation's hatred of nuclear weaponry meant that science and technology were part of the political agenda, even though initially science was privileged as in itself either good or at least neutral and thus susceptible to being 'used' or 'abused'. I was fascinated with the question of how the utopian promise of science had turned into the genocidic nightmare of Hiroshima. It was this fascination which led to me to get to know Steven Rose as one of the young scientists at the New Left meetings. It would be neat historically, given that we wrote *Science and Society* together before the decade was out, to say that we met listening to the Marxist crystallographer Desmond Bernal when he spoke there. But it would not be true, we met casually enough through overlapping circles of friends. I liked him immediately; there was a funny mix of cleverness, arrogance and a gentleness. I also fancied him rotten.

Anyway as our relationship is too long-standing and too precious for me to analyse, I will only say that Steven remains my best friend, lover and ally. Certainly getting here has not been a picnic. Like so many heterosexual partners we nearly broke in the height of the women's movement, when however much women and men thought they had worked for equality in their personal relations, they were revealed as little more than a painful joke. For a long time I envied lesbian friends, surely moving beyond heterosexuality would make relationships easier; now with the clearer eye that comes with age I more pragmatically suspect that, regardless of sexuality, building good relationships is almost impossibly difficult. If we get any part of the dream of love then we are lucky.

I finished my degree living with Steven and Simon in Oxford. He had finished his PhD, and had both a research and college fellowship. We talked about living either in London or Oxford, but biochemistry then entailed long hours in a laboratory, whereas my text-based social science was more portable. The trouble with this solution was Oxford, a provincial city likely be hostile to a couple, with her child not his, and 'living in sin'. Thus our main reason for getting married was to protect Simon, he had had enough hard things happen to him and leaving London was to leave our supportive alternative world.

The Oxford libraries were wonderful, and no-one discriminated then against a student from another university. Simon was happy and really pleased at acquiring a father. When he called Steven 'Dad' I wanted to cry. Initially the social events that I was invited to as the wife of a junior fellow were intriguing; college life was as mysterious as any exotic tribe I was reading about in anthropology. But as I finished my degree and wanted to become a social scientist the fictional career came hideously unglued. The one social scientist in Oxford who did good empirical research interviewed me for a job. The crudity of the sexual harassment at this one-to-one interview was at a level that I did not know was possible. I went home enraged, withdrew my application and wept. The next job interview I attended was when I was conspicuously pregnant. This produced a lecture about the impossibility of reconciling childcare with research. My insistence that I had already demonstrated that I could manage motherhood and get a good degree, served only to generate guilt, and I received an invitation from one of his colleagues to become a part-time badly paid research assistant. As there was nothing else in sight I took it.

These experiences combined with my growing recognition that I was not an anthropologist but was an integral part of a misogynist Oxford saga depressed me. Once it was inescapable that the separation of women and men at the end of formal dinners was not part of a comic period piece, I stopped being able to play. The problem was to steer a path between his employment and her personhood. We agreed the public fiction that on such occasions I would be staying in London because of work. In actuality I would usually be at home carefully not answering the phone. Compared with London, Oxford's treatment of women was in the dark ages. I had to get back to relative civilization or suffocate. We did but the price was that Steven had to work in Rome for six months. I refused to go with him as it was clear that I would be even more of a non-person in Rome than in Oxford. It was miserable being separated but suddenly a lucky break made the misery worthwhile.

I received a phone call inviting me to apply for a job as a research officer with the Milner Holland Committee on London Housing. The scandal of Rachman and the links with the Profumo Affair had suddenly put housing into political preeminence. The Fabian Society had taught me to recognize the studiedly informal manner of the very senior civil servant and I ran my end of the conversation as if I was part of that culture. It was when he told me the salary, £1500, rather more than the top of the junior lecturer scale, and would this be acceptable, that I had to struggle not to whoop but merely murmur that I thought so, that I began to feel that my luck was changing. The interview the next afternoon was with the Secretary of the Committee, and the inevitable LSE housing consultant. This was John Greve, then a lecturer in the Titmuss Department, who had taught me. As I seemed to be the only candidate, and a good part of the conversation was about how soon I could start, I began to hope that I was in a one-horse race.

Working as a researcher for a government committee of enquiry was brilliant; all those problems of access into formal institutions disappeared at the wave of an official letter, and because I was young and unimportant I had equally easy access into the shady world of dodgy estate agents and midnight flits. It was not hard to be convinced by a young single mother that going on the game, to pay her exorbitant private landlord rent, was less degrading than going on National Assistance. I also found that the reformer's belief that research would help make things better did not help me cope with completely appalling personal situations. I learned to use the magical formula 'I forgot to mention that there's an interview fee. It has to be cash and keep quiet about it because they' ('they' were very useful in such exchanges) 'forgot to do the paper work'.

Becoming a research civil servant was a great 'learning by doing' in the sixties. Training was best described as chucking young graduates in the deep end and seeing which swum. Not knowing there were any more effective and supportive techniques, I have to confess I rather enjoyed splashing around. One day John Greve told me he told me he was going away to Norway for a year's study leave and was I interested in putting in for his LSE job for the year? Suddenly that dream which had sat in my mind's eye of my being the woman tutor and some other younger person as the student sitting literally and metaphorically at her feet, looked as if it could actually happen. There were three candidates interviewed: a Harvard PhD who knew a great deal about particular Victorian committees but little or nothing about twentieth century Britain, a woman economist who had done important work on social policy responses to a restructuring labour market and me. While I could share the thought that the Harvard historian was too narrow, I was uncomfortably aware that the woman was much better qualified than me. Why was she not chosen? Working out an answer came very slowly and only as I began to understand both LSE and the department better. First she was left wing and there-fore dangerous so far as the taken-for-granted Fabianism of the department was concerned. In 1964 left did not mean, as it does now, left of centre. It meant she did not just seek to influence the 2,000 who mattered, but that she did dangerous democratic things like work with trade unions. Her other fault was that she was married to an LSE academic, and the unspoken nepotism rule came into operation. It is not exactly self-flattering to have to conclude that I was appointed at least as much because of what I was not, as for what I was.

As the sixties went on it became clear to both the Department and myself that I was changing, the balancing act between the ameliorative positivism of Fabianism and my longing for a radically new society was collapsing. Increasingly I was working with community groups trying to understand how social policy could be changed from below. The social and political theories which justified working with people outside the labour market were a fuzzy mix, and for the most part such anarchistic practices were deplored and ignored by Marxists. But the practices gave space to women and to innovative forms of community action, and gradually, the women's liberation movement provided the confidence to start theorizing com-munity action as a struggle for social reproduction. But in the first phase democratiz-ing welfare and education from below, was part and parcel of the appearance of new groups in society, demanding greater democratic control of their lives.

The 'troubles', as they were to be named at LSE, were for me pretty much a golden period. I shared the moral seriousness of the students, their commitment to building new and democratic forms of both the construction of knowledge and its transmission and their hatred of the genocidic war in Vietnam. As the student movement weakened and the right reasserted control, I saw numbers of my friends both in my own department and elsewhere at the LSE losing their jobs. In my department they were all women on short term contracts, who had been 'let go'. This euphemism covered the mismatch between their ideological stance with that of the Department.

These struggles around free speech, short-term contracts, tenure and promo-tion were reinforced by what I was learning in the women's movement. For example there were bright young academic men who needed approval, support and promo-tion but there was no parallel concept of bright young academic women. Academic women in LSE, not least in the Titmuss Department, were not supposed to be actual mothers. Thus one young woman academic on a one-year contract came in, looking green with exhaustion, to teach just ten days after giving birth. She is now an extremely eminent university administrator. We were supposed to be like the women in the social policy we taught — the self-sacrificing, disembodied and non-competitive partners of men.

In the early seventies universities were still expanding and the idea of fresh intellectual and pedagogic space coincided with the different difficulties both of our sons were experiencing with schooling. One who had been a star pupil suddenly dropped out of his over large and under-managed comprehensive, the other showed few signs of staying in school even when I managed to get him there. London was losing its charms. When one of my LSE male colleagues, whom I thought worthy but deeply boring was appointed to a chair in a new university, I remember thinking, well if he can get a chair maybe that is the solution for me too. I must find somewhere new and build the kind of department that, whether I was a student or a teacher, I would want to be in.

Retrospectively it is easy to see that I had very little idea of quite how tough a job I had let myself in for when I was appointed to Bradford; but I also suspect that ignorance can be an asset as a good number of problems can be overcome by not knowing how tough they are. I found Bradford, both as a university and even more as a city, as raw in its sexism as its racism. At the first appointment committee I took part in, one of the committee began to explain how Asian women's fingers were small and they were naturally good at repetitive jobs so Asian women were ideal for working in textiles. While I was thinking about how I was going to have to help take my new university to the Race Relations Board before I had met a single student, Sheila Allen moved in. I witnessed a demonstration exercise of how a skilled social scientist with political integrity could interpose herself between a candidate and intolerable racist questioning which denied the possibility of equal consideration. It was a useful training experience which was to serve me well.

Sexual harassment, despite my new (and I thought) august status did not stop, nor was it invisible. One of the university administrators who had been an undergraduate with me at LSE was trying to explain to me in my first weeks which of the suits was the Chancellor. Finally he said 'oh you know — the one who is always trying to grope you.' It was not very correct but we both giggled insanely. During the mid-eighties I used to go to the lunches organized by Miriam David for women heads of department, where we confidentially exchanged horror and even occasional success stories in our struggles to build good departments. Despite the variations between us as individual women and between our institutions, gender was compellingly present in our stories. Collective research on the dilemma of the woman head of department, therapeutic laughter and good food were a significant resource.

Of course by the end of my time at Bradford, the trafficking between the women's movement and the academy was, or more accurately was claimed to be, part of a success story of a now university system-wide commitment to equal opportunities. I took pride in our share of the feminist struggles which had brought this about. For example during the height of feminist consciousness in the department we actually managed for a number of years to create an environment where male academics could no longer coerce women students into sex. I was very discreetly told about the defining struggle and sworn to secrecy. A student had appealed to one of the most glamorous of the young women staff for help against a would-be seductive male colleague. (So much more explicable than coming to one of we battle scarred 40-year-olds.) The young academic then cornered her colleague, challenged him with the question whether, given his beer belly and his general lack of sexual attractiveness, he really thought that if he was not a lecturer the student would give him a second look at a disco. He faded.

I want to set this success against a biography where I had watched (to be fairs a minority of) academic men, both left and right, set themselves to score sexually with first year women, and where I had learned through the British Sociological Association's women's caucus of the widespread sexual harassment by so many men supervisors. But I was also to relearn painfully that the price of liberty is vigilance and our feminist vigilance had been weakened by reliance on policy statements. Thus in the last years before I took early retirement we had a case of sexual violence by a young male colleague against one of our women undergraduates. What was particularly appalling was that although he admitted his action to the Head of Department and there was an abundance of witnesses, he was not proceeded against. The most positive outcome, and it was a far from satisfactory, was that a small mixed group of academics committed both to ending violence against women and to professionalism in teaching suggested successfully to him that it was better to resign than be forced out.

Why do I finish on such an equivocal note? It is quite simple. Anyone who writes a biography located in a teaching and researching culture involved in the political and struggles of her time has to have a feeling of maybe never finished work. Many tasks which keep a house of learning fit for a diversity of human beings to study, teach and construct new knowledge are rather like keeping a house clean, so with some gentle irony I suspect that even academic women's work is never done.

But I have a second ending, equally unfinished but about new beginnings. One of my nicest Christmas notes came from a young woman I knew a while back. I had taken a liking to her alternative politics and her sharp intelligence, even while learning something of the devastating personal background which had made her quite frail. From having not an Ordinary Level to her name she is now in research, and planning to do a PhD. She told me that the story I had told her of my being an accidental academic was part of the how and why she was able to reinvent herself. Doing autobiography is politics too.

### Reference

TITMUSS, R.M. (1958) *Essays on the Welfare State*, London: Allen and Unwin.

# 9    An 'Interesting' Career in Higher Education

*Date of Birth: 18 December 1933*
**Dr Dulcie Groves**
Honorary Lecturer in Social Policy, University of Lancaster

In 1984, aged 50, I took early retirement from my post as Lecturer in Social Policy at the University of Lancaster. For the following five years I had a 'leaseback' contract for a substantial amount of teaching and some administration. Being substantially engaged in personal research and retaining my previous office and job title, my working life was little changed apart from the fact that I no longer sat on any university committees and could live life at my own pace, leaving more time for outside professional and personal interests. In a nutshell, thanks to Sir Keith Joseph (former Conservative Secretary of State for Education and Science) and his cuts, I was out of the rat-race.

One circumstance which affected my decision to opt out was the then minuscule prospect of being promoted within the traditional university sector. On arrival at Lancaster in September 1976 I had already gained unusual promotion (for a woman) within the polytechnic sector, to the rank of Principal Lecturer with Acting Head of Department status. But this was for administrative and teaching competence. Having seized the chance of transferring into the university sector so as to engage in research as well as teaching, I was rightly warned on arrival that any promotion would be reliant on a successful publication record. At the time I was embarked on obtaining my PhD by thesis.

My career-change coincided with a period of front-line caring for a terminally ill parent, an experience that I was later to turn to good account in my academic work. It took a couple of years to get going, academically speaking. However, by the time of the university cuts in the early 1980s, my teaching and research were going well and I had nearly finished my PhD. But what had become plain was that any woman aiming for promotion at Lancaster, with a better record than many other universities, would truly have to be 'academic superwoman'. Furthermore, in my department we actually had 'superwoman', one of my best friends. And it took her eight years to gain promotion, initially to Senior Lecturer. In fact, in my first twelve years at Lancaster (1976–88) I can remember only three women being promoted. Not for nothing did the 1990 *Hansard Society Commission Report on Women at the Top* describe Britain's universities as 'bastions of male power and privilege' (p. 68). However, by my final year of teaching (1988–9), things were looking up. No fewer than three women were promoted to Senior Lecturer and by then a couple of previous 'promotees' had got personal chairs. From then on, with substantial help from 'superwoman', whose internal career soared upwards, there was a steady trickle of female promotions.

At some point in the early 1990s I was discussing this fact with my best friend from school, first met in 1943. One of a handful of women accepted to read physics at Cambridge in 1953, married with four children, she typified our generation by starting out as a full-time teacher at two leading girls' schools, one of which gladly reappointed her after a lengthy career-break as a permanent low-paid part-time 'returner' until she retired. Informing my friend that things were improving on the promotion front for female academics, I confessed to feeling a bit guilty about throwing in the sponge at the age of 50, since I certainly identified myself as a feminist and had done from university days. In point of fact the then Vice-Chancellor had, in 1984, informed me that no member of staff over 50 would ever be promoted. My fond friend comforted me with the notion that while I might not have hit the high spots, I had had a really 'interesting' career. This was said with such conviction that I have carried on happily to this day, to the point where the editors of this book invited me to contribute a chapter illustrative of a 'good career' for a woman of my generation, born in the mid-1930s. My actual management experience came in the middle.

My good fortune was to be born to parents who valued education for girls and were in a position to encourage me to stay on at school, get a degree and a professional qualification. They firmly believed that women should, if possible, be capable of supporting themselves financially, married or not. It was widowhood or a husband's chronic illness which might necessitate a wife's earning, rather than divorce, then an uncommon event. My mother was a 'marriage-barred' infants' teacher, with seventeen successful years of work behind her. My father, well educated by the standards of the day, was in the wholesale textile trade, latterly in management. He died when I was 19. An only child, I had a happy upbringing, winning a scholarship from my elementary school in Penarth to Howell's School, Llandaff, an old independent academic girls' school, which I attended from 1944 to 1951. I did not on the whole enjoy this tough regime and least of all the four years I spent from 11 to 15 as a boarder. But it enabled me to get a good School Certificate, though as the very first Advanced Level candidates, my year did extremely badly. I lost interest in European history, thus failing an Advanced Level. Fortunately, two were sufficient for university entrance. Had I passed, my career might have been very different.

My original intention had been to read for a degree in English, with the possibility of becoming a librarian/archivist, but, sharing my parents' interest in current affairs, I was becoming attracted to the social sciences. Too young for university in 1951, I decided to go to Cardiff Technical College for a year, where I began three social science Advanced Levels. Once started, I knew that I would enjoy a broad honours programme in the social sciences at university. I applied to Nottingham, originally my second choice, for economic and social history, but ended up reading social administration, politics and sociology. Armed with three good 'A' level passes obtained in one year and having enjoyed the adult atmosphere of the 'tech', I took to university life (see Groves, 1993). A strong feature at Nottingham was the beautiful lake, with ducks: it fulfilled my personal requirement that any university I attended should be located near an international cricket ground, for easy access to Test Matches!

The University Careers Service seemed to take a very conventional line where women's choices were concerned. The vast majority of women graduates at that time became teachers. Most women on my honours social administration course became social workers or personnel officers, the latter occupation then being constructed as another type of 'welfare' career open to female graduates. Having become very interested in public administration via my Part I politics course, in my third year I sat and failed the administrative grade Civil Service examination by the then 'short' method. I did not have a subject to offer for the 'long' academic examination route. The prototype successful candidate was an Oxbridge male. Women candidates were examined on their own over a period of three days. I found that a number had been coached: I had had no idea what to expect.

Some women students took postgraduate secretarial courses (which I considered) while some scientists got laboratory jobs. In the end I decided to train as a Froebel teacher of junior subjects, since teaching was well paid and offered good holidays. This was a consideration, since my university vacations had demanded a substantial amount of field work. Early in my third year, my tutor did ask if I was interested in applying for a postgraduate scholarship, but I thought this an improbable option, since I had no reason to expect a really good degree. After seventeen years of unbroken education and with my father having died suddenly at the beginning of my second year at university, I fancied a 'fun' year in London on what was generally accepted as a cooling-out year! My tutor and, indeed, my mother and our professor expressed disappointment at my choice of what was then viewed as a 'non-graduate' career, but I saw it as the gateway to an enjoyable lifestyle which could lead on to other prospects. I was genuinely interested in the field of education. At this time I would have had no serious dedication to the idea of a lifelong career, which by definition would not have been seen as combining with marriage. A teaching career could however be interrupted and combined with marriage and motherhood. At that time the marriage rate for women was climbing, with a near-even sex ratio in the UK. There was considerable pressure on most (though not on me as an individual) to marry. I certainly wanted to marry eventually, but having parents who themselves had married late and who thought it a good idea for women to earn, travel and enjoy themselves before settling down to domesticity, unlike most of my women friends, I was not interested in marrying immediately.

I enjoyed my 'education year', split between Maria Grey College in Brondesbury and the Institute of Education, mainly for the pleasures of living in London! In January 1956 I saw a post advertised to teach 8 and 9-year-olds in the Preparatory Department of Nottingham High School for Girls (a Girls' Public Day School Trust school). It occurred to me that an interview would guarantee a free trip back to Nottingham to see friends. To my surprise, I got the job. The Trust later reprimanded the school for selecting an expensive graduate, rather than the cheaper product of a Froebel college! I stayed for three years. It was an enjoyable job, enabling me to branch out into adult life and take pleasure in having my own flat in a friendly family house. Although this part of my life quickly receded into oblivion once I went off to graduate school in the USA, I now see it as formative in that I had space to mature and think about what I wanted to do with my life. Marriage was a possibility but there was also a sub-text for some women of my generation around justifying the benefits of an extended education and helping to make the post-war world a better place. I considered myself a feminist and during the later 1950s, public debate was emerging about the role of women. I was particularly affected by reading Roger Fulford's *Votes for Women* (1957). I read about the early twentieth century suffrage struggles in detail for the first time and it made me think.

Having benefited from time off from serious study, I began to contemplate postgraduate work. My old department at Nottingham had encouraged me to register for a higher degree part-time, but the Girls' Public Day School Trust would not permit this! My first degree had been good. I had enjoyed comparative social policy and politics on my degree course and had become interested in the USA. Studying there was fashionable. Social policy did not exist, as such, as an academic subject in the United States. My best option was to take a Master's degree in social work. In due course I applied for graduate scholarships and was successful on the English-Speaking Union programme, being accepted for Bryn Mawr College, whose Graduate Department of Social Work and Social Research was small and flourishing, one of the first five schools ever recognized for doctoral studies.

In 1959–60 I was in the initial year of the Master of Social Service programme, with a placement in psychiatric case-work. That summer I had a well-paid job in a children's camp, equivalent to a supervised group work placement. Exchange regulations for taking money from the UK to the USA were extremely strict at that time. I needed more pocket money and discovered that I could earn it in an interesting way by deputizing for hall wardens. These were advanced graduate students who, on a system devised early in the century and unique to Bryn Mawr, did half-time academic work and held a half-time academic post as an Administrative Assistant in the Dean's Office. In return for a furnished suite of rooms, free board, free tuition and a generous stipend, the duty of a 'warden' was to act as moral/personal tutor (in the British terms of the day) to those fifty to eighty undergraduates resident in each hall, with no domestic or financial responsibilities. There were weekly seminars covering all aspects of the work of the Dean's Office and college management. It was a well-known route to eventual deanships and indeed, presidencies of colleges.

Towards the end of the first year, the College Dean asked if I would like to become Warden of Denbigh Hall, continuing my studies half-time. My four-year student visa permitted this. My Department, knowing that my main interest lay in social policy, suggested that I should substitute doctoral courses for some Master's courses. I did in fact graduate with a major in community organization, including the appropriate fieldwork. This covered both grass roots community work skills and what would now be thought of as management skills appropriate for voluntary organizations. We learned, for instance, how to conduct and minute committee meetings, work with board members, how to 'network', develop and see through projects. We had to document and present our academic work meticulously. The only real academic disappointment was an experimental requirement that all students should complete a group master's thesis as opposed to individual theses. My group was assigned a very boring project in the health field, using factor analysis. We had no choice of topic or research methods. This exercise succeeded in putting me right off academic research for some years. I did well on the course and emerged with the equivalent of a taught Master's in social policy with a professional degree in community work. In four years at Bryn Mawr I met many able scholars and travelled extensively, making many friends. I learnt to be more assertive and hold my own in group discussions. But I had no wish to settle in the States.

When I got back I was nearly 30. With a Bryn Mawr friend, I spent a month youth hostelling. Sitting on a rock above the sea in the North of Scotland, I opened a cache of mail and found a letter from the Organizing Secretary of a Peckham settlement where I had enjoyed a short period of field work in 1954. They wanted a 'qualified' settlement head and had heard about me from my university tutor. The salary (£1000) plus room and board was attractive. The contract was an initial six months with an option to discontinue, on both sides, on two months notice. At my interview (wearing a hat of course), it became obvious that the place had fallen on hard times. Two successive heads had left within six months following the lengthy tenure of the successor to the young head of my student days. They were short of money and staff. The Executive Committee, composed largely of the heads of well-known girls' schools, by whom the settlement had been founded in the 1890s, believed that salvation lay in the appointment of a 'qualified' person, like me. I was doubtful, but accepted the challenge in the knowledge that it might well be very useful experience and would also allow me to establish myself in London, replenish my wardrobe and decide what I wanted to do. 'Professional' community work was new to the UK. In retrospect I see deep significance in the fact that the (concrete) ceiling in what was designated as my office came cascading down a few days before I was due to take up the post in October 1963.

The activities of the settlement consisted of youth and old people's clubs, a lunch club, meals-on-wheels, a nursery school, a second-hand clothes store and much visiting of elderly people. There were usually a couple of students filling in a 'gap' year and other residents, helping in the settlement, plus volunteers and paid staff. However, the poor condition of the building precluded many residents at that time, though there were two full-time students, one of whom is now a professor! The full-time staff, paid by the settlement, had left, apart from the Organizing Secretary and her assistant. But quite soon I was able to appoint a domestic bursar and a part-time secretary. I took fieldwork students in due course, one of whom found a pair of false teeth stuffed down the side of her bus seat on her very first visit. After a few months it became clear that the Executive Committee (of which I was not a member) needed to take a good look at what the organization was doing, various former activities having run down. The finances needed appraisal. Although it was believed that the remaining projects ran on money raised from the supporting schools, the greater part of the finance was, actually, coming from the local authority and the London County Council. Furthermore, local people were virtually unrepresented on the governing body, chaired by an 80-year-old retired bishop. The treasurer was an 87-year-old retired schoolmistress. She was dismissive of my new part-time secretary who 'comes from COMMERCE', having had a good job in the City before marriage. My secretary's efficiency was not appreciated by the Hon. Treasurer, who once descended regally into the dining hall exclaiming '*Ay* don't know *whay* she thinks she can speak to me like *thet*: for *ay* am a *voluntary* worker and she is only *paid*.' Even more problematic was the fact that the jobs of the Head of the Settlement and Organizing Secretary, which were meant to be distinct, had for some reason become entangled, with blurred lines of responsibility. In due course it became clear to me that the incumbents of the later 1950s had in all probability enjoyed a close partnership domestically as well as professionally and had been doing what we might now understand as a job-share of both positions. It was little wonder that succeeding settlement heads could not make things work and exited speedily, not helped by the fact that the new Organizing Secretary definitely saw herself as ruling the roost besides liaising with schools!

At this time there were the beginnings of interest in the development of community work in the UK and I got to know other settlement heads who were working on the cusp of change. Overshadowing activities at Peckham was an extremely distressed wall, requiring about £3000 to be made safe. It promised to eat up any spare financial resources. By the late spring of 1964 I was in a position to offer the Executive Committee a discussion document on options for the future work and finances of the settlement. It was the sort of document that I had been taught to prepare at Bryn Mawr. However, the Organizing Secretary hit the roof on reading it, on the grounds that I had no business to prepare such a document. In the event the Committee saw sense in my observations and were prepared to give serious consideration to the issues. However, it seemed likely that the main effort for the immediate future would be taken up with finding remedies for the parlous physical state of the old building, not least the infamous wall. I decided that this was not a good use of my time and energies and felt that the Organizing Secretary was likely to try and obstruct any change. I heard that she had been sacked from her previous post, a fact about which, if true, the Settlement Committee may well have been unaware. They were genuinely surprised and disappointed when I said that I did not want a permanent job and offered to sack the Organizing Secretary, a

Cambridge graduate in her 50s, who did actually leave quite soon after me and died at a great old age — a millionaire, as it turned out! It was decided to set up an Advisory Committee to discuss the future of the settlement. I resigned after much careful thought and, in a good job market, felt it a wise decision, which I have never regretted. The settlement eventually staggered back on to its feet. Thus ended my first foray into management.

Before I had worked out my notice, I heard of a job teaching social administration on a new external London degree course in sociology at Kingston College of Technology. The College had an excellent reputation, I liked the staff in post and was offered the job, where I stayed for seven years. The teaching conditions were primitive to start with, but the mature students were wonderful and, being a section of a large department with a head whom we never saw, we ran the course ourselves as a collective. After two years I was promoted to Senior Lecturer and could have been Course Tutor had I wanted, which I did not. It was a creative job in many ways, despite having to follow an external syllabus. Outside the College, I was increasingly involved with the development of a professional association for community workers and served on its council for some years. By the early 1970s, regional colleges were becoming polytechnics and external London degree courses being replaced by new degree courses validated by the Council for National Academic Awards (CNAA). In the summer vacation of 1970 I had appendicitis and, returning for the autumn term, neatly sewn up, in due course caught glandular fever, almost certainly from the rather unsavoury coffee mugs we all shared in the School of Sociology. Much was changing in higher education and I was approached to apply for a principal lectureship at the Polytechnic of the South Bank. This meant less travel to work from home in Hampstead. The four years I spent at South Bank (1971 to 1975) constitute the major management experience of my career. I had really enjoyed Kingston, but felt ready for a change.

I was the first woman to be appointed from the outside to a principal lecturership at South Bank: one internal female promotion had taken place at the same time in business studies, as had occurred in maths, at Kingston. At South Bank, a new CNAA degree course with branches in sociology and social policy had already been approved to replace the external London courses. There was an external London Social Studies Diploma running part-time in the evenings and a course for sister-tutors involved in nurse education. The intention was to expand into social work. This proved to be a very demanding job since, initially, the core social policy staff were few in number. The major weakness was lack of secretarial and administrative support. I did a substantial amount of teaching, but was also heavily involved in the development of a new postgraduate CNAA social and community work course. I was also involved in the validation of other CNAA courses along with the committee and management responsibilities that went with a senior post. In addition, it was essential to make good contacts locally and nationally. At some point the Head of Nursing Courses and I got together and kept a complete record of how we spent our time by the quarter of an hour, a ploy I had been taught at Bryn Mawr. By then, the autumn term of 1973, the Head of our very large department had left, as had the Faculty Assistant Director, so I had Acting Head of

Department status for social policy, social and community work. 'Gentlemen and lady' was how the Director opened 'heads of department' meetings! The Polytechnic was contemplating an administrative restructuring, but, with some genuinely democratic procedures in place, the staff were able to make it clear that the proposals were seriously inadequate: they were eventually abandoned.

In the autumn term of 1973 I was working more than sixty hours a week. At this time my 80-year-old mother, living in Newport, Gwent, began to show the first signs of her final illness. I can remember feeling sorry that I, as the sole relative, only managed to visit on one Saturday, for the day, in the whole of that term. I did successfully get the postgraduate social and community work professional course validated as the first one of its category to be approved by the CNAA. More secretarial and academic staff were appointed, though it proved hard to attract social work staff, given other professional opportunities which were opening up. We certainly got good students. The one area that always remained problematic was the ultimate responsibility for the social policy branch of the undergraduate degree. I had been appointed on the understanding that there were to be two principal lecturers, one for social policy and one for sociology and that the two branches of the CNAA degree were to be run rather independently. However, the sociology post had not been filled, despite the availability of a distinguished internal female candidate. Some months later, an outside (male) appointment was made and in due course it became clear that he had been appointed Course Director for both branches. I lodged an objection and there was a formal enquiry: it was clear that my job description had been altered subsequent to my appointment. I have never been sure whether the explanation lay in sex discrimination or sheer incompetence. It could have been the case that the Appointing Committee baulked at the notion of having *two* female principal lecturers in post. Or it may have been that the successful male candidate insisted on control of the degree courses. I am happy to say that the disappointed candidate went on to an extremely distinguished academic career! The confusion was a source of annoyance throughout my period in post. It diminished the standing of social policy as a subject.

With subsequent experience of the 'traditional' university system, I realize that my foray into public-sector educational management was quite a gruelling experience. I certainly learned a great deal and always viewed it as a 'development' job, where my community work skills would come in useful and I reckoned, on arrival, that I would stay about five years. I found that I had the skills to get a major new course under way and that I could motivate colleagues. And in terms of career development, I had one exceedingly useful experience. There was of course no such thing as staff appraisal. However, we had an Assistant Director in post and leaving, at the point where the head of our very large department also left. Contemplating the restructuring possibilities then under discussion, and the interim regime in which I would have 'Acting Head of Department' responsibilities, the Assistant Director praised my work and, to my surprise, said that the Directorate had me in their sights as a future Head of Department. On reflection, with polytechnics expanding, this indicated an upward career path into administration (i.e. management), possibly to an Assistant Directorship, the likely ceiling for a woman.

But, on consideration, I did not fancy an administrative career. What I had not engaged with was academic research and writing, where I felt I had some potential. Approaching 40, I thought I needed a challenge! At the end of that (1972–3) academic year I applied for a couple of lectureships in traditional universities, was called to interview, but was not successful. Transfer to the traditional university sector seemed advisable if I was to have the space for research. My interview confirmed my belief that I would not be taken seriously unless I had some publications, quite apart from the fact that universities then regarded polytechnic staff as distinctly inferior! It was true that the ethos of the two sectors was substantially different.

Throughout 1973 we got the Postgraduate Social Work Diploma up and running but meanwhile my mother was becoming increasingly infirm. My work was extremely time-consuming and I was in line for further responsibilities. It was difficult to put in as many weekend visits to my mother's house as I would have liked, though she had good neighbours and a home help. She had been a first-class parent and made no demands: however, I felt she deserved some time and consideration from me. In the event, with polytechnic restructuring in the offing and a likelihood that my mother could be ill for some time, I decided on a career change. Late in 1974 I told the Polytechnic that I intended to leave at the end of the following year, when the new post-graduate course had run in and we had completed the revalidation of the new degree. This made clear my dissatisfaction as to the status of social policy on the degree course. As more staff came into post, I became more free to increase the input of help to my mother. By the autumn of 1975, I had identified an engaging thesis topic and registered part-time for a PhD with an internal University of London college. My mother was by now suffering severe physical disability, though mentally astute. She decided to give up her house and accept my invitation to create a 'geriatric commune' in my London flat, with me as carer and part-time student. However, before I had left South Bank, I had had contact with staff setting up courses in a new Department of Social Administration at the University of Lancaster, as a result of which I was invited to apply for a lectureship in social administration, specializing in income maintenance. I duly sold my mother's house, bought a new one in Lancaster and shut my flat. I did very little academic work in my 'caring break' for January to August 1975. My mother lived with me in Lancaster for four months, dying early in January 1977. She had offered to go into a nursing home, but I felt we could manage, as we did.

Perhaps it was not surprising that I succumbed to a colossal attack of flu and bronchitis the following April and was not really well for the first couple of years at Lancaster. I made a slow start, but made good use of my caring experiences in research and writing (with Janet Finch) on feminist issues in community/informal care as well as eventually obtaining my doctorate for a thesis on women and occupational pensions. There was indeed more space for research at Lancaster, which also rightly prided itself on its teaching and the encouragement it gave to mature students, features which had attracted me there in the first place.

But, as recorded at the beginning of this chapter, women then had limited chances of promotion. The University, by the early 1980s, was facing substantial cuts. I was the junior member of a Senate Sub-committee charged with looking into the future and making recommendations. I did not like what appeared to be on the horizon. In due course I took an 'enhanced' early retirement, though I carried on with a low-key academic career. Once I managed to sell my house, I returned in 1991 to my London flat and continued to research, write, do interesting part-time teaching, edit an academic journal and campaign for better pensions with voluntary organizations and pressure groups. I probably do the equivalent of a half-time job, though my earnings are modest. I could carry on like this for a long time yet — an academic 'third ager', still formally attached to the University of Lancaster, who have been most supportive.

Contemplating my working life, I recognize that I was advantaged by having parents who believed in giving daughters a good education, though my upbringing was of course constrained by the effects of war and subsequent austerity. Post-war South Wales was an egalitarian if patriarchal society. More Welsh children by far attended grammar schools than in England and more women went to university. My school, unusually for Wales, was independent and founded in 1860 to give girls who had lost one or both parents a good education, thus enabling them if necessary to earn their livings as governesses! The tradition of being able to earn your own living survived the school's transition to the public school ethos which developed in the late nineteenth century. By the early 1950s, most leavers continued their academic education or took a lengthy vocational course: nearly everyone else left with a School Certificate for a 'job with prospects' requiring more exams.

Since my parents were English by extraction and in no way involved in the Welsh culture, we did look to England for our recreation and travels. I always assumed that I would leave home at 18 for post-school education or training in England, never to return apart from visits. Being at a selective school, I never thought of myself as particularly bright, even if I had once come top of the county, aged 10, in the 11+ examination. At home we regarded this as a joke. At a school like Howell's, post-war peer culture applauded prowess at games rather than school-work. The school assumed that everyone could pass the School Certificate: the Head decried unnecessary chasing of matriculation exemptions. Many went to a university, but little emphasis was laid on getting into Oxbridge or winning a state scholarship. There were no honours boards. Perhaps just going to a school like that was deemed sufficient. When I was interviewed for my English-Speaking Union award to Bryn Mawr, I can recall that the Chair looked at my application form and remarked that I had been to Howell's, a very good school, which probably com-pensated for my degree from the deeply unfashionable University of Nottingham! At school we were not encouraged to be competitive as individuals: there were no numerical end of term form positions. All internal competition was for the honour of the house or, less usually, form. This was not a good preparation for middle age in Thatcher's Britain!

I viewed my university studies as a good general education for adult life, to be followed by professional training leading to reasonably well-paid (for a woman) employment of far greater interest than a non-graduate job. I think we all assumed that we would get married at some time and would in due course give up work or go part-time. Career opportunities for women graduating in 1955, barring teaching, were very limited. Careers advice was lacking. I certainly thought it very likely that I would give up work at some point and agreed with my parents that it was a good idea to enjoy the fruits of earning your own living and to travel before settling down to what could be mundane domesticity, as a choice.

My study in the USA was embarked upon as much from a spirit of adventure as from a desire for further qualifications. From undergraduate days I had had a keen interest in education, so I enjoyed getting to understand the American education system as well as US welfare provisions. It is not surprising that I had a career in education. I never wanted a profession in which women were unusual or treated with hostility. When I went as a lecturer to Kingston in 1964, I made the sixth woman on the staff. I was made welcome and was always conscious that I was a role model, as the only woman in my section until my final year. In the course of my working life I seldom applied for jobs: the ones I took up were put in my way by people who knew me and my work. Of course I was launched on to a buoyant job market and am one of a small age cohort. Few women of my generation went to university, let alone got higher degrees. I enjoyed having interesting and well-paid work, but resented the periods when work took over most of my waking hours, as I liked to keep some outside interests.

Many of my school and university friends had parents who had married 'late' like mine, and I assumed that I could do the same. However, when we reunited our year at school recently, it was clear that those who did not marry by their mid-twenties were unlikely to do so. We seemed to have roughly an 85 per cent marriage rate. Certainly by the time that I returned from the USA, most of my female contemporaries had married and eligible men appeared to be a scarce commodity. Divorce was rare and still stigmatizing. In my thirties, I found that I was enjoying my work and, able to observe my domesticated female contemporaries, as I developed teaching on the position of women as the second wave of feminism got going, I became more aware of the legal disabilities suffered by wives. Because I had grown up knowing a number of career women in that age-group whose marriage prospects had been severely impaired by the First World War and who were subject to marriage-bars to employment, I think I grew up accepting a career or marriage scenario. And we had sufficient teaching on maternal deprivation at the university for most us to accept unquestioningly that having children would of necessity involve a lengthy career break.

I think that my generation of women, children of the depression and the war, have asked rather little for themselves. We never expected to 'have it all'. I was unusual in having parents who always encouraged me from an early age to look beyond home and family. But 'pushy' or 'ambitious' were negative terms. It is not perhaps surprising, given my background, that I achieved an 'interesting' career: it would have been much more unusual had it been really high-flying. For that I would have needed much more ambition and motivation. There were no circumstances in my early life to set me on an upwardly competitive career path. I was a feminist, keen to see women in public life and keen to do my bit on a limited stage. One of the great pleasures of my working life has been to encourage women students: helping to develop academic women's studies and doing feminist research have been other highlights. But I doubt that I would be any happier than I am now had I ended up in a really senior job. I am sure my lack of ambition has exasperated some of my younger female colleagues, among whom there are certainly some high flyers. As a pensioner, I think I would have more regrets about not having a career than I have about not having had a husband and children, given that I am of my generation. But as my late father was fond of saying, 'It's all the same a hundred years hence'.

### References

FULFORD, R. (1957) *Votes for Women: The Story of a Struggle*, London: Faber and Faber.

GROVES, D. (1993) 'Dear Mum and Dad: Letters home from a women's hall of residence at the University of Nottingham 1952–55', *History of Education*, **22**, 3, pp. 289–301.

HANSARD SOCIETY (1990) *The Report of the Hansard Society Commission on Women at the Top*, London: The Hansard Society for Parliamentary Government.

# 10    Luck, Hard Work and An Unplanned Career

*Date of Birth: 28 March 1930*
**Angela Crum Ewing**
formerly Deputy Registrar, University of Reading, and national
president of the Association of University Teachers, 1991–2

My career depended on chance and luck, or the lack of it. It was not planned. But when I began to think more carefully about the way it had developed, I found that I could not consider it separately from my life as a whole. It has been part of my life, and it is my family background that has been the most crucial, though not perhaps at first sight the most obvious, influence on it. I was born in 1930, the youngest of three children in a prosperous middle-class family in Leicester. My father, who was 50 when I was born, had hated his schooldays and had left school at 14 and gone into his father's business. By the time I was born my grandfather was semi-retired and my father eventually succeeded him, keeping the business profitable even during the depression of the 1920s and 1930s. My mother, twelve years younger than my father, had trained as a teacher. After a brief and very unhappy period teaching in a small school in a South Yorkshire mining village she had joined the Bank of England as a clerk just before the outbreak of the First World War. In the absence of so many men who had joined up she was promoted rapidly, reaching a position that had never previously been held by a woman, and managing to retain this even after the end of the war until she left the bank in 1920 to marry.

My father, despite his own unhappiness at school, had a great respect for education and unusually for his generation believed that his two daughters should have just as good an education as his son. He may have been influenced in this by one of his sisters, a professional violinist, originally a member of Sir Henry Wood's orchestra which was the first symphony orchestra in Britain to employ women and men on equal terms, and later a founder member of the BBC Symphony Orchestra. Her husband had been shell-shocked in the First World War and was unemployed for lengthy periods, so my aunt had to support the family. As a child I was deeply envious of my cousin who as a baby had been parked by his mother in a wicker clothes basket in the greenrooms of the Albert Hall while she performed during the 'Proms' season (BBC Promenade concerts). This seemed to me very romantic. Looking back, I am now filled with admiration at the way in which my aunt ignored the conventions of the day.

My mother was the third child of a family of five. Her father died when she was about 5-years-old, and her mother managed to continue to live a life of painful respectability in London, locking the children into the house each evening and going to work in West End theatre box offices, returning in the small hours to snatch a few moments' rest before getting the children up and off to school. My mother remembered her mother washing the front doorsteps during the night so that the neighbours would not realize they had no servant. She inherited from her a belief in the independence of women and the importance of seizing opportunities. My mother had profited from (and perhaps deliberately seized) the opportunities for promotion at the Bank of England during the First World War. Some twenty years later her life was transformed by seizing the opportunities presented to her in the Second World War. My father was not in any sense a demanding man; but my mother undoubtedly must have felt an obligation between the wars to provide the usual comfortable domestic background for him. But in 1939 it became respectable, indeed praiseworthy, for women to support the war effort and work outside the home. My mother embarked at the age of 47 on a life of public service, and for the first time was able to demonstrate publicly her enormous drive and organizational skills. She ran the Women's Voluntary Service (WVS, now WRVS) in Leicester throughout the war. She became a magistrate, and chaired the Leicester City Bench for many years. She was elected to the Leicester City Council as a Labour member, immediately becoming Chair of three of its committees (Health, Education, and Maternity and Child Welfare), and then refusing to stand for reelection because she disapproved of 'party politics in non-political affairs' *(sic)*. Her many other activities included being involved in planning the National Health Service, chairing the Management Committee of a group of hospitals in Leicester, serving on a Regional Health Authority and being appointed to a Royal Commission on Prisons. From the age of 9 I became used to my mother being engaged in a huge variety of interesting jobs which she obviously enjoyed. Many years later, when I married for the second time, I found that my new mother-in-law was also a strong-minded woman who had seized the opportunity at the outbreak of the Second World War to escape from the traditional home-making role of the middle-class married woman and embark on a fulfilling career outside the home.

The outbreak of war in 1939 led to my being sent away to boarding school, rather earlier than my parents had intended, and I joined my elder brother and sister at Bedales School in Hampshire, regarded by many people at the time as a very unusual institution. It was coeducational, success in sport was not regarded as any more important than achievement in the arts or sciences, cooperation rather than competition was encouraged, and great stress was laid on the importance of friendly relationships between everyone in the school, teachers and children alike. Today these principles are for the most part generally accepted, and it is difficult to realize how unusual they were in the 1930s and 1940s, and how they were seen by many as positively dangerous. Bedales was a 'progressive' school, a pejorative term for many at that time. I was very happy indeed there — so happy that I did not work particularly hard, failed to get in to Oxford (my first, and only, academic failure), and went on to the University of Edinburgh without any clear idea of what I wanted to do subsequently.

My smooth passage on to university was possible only because my father could support me financially. There were no mandatory grants in 1949, and looking back I now realize how lucky I was. Without that financial security perhaps I might have worked harder at school. I would certainly have had to give some thought to a career — or at any rate a job. I was the first member of my family to go to university, and I went with high expectations. Sadly, for the most part they were unfulfilled. Edinburgh was a beautiful city in which to live, and I made many good friends, almost all of them English like myself. My English friends found it difficult, as I did, to adjust to a university in which most of the students had entered from local schools at the age of 17, continued to live at home and apparently came in to the university only for lectures and classes. I also found it particularly difficult, after my friendly and relaxed schooldays, to come to terms with a totally impersonal environment. The smallest 'tutorial' *(sic)* group I was in had twelve members. Teaching was geared to a remorseless round of examinations, since we sat these four times a year. At the end of my time at Edinburgh, not a single member of staff knew my name. I emerged with no idea that I would spend my working career in universities, indeed no idea about a career at all, but with my view of the importance of friendly relationships reinforced.

Then I got married and took what work I could get until, after two years or so, we had saved enough money to have a baby. My career was chosen for me, or rather I had again been fortunate enough to fall on my feet: at the back of my mind, whenever the thought of life after school and university had cropped up, I had known that what I hoped for was a family and this for me excluded any serious thoughts about a 'real' career. For the next ten years, the late 1950s and early 1960s, I was fully occupied in producing and caring for our four children. It never crossed my mind to do anything else. In those days there was no maternity leave and no expectation that middle-class women might return to work after their children had been born. But questions were beginning to be raised about the traditional role of women as home-makers. Mary Stott was editing the new women's page in the *Manchester Guardian,* as it then was, and I read in that, with some amazement, references to frustrated women graduates tied to the kitchen sink and to the demands of toddlers. My amazement arose because I was not at all frustrated and at that time felt I would have been quite content to remain at home indefinitely.

However, when my youngest child started school we needed more money and I decided, with considerable reluctance, that I must look for a job. I tried teaching and found, as my mother had done, that I hated it. Our house was on the edge of the campus of the University of Reading, so that seemed an obvious place to look for work, and I managed to get a part-time job there as a secretary. A few years later there was a vacancy at the University for a full-time Administrative Assistant and after some thought, and consultation with our children, I applied for it, got the job and in 1969, at the age of 39, finally started my professional career.

Up to that age my motivation in seeking a job was solely the need to earn money. But my move to a full-time career post was prompted not only by the prospect of more money but also by the fact that I was frustrated with an undemanding, though perfectly enjoyable, occupation as a secretary. I began to be ambitious: but I continued to put my family life first and was determined that my work at the university should never interfere with the demands of my family. Some years later, however, I reached a turning-point in the development of my career. My own children, and the two step-children who had arrived on my recent remarriage, had become relatively independent. My second husband, who had grown up as I had with a working mother, assumed, correctly, that I was ambitious to progress in my career. I had become by this time bored and frustrated with my job, which had become routine. There seemed no possibilities for internal promotion; having started my career late I was now probably too old, at 50, to succeed in getting promotion elsewhere, particularly since the whole of my career had been in a single institution; and the management style at the university at that time was one which I found rigid, old-fashioned and unsympathetic. I had been appointed in 1969 as a university administrator. In 1980, despite the huge changes that had taken place in higher education, 'management' was still regarded as a dirty word and any attempt to manage by 'the administration' was fiercely opposed. I was interested in the work of the Association of University Teachers (AUT) and would have liked to become more actively involved; but it had been made clear to me by the university that as a member of 'the administration' this would not be acceptable and that if I did so this would be held against me.

I concluded, however, that this need not prevent me from becoming an active AUT member outside the university. So in 1981 I stood successfully for election to the AUT National Administrative Staff Committee, subsequently becoming its Chair, then being elected to the Executive Committee of AUT and becoming National AUT President in 1991–92. These new activities opened the door to a whole range of other opportunities for me. My decision to seek some more fulfilling and interesting work outside my job at the university was the only occasion when I have planned a career move, and I have never regretted it. Besides enabling me to find new and rewarding interests outside the university, there was also an unexpected bonus as far as my job inside the university was concerned. To my pleasure (and, in private, slightly wry amusement) I finally achieved promotion to the professorial salary range at the university during my year's leave of absence when I was AUT President. Was it perhaps because in my absence someone finally noticed what I had been doing, when I was not there to do it? Whatever the reason, when I did return to the university for the last three years of my career before retirement, it was to a new and rewarding job and to find a welcome change in the university's management style. I was able to return with renewed enthusiasm to a position I might not have reached without my decision ten years earlier to make a positive attempt to get out of a rut.

The fact that I am a woman has undoubtedly had an important influence on my career, both positive and negative. My parents' attitude, and the general ethos of the school I went to, inculcated in me an assumption of gender equality that I still find it surprising to have to explain or defend. In some respects this has been a handicap, since I still do not always immediately consider when a woman is disadvantaged that it may be precisely *because* she is a woman and I may waste a great deal of time seeking some other explanation. An example of this lack of awareness on my part arose when I started work as an Administrative Assistant in 1969. I had no secretary, and so that I could get on with dealing with my correspondence I was eventually found a very old typewriter which had been stored in a cupboard when its previous owner had acquired a new and improved model. It was a year later before a (woman) secretary explained to me that the other Administrative Assistants, all men, had all got secretaries and therefore no typewriters had had to be found for them. I still remember my initial astonishment, and then my anger, when I finally became aware of this discriminatory treatment. It is usually difficult, however, to establish with any precision whether some things have, or have not, occurred because of one's gender. Like many women, I am uncomfortable about being assertive, for example in pressing a case for promotion or extra pay, although I have discovered through painful experience that it may be necessary. Yet while pressing one's case in this way is regarded as normal for a man, women are still finding, as I have done throughout my career, that for them this is not seen as normal behaviour, but as being aggressive or 'difficult'. In the mid-1970s, for example, I was offered a newly-established post in my department, with no regrading, and then found that the post I had vacated was being advertised at a higher grade. At that time I had no experience of pressing a case for myself, but I did screw up my courage to protest, and was told that 'they knew they could not get anyone as good as me to do the job without raising the salary'. My continued protest was greeted with amazement because it was assumed that I would understand that this was a compliment to me. The amazement became embarrassment when I rejected the compliment, and it was then made clear to me that I was being 'difficult'. I did win the argument and got regraded; but would a man have been treated in the same way? I cannot be sure, though I think I know the answer. In the 1990s examples of such patronizing and insensitive management may be more difficult to find, but the underlying attitudes, though hopefully less common, do unfortunately still persist. The uncertainty remains, as it does for so many women: if I do not get promoted or more money, is it because I am a woman or is it because I am not good enough? When a colleague unexpectedly resigned and I ran his office as well as mine for four months, I received no monetary reward. When my (male) colleagues covered for me when I was on leave of absence, they did. Was gender involved here, or other factors? Should I have asked for an honorarium? It never occurred to me to do so, but should it? The answers are not clear: but what is clear to me is that those who make the decisions on promotion, pay or anything else should themselves be clear that gender plays no part in their decisions. Years ago it would never have occurred to me that it was necessary to state this explicitly; now I have learned that it is, and that merely stating it is not enough either. Procedures to ensure equality need to be embedded in the management process.

A major constraint which has affected my career is due to my own personal choice. My own family life has always been of overriding importance to me and I have deliberately chosen never to be prepared to sacrifice any aspect of that in order to promote my professional career. When I returned to full-time work, in 1969, there were still plenty of jobs available in the expanding, and relatively prosperous, higher education sector. No doubt if I had been prepared to do so, I could have moved up the promotion ladder by being job mobile; but that was not something I wished to do. I could, too, have started my career fifteen years earlier, though it would have been more difficult in an era when maternity leave did not exist. I have had an easier life than my daughters, who have taken their maternity leave and then returned to work. I did not have to make that choice, but accepted the traditional life-style of the middle-class mother for the ten years that I spent at home in the 1950s and 1960s. But when I returned to work, I wanted a balanced life, with an interesting career and also the time to spend with my family, to have some leisure, to follow my own personal interests. This was my own choice, but it is also a very typical choice that many women make, or would like to be able to make if financial and other pressures permitted. It is not one that many men have made in the past, though some are now beginning to do so. And it is not a choice that is recognized or rewarded by promotion or selection committees. Similarly, late entry to careers, or career breaks in order to bring up children or care for sick or elderly dependants, are not taken into account by employers. Yet the breadth of experience gained by women in these sorts of ways can enhance and enrich their performance as managers.

Another constraint on my career development was my late entry into full-time work. I was fifteen or so years older than the usual entrant to university adminis-tration and by the time I reached the stage in my career when I might look forward to promotion to a senior position I was about 50. High flyers, who are seen as appointable to heads of administration posts, are almost always in their early to mid-forties. Ageism is a particular handicap for women, many of whom have inter-rupted careers. I was contractually required to retire at 65 and my career therefore lasted only twenty-six years. The implications of this for pensionable service are obvious. Many men are ready to take early retirement after a long and uninterrupted career: many women might be happy to continue after the normal retirement age, and would still have a great deal to contribute. There are strong arguments for a flexible age of retirement.

The positive aspects of being a woman, as far as my career are concerned, certainly exist but are less obvious. I am convinced, for example, though I cannot produce hard evidence, that one of the main reasons for the ease with which I rose through the ranks of the AUT to become President was because women members voted for me simply because I am a woman. As even my own university began to recognize the underrepresentation of women, a number of interesting jobs came my way. Being the 'statutory woman' has its disadvantages: but it certainly provides opportunities that would otherwise not arise, most importantly the opportunity to demonstrate that women perform possibly differently from men, but just as well as them, and often better. My middle-class background, too, has been an advantage to me. This would not, I believe, be the case today, or at any rate not to such an extent: but there is no doubt that for women and men of my generation being middle-class, and of relative prosperity, opened up opportunities that were denied to the working class. When I was a child, free secondary school education did not exist except for a tiny number of 'scholarship children'. My father had the means to pay school fees, fees for my music lessons, and my tuition fees and living expenses while I was at university. My school education introduced me to principles of equality and the importance of human relationships which are fundamental in the practice of good management. Perhaps my career has suffered because of the lack of emphasis at my school on competitiveness; but it did teach me the importance of team-building. I do not believe, in any case, that competitiveness should have a place in collegial institutions such as universities: although I did discover a streak of strong competitiveness of my own when I was running for election as AUT President, and I campaigned hard, since I believed my opponent was an unsuitable candidate. Among the many advantages I gained from my unusual school was that, along with all the children in the school, I was professionally trained in public speaking. This useful skill, particularly important for women, should be included in every school curriculum, and I remain grateful that my school recognized its importance. My rather unhappy time as a university student has also contributed in a negative way to my career development, since it has left me with some clear ideas from a student's point of view about how a university should *not* be managed.

Looking back now the crucial influence of my family background becomes evident. My father was a businessman, and I remember with some amusement the very clear distinctions made in my childhood between middle-class 'trade', which we were, and 'the county'. Each looked down on the other. We regarded 'the county', almost certainly unfairly, as rather idle people who lived off their inherited money and engaged in dilettante occupations and/or field sports. I see in myself, and in my approach to management, many of the attributes of 'trade' which seem to me estimable qualities and of great practical use: a pragmatic approach, careful planning coupled with attention to detail, flexibility, financial probity, risk assessment, evaluation of cost effectiveness, good recording systems, innovation when justified. My father applied all these in his business and in his family life, together with a warmth and sensitivity in his personal relationships which is less obviously typical of the successful business world. He knew the names of all his 200 or so employees, and their family circumstances; but he was capable of taking hard decisions when necessary in order to keep his business afloat. Years after his death, I still find myself wondering how he would have approached a problem: once I have decided that, it almost always seems to me correct.

How can one be sure what is due to heredity and what is merely coincidence? The pattern of my career closely matches that of my mother. She started by teaching, disliked it and gave it up. So did I (though I lasted only half a term, whereas she survived for two years or so). She worked at the Bank of England as, initially, a clerk and gave it up when she married. I had a couple of secretarial jobs and gave up work shortly after marriage. She began a fulfilling career at the age of 47, nineteen years after she had got married and when her youngest child was 9-years-old; I began my career at the age of 39, seventeen years after I had married and when my youngest child was 9-years-old. I share with her (or have inherited from her?) a belief in the absolute value of good organization and that once it has been decided that something must be done, a way has to be found to do it. Like her, it was chance that determined my profession. Running the WVS in the Second World War enabled my mother to demonstrate her considerable abilities at running an organization and turning her hand to anything, from decontaminating and reclothing a trainload of (literally) lousy bombed out evacuees (she persuaded the local Marks and Spencer to open their doors after hours and let her have the free run of their clothing stock, as a contribution to the war effort) to persuading internationally known musicians to give their services free for free lunchtime concerts in the local museum. My abilities were much less spectacular: but I had the luck to find that university administration (later management) was something I enjoyed and to which I could bring many of the qualities which I had inherited, or which my education had inculcated in me.

My unplanned career would not be possible now. I became a university administrator, and subsequently a manager, by accident. I started working as a secretary with no secretarial skills (apart from self-taught typing) and bluffed my way into my first job with a temerity which still surprises me. Jobs were plentiful in universities in the 1960s and early 1970s. My interview for a permanent post in the administration, with tenure after an initial probationary period, was an informal one and I was the only candidate interviewed because the two professors for whom I had been working 'had a word' with the University Registrar in advance. By the time I retired, in 1995, jobs of this kind were attracting literally hundreds of applications from graduates, many with PhDs and almost all of them meeting the criteria for appointment. I was fortunate to start what was to become an interesting and fulfilling career for which I turned out to be well-suited at a time when it was easy to get a start. Yet the job to which I was appointed, with tenure until retirement, bears little resemblance to the job I was doing on retirement. Administrators had become — even in the most old-fashioned institutions — managers; the large mainframe university computer, on which we had to give priority to academic research and which depended on batch processing and punched cards, had been replaced by interactive computing with a PC on everyone's desk; performance indicators, quality assessment, audit and accountability in its widest sense were part of one's day-to-day business; tenure had disappeared; money was becoming steadily scarcer; and universities were no longer elite institutions — we had become part of a mass education system. If I were applying for a job on the bottom rung of university management now, at the age of 39 and with the experience I then had, none of which would be seen as directly relevant, I would not stand a chance. Yet, to return to a point previously made, the apparently irrelevant experience of childcare and managing a family ought to be taken into account and regarded as just as relevant as, for example, experience gained from paid employment either within or outside higher education.

The development of my career, for the most part unplanned, has been based almost entirely on luck (and hard work, if I am to be honest): luck that I was middle-class, that I had enlightened and supportive parents, that I went to an unusual school, that when my children were young their father was a teacher who could care for them in school holidays, that my second husband urged me to break out of a rut (and thus for the first and only time to engage in positive career planning), and even — just possibly — luck that I am a woman. If I had been a man, would I have made a success of my career? It is pointless to speculate. The conclusion I come to is that the qualities of my middle-class 'trade' background, so useful to me when I began work as a university administrator, were supplemented as I developed later on into a higher education manager by a whole new range of essential skills. The old, macho style of management traditionally associated with men, who still predominate in the top managerial positions in higher education, has become less and less appropriate, and is being replaced by a style that encourages teamwork and seeks consensus rather than confrontation. This is my style of management, though I resist the opportunity of calling it a female style. It is, nevertheless, a style that many women besides me instinctively prefer; and so, on balance, it was luck that as a woman I was able to survive my development from an old-style university administrator to a modern higher education manager.

# 11    The Road not Taken

*Date of Birth: 6 September 1931*
**Mavis Ainsworth OBE**
Formerly Director of the School of Cultural Studies, Sheffield Hallam
University

I decided in my late thirties to go for promotion. I had a Senior Lectureship in a College of Education that left me free each day after 4pm, every weekend and all the student holidays. Not a bad deal. I had plenty of time to concentrate on my house, husband and two small children. Now I have just retired at 65 from a senior management job in a new university. I have been responsible for the academic leadership and resource management of a school with over 2,000 students and 200 academic and support staff. In my earlier career I was Head of Department, first in the College of Education and then in the Polytechnic that later became the University. I have spent twenty-six years as Head of Department, Dean, Director of School. Over the past few years I have worked weekends and evenings and had thirty days holiday a year. I look back and think did I make the right choice? Yes, most definitely, I did. But how much of my career has been determined by free choice? Let's say that I reacted to circumstance and tried to steer a course in roughly the direction that I wanted to take. This mode of travel seems to reflect the common experience. 'It cannot be denied, but outward accidents conduce much to fortune' wrote Frances Bacon' . . . but chiefly, the mould of a man's fortune is in his own hands. Therefore if a man 'look sharply and attentively, he shall see Fortune: for though she be blind, yet she is not invisible'.

   I was fortunate to be an only child with a mother who had ambitions for me. I came from a working class family; my father was a compositor in a printing business: no one in the family had any experience of grammar school education, let alone university. My mother made sure that I went to a primary school in a middle class area, from which I gained a place in a girls' grammar school and from there, at the suggestion of the headmistress, I applied to university. This came as a surprise to my family, who had teacher training college in mind for me. My father was reconciled to the idea when he found out that I could get a grant if I signed up for a degree course followed by a teacher training year. So was my future career decided.

I still look upon my years at university as among the best. I loved studying English and thought that perhaps school teaching was not such a bad idea if I could continue contact with the subject. But the reality of teaching in a girls' grammar school was not finally to my taste. I did not so much want to teach literature as to explore it with people who could expand my own understanding. I began looking for a way out after four years. By then I was married and my husband was having difficulty landing a permanent university lectureship; then we were refused a mortgage on a house because of inadequate earnings. This worst of times turned into the best of times when we decided to emigrate to America. My husband secured a post-doctoral fellowship at the University of Illinois and I signed up for a Masters degree and teaching fellowship. I loved every minute of it. This was 1956. After the post-war austerity of Britain, America seemed a wonderland of excess, with mountains of food in the supermarkets (at that time unknown in England), oversized cars and a vast continent to explore. All the young men were six foot tall with gleaming teeth and charming smiles. The young women were confident and self-assured. I secured my MA, embarked on a PhD and began planning a university career. Everything seemed possible. The snag was that my husband needed a permanent job and the one he chose was at a British university. So we returned to England and have spent the rest of our lives wondering whether we would have been better off staying in America.

On my return to England, I had no job and this seemed like a good time to start a family. My two sons were born in quick succession (for two weeks of the year they are the same age) and I switched my energies to home and children. I knew that I had to go back to work when all conversation with my friends turned on baby rearing and ways of cleaning the cooker. I was 33. I did not have a PhD and a university job seemed out of the question. I went for what I felt was the next best thing and sent a circular letter to the regional colleges of education offering to teach English part-time. I struck lucky and was appointed to a newly-established College of Education. When I found out that a full-time job required ten hours teaching weekly as against six hours part-time (for less than half pay), I took the first full-time lectureship that came up: I felt that this was the sort of job that would combine nicely with home life. And so at 34 I started my full-time career.

Even then I had not settled on the way forward. I had a choice between settling into a congenial teaching job compatible with family life or going for promotion and taking on responsibility with its attendant problems. In looking back I can see that the decision to go for promotion was in part influenced by my background and in part an expression of my personality, although the support of my husband was a crucial factor. As an only child with an ambitious mother I had been expected to do well. My mother, at the age of 45, had enrolled, with the support of my father, on a three-year full-time nursing course, after working unqualified in a nursing home for several years. She learnt to drive a car when she was 48 and worked as a district midwife and then as a general nurse until she was 70. This was a remarkable achievement for a women of her time. My girls' school was similarly influential. I had not been exposed to gender conflict; it was assumed that the girls would go on to university and careers. I guess also that the grain of my character is against settling for the soft option. I have always liked to influence events and make things happen. I was the one who between the ages of 8 and 11 had organized the neighbourhood kids into projects to support the war effort. We went from door to door collecting aluminium pans for making munitions, knitted scarves and gloves for the troops, sold our handicrafts to indulgent parents to raise money for the war effort. Later I became quite prominent in a fairly small grammar school for girls, head of house, prefect, head girl, all that stuff. In short, I found it difficult to take a back seat. I had ideas that I wanted to put into practice about teacher training and I felt frustrated by a traditional and half-hearted head of department. I decided to try for a head of department job.

It was then that I had to face the obstacles placed in the path of aspiring career women. Moving to a new job involves either living apart from partner and children or staying put and hoping for something to turn up. I decided that in my scheme of things my family was more important than the job. I realize that men down the ages have faced similar obstacles. Francis Bacon writes 'he that hath wife and children hath given hostages to fortune. For they are impediments to great enterprises either of virtue or mischief.' But men usually manage to fit the family round the career if only because they can earn more. It is not so easy for women. I notice that many women who have broken through the glass ceiling are single, divorced or childless. Nevertheless, I had by now chosen the career path so I stayed put and waited for something to turn up. There were more gender obstacles in the way. This was in the late sixties before equal opportunities' legislation, and discrimination was blatant. I was told after an interview for a Head of Department job by a female College Principal that a less well qualified male had been appointed because, unlike me, he had a wife and children to support. At another job interview I was told, this time by the male Chairman, that because I had young children the panel considered that I could not devote the time necessary to succeed in a high profile and responsible job. I decided that the best strategy was to demonstrate how good I was at my job. I took on as much responsibility within the Department and College as possible, far beyond the grade for which I was paid, and also became Chair of the Regional Colleges' Board of Studies. A new male Principal recognized my contribution and when I was 39 appointed me Head of the College's English Department on its merger with another college. I played a high profile role in the subsequent merger with the Polytechnic and was appointed Head of a newly-created English Department formed from the staff of three colleges of education. I was 44-years-old. I was Head of Department for eleven years, and for the last ten years I have been Dean of Faculty and, following reorganization from faculties into schools, Director of the largest school in the University.

From my appointment to the Polytechnic I do not believe that being female has been a serious disadvantage. By the 1970s equal opportunities concerns were permeating employment practices and the discrimination that I had experienced, based on unthinking acceptance of stereotypical male and female roles, was diminishing, or at least becoming less overt. Employers were beginning to accept that women were serious about careers and could do a good job. In some ways my gender was an advantage. I had a rarity value. I was the only female Head of Department, the only female at senior management conferences, the only female member of the Academic Board. Here I gained advantage from being regularly elected to the Board by the other male heads of department who preferred to trust me rather than each other. My problem was that I did not have any female role models, and I had to pioneer a way of behaving both with my departmental colleagues, who were mostly male, and my fellow heads of department and top management. Similarly they had to adjust to working for a female head or, in the wider organization, to relating to a woman as a senior management colleague. Male/female relationships are well established for family and social life; these had to be modified to fit the requirements of professional life. The feminist stance at that time was to insist that there were no significant gender differences and the female persona as constructed by men should be abandoned, particularly in the workplace. I found this difficult to accept; the female persona whether biologically or culturally determined was too much part of what I was. I liked to look attractive and shopping for clothes was a favourite leisure activity. I liked to pay attention to the personal and caring roles that were expected of me. I liked to work collaboratively with others and be open to what my colleagues wanted to do. I thought of myself as an enabler, someone who creates an environment in which those for whom I was responsible could flourish. I was a good listener and a good communicator. These may be culturally determined female characteristics or inborn aspects of my own personality. Either way I did not feel the need to play down these qualities. Rather I found them supportive of the leadership and managerial roles.

But there are aspects of the leadership and managerial roles that do not fit so well with the female persona. Essentially the head of any group has to promote the interests of that group and ensure its success in a competitive environment. Men have dominated public affairs for centuries, and their mode of leadership is the norm. This they have fashioned from their innate and socialized characteristics but the way of working has been crucially determined also by the task itself. I think that the nature of the task as much as the way men approach it deters many women from taking on senior roles. The task itself requires women to act in ways inconsistent with their socialized identity. Certainly individual women have the personal qualities required but are constrained both by their own and other people's sense of appropriate feminine behaviour. In promoting the success of the group within the larger organization one has to work collaboratively and promote the institutional purposes but at the same time secure advantage for the group. Men have the advantage here because they are brought up to bond together in a continual flux of companionship and competition. They work collaboratively and competitively at the same time and use humour to lower tension and establish camaraderie. Women are not nurtured in this tradition and have to learn how to be effective on behalf of their group. They need support but do not have the entrée to informal male networks. That is not to say that women cannot get support from individual male colleagues, particularly where mutual advantage can be identified, but the way to secure this support is uncharted. It is more readily secured through making alliances with individuals rather than through gaining entry to informal groups. One crucial requirement of successful leadership is to be prepared to back one's own judgment in face of opposition. My membership of the Academic Board and other major committees gave me knowledge of government and polytechnic policy that I was able to exploit in making strategic plans for the development of my area. To be effective I had to secure support from colleagues who often preferred no change at all, and, having persuaded colleagues, I had to secure support and resources from the wider institution. I tried to work through consultation as being the only sure way to a sound plan. But no matter how democratic you are and how much advice you take, in the end you have to accept responsibility and accountability for making decisions that are opposed by some staff. I also paid attention to implementation. I tried to balance strategic planning with managerial effectiveness and insisted on thinking through grand designs in operational detail. This was regarded as a female weakness in comparison with the masculine capacity to think big and build castles in the air. I could dream castles but also wanted to examine the foundations. The head of a group is also required to make decisions that affect other people's lives. This is not a task associated with femininity. It is necessary to promote some people and not others, to take up some ideas and soft peddle on others, to spend money on some projects and not on others, to undertake disciplinary action and judge performance. None of this comes easy.

I also had to contend with my male colleagues' stereotype of the female, based on their experience of women in family and social roles. Remember, at the start of my career I was the only female in a senior position in the organization. Women are not traditionally given floor space to express opinion. There was the problem of being listened to in competitive male groups. I had to work hard at claiming attention: I prepared meticulously for meetings and tried to speak clearly and to the point. I did not enter into conflict unless I had carefully researched my case and was sure that I could win. Words like 'formidable', 'determined', 'persistent' began to be attached to me. These characteristics went unnoticed in my male colleagues and were certainly required for success in the job, but they were at odds with traditional notions of femininity. At the same time I had to work hard to combat stereotypical expectations of female inadequacies. I always tried to keep my cool and argue in a civilized and logical manner even when surrounded by men banging the table and being generally unreasonable and emotional. I never gave colleagues any cause to suppose that the job was playing second fiddle to my personal life and I set myself very high standards of professional behaviour. I felt compelled to prove my competence. While some of my male colleagues could get away with slipshod work and pass it off with a joke, I could not indulge myself in this way. Above all I tried to keep a well balanced, relaxed approach and maintain informal, friendly and good humoured working relationships. I am sure I was too demanding and too anxious for too much of the time but I constantly tried to modify this behaviour which I am sure springs from lack of confidence and uncertainty in the leadership role.

I suppose the job was stressful and the stress was somewhat increased by travelling as a female in male territory. But I now realize that I quite enjoy stress and have a low boredom threshold. I return to the contention that the nature of the job imposes its own demands on male and female alike. I think that it is up to women to take on leadership and management roles and see how far we can use our inherent characteristics to improve the experience for all concerned. We should not back off senior jobs because the male way of working is uncongenial. I have enjoyed working with men, I like their humour and relaxed way of working and their ability to fudge and compromise when the going gets tough. I felt that I had to prove my worth and to some extent I have had to learn to play the game according to their rules, but the rules were on the whole appropriate to the nature of the job that had to be done. I was also able to introduce my own ways of working more in tune with female values, and these were welcomed by both my male and female colleagues. What I experienced towards the end of my career was an immense relief to have more and more women coming into senior roles and being able to identify with their perspectives and struggles. I think that the situation for women now is light years ahead of when I started my career. Women have established themselves as significant players in the workforce worldwide. There are now many more women in senior positions in universities as demonstrated by the growing membership of the Glass Ceiling organization. The six women Vice-Chancellors are a significant cause for celebration as are the numerous women Deputy and Assistant Principals and the growing numbers of women in senior administrative posts. The battle for recognition will not be won until there are equal numbers of women staff and equal numbers of senior women staff to match the 50:50 student gender balance. Discrimination remains but is more difficult to conceal. I think that the barricades are down and it is up to women to take the opportunities that are there. Not all women want the hassle of a senior job but then neither do all men. In my experience women hesitate to take on responsibility because of their compulsion to do everything well. They cannot envisage operating successfully across the necessarily wide range of responsibilities. Men take the job and then figure out how to make it fit their requirements. Women need to be at the centre of public life. Organizations benefit from drawing on different male and female perspectives. Anyway it is simply not reasonable to suppose that the best candidates for senior positions can be chosen from only 50 per cent of the population or that they have the best approach to running the affairs of the world. History does not bear this out.

I have written about the difficulties, or should I say challenges, that I have encountered. I also want to write about job satisfaction. What I enjoyed most was being in a position to influence the direction that higher education was taking away from the education of a narrow elite to a multi-layered mass education. I had been fortunate to break out of a working class background through the educational route. I had experienced a mass education system during my two years at the University of Illinois in the 1950s, and I saw this as the key to breaking down class barriers and giving more people the chance of a better life. I liked the type of education on offer in an American university. The American undergraduates were more widely read than our school leavers and well prepared for less specialized courses. Their school and college education develops social and personal skills as well as contact with a wider ranging curriculum and prepares them better for success in the outside world. I did not have any qualms about seeing education as a passport to a decent job; that was the way it had worked for me. I think that our specialized undergraduate degree courses are too narrowly targeted both in their subject matter and the skills that they develop. They provide an excellent foundation for an academic career when they should be developing the capabilities that students need to function in the fast changing employment markets of the future. American students who decide on an academic career are not disadvantaged. Rather, they are very well prepared by a broad-based degree followed by a professionally directed postgraduate education.

The polytechnics were established to provide exactly the sort of education I had in mind. I was able to contribute to policy formulation at senior level and translate this into action in my area of responsibility. With my colleagues in the English Department I facilitated access for mature students by developing concurrent full-time and part-time degree courses, underpinned by mature student preparatory courses. The preparatory courses were eventually transferred to the further education sector but I can remember a number of mature students who started on our New Opportunities for Women course, progressed to the English Studies Certificate and from there to either the full- or part-time BA, or a mixture of both. A few went on to postgraduate work. We maintained links with the further education colleges and the route remains open. In the faculty and school we implemented university policy on semesters, unit structures and staged awards. We combined separate degree courses into programmes with some common teaching. We opened up choice beyond the confines of the individual degree course. The university introduced the combined studies scheme that gave students the option of constructing a wider ranging curriculum from units in different degree courses to suit their needs and interests. My school attracted about 40 per cent of the university's combined studies students.

I welcomed the structural changes and worked hard at effective implementation. I was in tune with a system that provided lifelong learning for the mass of people through flexible and accessible structures. But I was also concerned with the nature of the curriculum. I had opportunity in a school that spanned the humanities and art and design to call on relevant traditions in each area so as to provide a model curriculum, one that called on a wider range of people's capabilities, the practical and creative as well as the intellectual. By this means their personal and social lives would be enriched and they would be better able to find a place in a rapidly changing job market. There was such a curriculum in art and design but it had too little exposure to the range of thinking in humanities. Humanities had suffered from inclusion in the academic focus of the traditional university and was separated from creative practice. I believed that curriculum design should emphasize the educational needs of the individual before the demand for comprehensive coverage of a subject field. I felt that it was possible to include curriculum components that were valid in terms of the study of a subject field but gave students opportunity for practical and creative work and exposure to the modes of thought of different subject areas. I also felt it important to offer work-based or work-related projects as part of the curriculum to provide an added vocational emphasis. I tried to ensure relevance by appointing professional practitioners to teach the practical and vocational components. One of the satisfactions of my job was that I was able in a small way to put my educational ideals into practice. I had to gain acceptance and resources at university level and I had to convince my colleagues that the proposals made sense educationally and would be attractive to students. It was they who did the detailed work and ensured the success of the courses; I was only the enabler. In the English Department we developed an English degree that included creative writing as an essential component and employed well-known professional writers to teach it. Recently a professionally focused MA in Writing has been added. As Director of School I was able to initiate media studies, film studies and film and literature degrees that had practical, creative components. We extended into professional postgraduate film and media degrees taught and developed in collaboration with industry practitioners. I should like to see the practical components of courses given GNVQ/NVQ (General/National Vocational Qualification) accreditation within a degree structure that dispenses with honours classification and provides transcripts of course content and skills acquisition. But that is for the next millennium to achieve.

These have been the chief satisfactions of the job: working with colleagues to develop a view on the strategic direction we should take and then making things happen to translate vision into practice. Much of the job has been concerned with problem solving. To translate vision into practice, especially in a large faculty or school, means solving the problem of creating an organizational structure that will give people the space to work effectively in small peer groups. I chose to work with an executive group of six senior academics, necessarily composed of men because there were no female senior academics when I took over, although that did change later. Through extensive consultation within the school, we developed and refined an enabling school structure. School staff were divided into subject groups led by principal lecturers with executive group members having oversight of one or more subject groups but having cross school roles as their major responsibility. We gained recognition at university level for our Research Institute led by a member of the executive. In implementing change I delegated widely and kept open lines of communication. I was always prepared to inform and discuss; yet the expectation of management secrecy was such that I had to work very hard to communicate. Staff saw some of the changes as imposed by the university and I had to be mediator to justify their relevance to our school. My male colleagues on the executive did not put the same value as I did on continuously informing and discussing issues with their subject groups. In the end I sent round detailed monthly news bulletins to all academic and support staff; made myself available to any individual or group who wanted to consult me, organized annual staff conferences, held regular meetings with subject group leaders and visited subject groups at least once annually. I was striving to establish a sense of school identity but I am not sure how far we managed to create it. I think we managed it on the Executive Group. But in a large school I learnt to accept that subject group identity is the bedrock and each group has to be convinced that changes would not be detrimental to their concerns. The pace of change has accelerated and problem solving became dominant. Each day brought its own crop ranging from the trivial to the catastrophic. I quite enjoyed solving problems; it was the need to deal simultaneously with so many that sometimes weighed me down.

I have gained great satisfaction from promoting the cause of women. As the only senior woman in the organization at the beginning of my career, I felt a responsibility to do this. But it had to be done without alienating the men. I have gained great support from being a member of women's organizations: first the Women's Group of the Society for Research into Higher Education and for the past eight years the Glass Ceiling organization for senior women in universities. It has been a great comfort to discover at these meetings that my failings and inadequacies were not totally personal but the common experience of other women working in a predominantly male environment. I learnt about equal opportunities issues first hand from the people doing the research. I learnt coping strategies and at the same time had fun. I had great pleasure nominating women I had met for external membership of our committees. In particular, when my school came up for a comprehensive review, I put forward an almost exclusively female group to do the job. I began influencing opinion at the Polytechnic in collaboration with women colleagues who wanted to set up courses for mature women entrants to higher education. My membership of the Academic Board enabled me to gain support for such courses, in particular male science and engineering staff became interested in ways of attracting women students. There was a strong and spontaneous grouping of women academic and support staff that had grown up quite independently but which from time to time I was able to help. Together we got Academic Board agreement to form a sub-committee to examine the role of women in the Polytechnic. We produced a weighty and comprehensive report on the position of all grades of women staff and students, and the physical and psychological environment. We included statistical evidence of the clustering of women in the lower status jobs and the gender bias of certain courses. We made about thirty specific recommendations for action to improve the situation that were all agreed by the Academic Board. We had gained credibility from having one of the male Assistant Principals included as a member of our group but there was no serious opposition. The report was the groundwork for the official equal opportunities policy and strategy promoted by the senior management executive and which all senior staff are now required to implement.

There is, of course, one ineradicable drawback for women who embark on a demanding career. For most women a successful partnership that includes child rearing is central to their lives. This is both a strength and a potential weakness. I was totally committed to the job but could distance myself from success and failure because in the final analysis I cared more about my family than I did about the job. What matters most to me is that my sons have turned into pleasant and mature adults with successful careers. I thought of my home and personal life as a separate world in which I could interact with family and friends in a supportive environment. I had started a family before I stepped on to the career ladder and the early stages of my career did not require the work overload that is the common experience of professional men and women today. My husband was also an academic and totally supportive of my career aspirations; he encouraged me to go for promotion. He did not want me to fit into the stereotype of the perfect housekeeper. We coped by accepting a considerable reduction in income by buying whatever labour saving devices were available, employing maximum help in house and garden and sharing what remained. I did not try to excel in traditional female pursuits; I never owned a sewing machine or a pair of knitting needles. My cooking skills remain rudimentary. This strategy did not, of course, free me from the sense that every woman has of being at the emotional centre of the household. I was the one who remembered birthdays and set up visits to friends and relatives; I knew when the children were having difficulties. I felt guilty when I had to spend too much time on my job at the expense of my family. There have been times when job and family demands have combined to weigh me down. There is no doubt that in recent years government cuts and the requirement to be accountable for quality in research and teaching have imposed a greatly increased workload, much of it bureaucratic. I think it is very difficult these days to have a balanced professional and personal life. I am sure that this is equally true for men in senior jobs. I found that if I felt reasonably on top of the job I slept nights. So I chose to work when I would have preferred to do other things just to be sure of a good night's sleep. I would have preferred a little more time for myself. In comparison with women friends with less demanding jobs, I have not had enough time to indulge myself. But to compensate I have had the excitement and satisfaction of working with colleagues to build a vigorous and successful institution that matches my ideals of what a university should be. I have now retired and am looking to redress the balance in favour of my personal life. I am aiming to become a hedonist. A whole new career is opening here.

# Part Three

# Reflections on Current Careers

# 12    Health and Efficiency

*Date of Birth: 26 June 1950*
**Professor Elaine Thomas**
Director of the School of Cultural Studies, Sheffield Hallam University


I don't go in for hobbies. I'm inclined towards obsessions. Regular exercise, provided by walking, aerobics, swimming or working-out, is a good example. It is not gentle or comfortable. It is strenuous, demanding and repetitive, stimulating, exciting and ultimately, relaxing. And I do it compulsively as this gives me pleasure. I'm also a vegetarian and have been called obsessive in my dependence upon porridge and molasses, and my love of broccoli. When I read novels, I become consumed by a narrative and can't put the book down. Once completed, I then seek out another work by the same author until I have consumed all her work. I have collected frogs, hands, and cacti. I can also be obsessive about clothes, and spend compulsively in a short burst. At the same time, I am a frugal person. I like to save money and to manage on a little. This tendency is quite helpful when managing a School budget in today's financial climate. Evidence of sharp contrasts between types of behaviour and attitudes emerges as I consider my life and career to date. Effecting a balance between the public profile presented to friends and colleagues and the private person revealed to few is inevitably difficult, and the public persona is likely to dominate. Other contrasts emerge: being both bossy and conciliatory in nature; being creative and expressive while methodical and well organized; seeking approval while wanting to be naughty; fiercely protecting my privacy and independence while relentlessly projecting a gregarious and strong public image.

I was born and brought up in Lancashire, mostly in and around Accrington, famous only for the demise of its football team, Accrington Stanley. My background can be described as working class, Northern and Methodist. My father was a policeman, my paternal grandfather had a military history; strictness and discipline underpinned a kind and supportive family environment. My mum did not have a career, and has always expressed a view of herself as unintelligent. However, she always seemed to have a job; in the market; in school canteens; various shops. Both my parents worked hard to sustain a small family of two daughters, of which I was the elder. My dad is a sensitive and kind man, with musical and artistic interests. We used to paint together until, around adolescence, I became a little more skilled than he was, and he abruptly stopped. We have always been competitive, as if each of us needed someone to provide that kind of stimulus. He would have liked a son, but his elder daughter fulfilled some of the requirements, except that she was very soft. In the early years, we used to wrestle, in a light-hearted way, but I wasn't up to it. I've always had a strong fear of physical pain. Methodist chapel was a regular feature, as was the Sunday school, and, for a short time, the church youth club. The Methodist influence was inherited from my mum's family, who came from Cumbria. My nanna, her mother, was a good, practising Methodist who saw no evil in anyone, and was gracious, kind and generous in a context of relative poverty. My mum's attitude to the church was more wary, and she influenced me substantially with her impatience and intolerance of the hypocrisy of church elders. My dad did not go to church, and has been pretty agnostic and critical for most of his life until recently, having begun to search for a faith in 'something'.

I was the first in the family to go into higher education. My mum and dad never tried to influence me in the way that middle class parents do. If anything, they always seemed a little in awe of me. They would, I know, be happy if I were a school teacher with a family, close by them, providing grandchildren and respectability. My career route has been to them excessive and not entirely necessary. Although perhaps puzzled by my chosen pathway, they have always been supportive. They never discouraged my interest in art or drama, coped admirably with my eccentricities, and, I know, are proud of me. My father displayed, during his working life, a strong resistance to career development. Opportunities arose for promotion fairly regularly as he is a bright man. He was fairly anti-authority for a policeman, and, like me, has a strong awkward streak which, unlike me, he was never able to channel constructively. I regard him as probably the single strongest influence in my life. I was fortunate to gain from my mother the female capacity for socialization and gregariousness. My father's intelligence and sensitivity were awkward strengths for him to handle in his male policeman's world, whereas I was able to develop and handle these traits in a context of support. My dad's generation did not have the opportunity to go to grammar school unless able to pay for it, and this was not possible for his family. I, on the other hand, benefited from a state education which provided me with expectations as well as opportunities. I was born in 1950, and neatly coincided with the decades, which have since provided useful descriptors of periods in my life. To be a teenager in the sixties after a warm but austere upbringing in the fifties presented a distinctive contrast. The onset of puberty coincided exactly with the rise of the Beatles, and the two phenomena have been inextricably linked for me ever since. Even now, a photograph of the young Paul McCartney has a strange effect upon me. My mum and dad also liked the Beatles, although I did not notice this at the time. Like many working class parents, they were young when they had their children, and, in the sixties, they were both in their thirties and receptive to the changes taking place. As I have got older, I have become more aware of the youthfulness of my parents. At quite an early age, I began to feel older than them.

Looking back to my teenage years, I can recall my parents' interest and support, my passion for the Beatles, a consuming interest in clothes and boys, and some key friendships. However, memories of this period are dominated by school.

*Let us now praise famous men*
   'Let us now praise famous men,
   and our fathers that begat us . . .'

These were the first lines of the school hymn at Accrington High School for Girls, where I was a pupil from 1961 to 1968. Not once did I encounter or consider any questioning of the appropriateness of this hymn. Rather, we all sang our hearts out in an assembly hall containing 600 female pupils, a large majority of single female staff and, at any one time, a maximum of four male teachers. The female teachers are worthy of particular mention. Anyone whose career is in education reflects upon her own teachers in a search for role models or influences. Alongside many women of my generation, I was taught by a large number of portly single women, regularly openly referred to as 'spinsters', many of whom had lost male partners during World War II. They were admirable and frightening and I did not want to be like *them*. Rather, I chose to identify with the younger married teachers who somehow seemed less lofty, more normal and accessible. A yearning for normality and acceptability is evident to me in retrospect, although this was constantly in conflict with a need to be different which manifested itself mostly through a strong interest in art and drama, the adoption of the role of joker, and an awkward questioning streak. Although endowed with an excellent memory which contributed to a capacity for exam achievement, and a very strong streak of competitiveness, my role was, to a degree, that of a rebel. This became clear when I was not made a prefect — the consequent feelings of rejection, as I aspired to a position with status, were at odds with my instinctive yearning to be different.

At the age of 18 I went to art college and everything changed. Here it was conventional to be weird. Dressing and performing in a particular and individual style was, in its own way, standard, and thus one replaced the school uniform with the art school uniform. I was, for the first time since puberty, being educated alongside men and consciously competing with them. My four years of studying art brought with it academic success, pregnancy, termination and marriage. As an artist I was aware that I was equal to and better than many of my male peers, although I did notice that their behaviour was rather different from mine. Conversations were always 'serious', and somehow represented the status quo. I adopted and adapted appropriately, both in artistic style and behaviour, but kept much private. During all my time there, it never occurred to me as odd that almost all the tutors were

GOODY GOODY

TWO SHOES

male, and all the people in senior positions in the institutions were male. This was 1968 to 1972 and I knew nothing of feminism, but I knew that I intended to be a success of some kind.

A one-year Postgraduate Certificate in Education broadened my artistic horizon and my attitudes. To become an art teacher in a secondary school seemed a worthy route and quite a normal and acceptable thing for a young woman to do. When an opportunity arose for a lecturing post in fine art in Belfast, I applied for it and was successful: I was thrilled but somewhat surprised. It had never occurred to me that women could be lecturers. In retrospect, I can place this underestimation of my own capacity in context. Although I considered myself to be ambitious and competitive, I had initially established safe, modest and achievable targets. The seeking of approval through good behaviour implied acceptance and modesty. As for most women, the 'goody-goody two shoes' syndrome continues through life, compromising and inhibiting women. I was always careful to compete only in areas where I thought I would win. Modest expectations also combined with a clear lack of role models in 1973. These factors recur in discussion with other women since then and, although I have changed since 1973, I regularly make a conscious effort to remember my perceptions and expectations at that time, in order to understand the nature and depth of the problem. I find it difficult now to admit to others that I applied for a lecturing post because my husband had already done so, with success. He gave me encouragement too. We were, after all, equals. We both got 'firsts' (First Class degrees), were both practising artists and both ambitious; but clearly, when it came to the job market, men's jobs and women's jobs were different.

Once I began teaching in higher education life was wonderful. Teaching highly motivated fine art students was a delight, and the expectation that I sustain my own practice was a gift rather than a requirement. Once teaching, my real learning began, and I have many cohorts of Northern Ireland students to thank for the stimulus and enlightenment they gave me. As well as thriving in this exciting and creative context, my capacity as an organizer began to emerge. During my thirteen years as fine art tutor, I was, for twelve of them, the only woman in the Department. I enjoyed working with my male colleagues, and the conscientiousness and attention to detail that my 'goody-goody two shoes' nature offered were appreciated in a male world. This male world was an artistic one, and it had its own characteristics. While it would be easy to stereotype some of the male staff using existing models for the artist or the teacher, most were much more complex and interesting. Becoming a leader in that world, as a female, was perhaps, in retrospect, predictable, even inevitable.

The particular male world described above included my husband, Mark, as a fellow lecturer and artist. We were colleagues at work, shared a studio as artists, and as a married couple, had made a home together. In 1977 we ceased living together, soon afterwards we no longer shared a studio, and, by 1980, we were divorced. Finally, Mark left Ulster and we no longer worked together. I responded well to living alone, which suited my need for independence and privacy, and I channelled my energies and feelings into my artwork during this period of change. Looking back at my career development, my aptitude for leading and organizing came to the fore once I became single, although I was never conscious of being inhibited or prohibited during my married years. Rather, I was confused about the expectations of others (family, in-laws, husband, friends) and my own deeply felt but unacknowledged frustration and ambitions.

I became Head of Department in 1986. However, on examining perceptions and expectations on my part, they are strikingly similar to those experienced in 1973. Description of the events and process whereby I became Head of Department reveals some familiar tendencies and some new factors which may strike a chord for other women. In 1984, the existing Head of Department vacated his post, and a newly-appointed male professor took up the position. The early eighties was a significantly fraught period when the impact of change was beginning to be felt. The institution in which I was based, Ulster Polytechnic, merged with the New University of Ulster to form the University of Ulster. Unitization of courses was placed on the agenda. 'Research' was emerging as a significant term. In this context, the newly-appointed professor experienced some difficulties, and eventually became ill. We then had a vacuum and various crises. When the post of Head of Department was vacated, it was advertised internally, and I was surprised to receive encouragement to apply for the post from both senior Faculty staff and colleagues in the Department. Again I recall very strongly the realization on my part that I thought Heads of Department were men and, really, I thought bosses were men. Needless to say, at this time, there had been only male HoDs (Heads of Department) in the Faculty, and the senior management of the University was predominantly male.

The importance of encouragement; the need to be needed; a context of crisis; these factors played their parts in my aspiring to and achieving the role. I have, in recent years, heard several references to male and female attitudes to career development, giving a clear message that men have far more confidence than women, in terms of natural expectations, Apparently, women will not apply for jobs until they are 80 to 90 per cent certain of gaining success, while men need a much lower level of expectation to encourage them. Rather than overtly aspire to a senior post as a good career move, my way of projecting myself forward was by adopting a 'Joan of Arc' or heroic female model. I applied for the job in order to do good for others; to serve their needs; to help to make things better.

On taking up the post, departmental staff were supportive and, without any focussed training, I found that I adjusted quickly to management, and a chance to champion the subject provided fulfilment. In order to be helpful, the Dean of Faculty encouraged me to attend a leadership course for university heads of department at Farnham Castle in England. This course proved to be a rude awakening. There were approximately forty senior managers on the course, four of whom were female. While I had no problems with the skills acquisition aspects of the course, the underlying philosophy was overtly masculine and evidently inappropriate. All references to leaders used masculine gender terms and the basic concept of leadership could be summed up as 'over the top, chaps'. I was so appalled and provoked by this course that, as soon as I found a course designed for women, I booked a place. The course, which was titled 'Women managers: Doing it our way' was organized by Sheffield City Polytechnic, and it began by asking all the women participants (approximately twenty-five) to sit on the floor in a circle, and introduce ourselves by first name only and identify our favourite colour. Other sessions included lying on the floor envisaging dreams wherein we met significant goddesses. I returned from this course truly confused. It made me feel impatient, competitive, and frustrated by soppiness and floppiness.

Thus, regarding role models, leadership styles and approaches to management, I relied on my own instincts and judgments, made plenty of mistakes, and learned fast. In 1988, faculty reorganization resulted in new, larger departments, and I applied for the post of Head of the Department of Fine and Applied Arts. There were no other applicants for this post, which provided me with the right kind of challenge early in my career. More female lecturers joined the Department, as the applied arts subject area was not a totally male domain. The department provided a new mix of both staff and subjects which created opportunities to question boundaries established on the basis of academic tradition and gender. A year after taking up this post, the Dean of the Faculty announced his forthcoming departure, and the University put in place procedures for reappointment internally. I expressed no interest in the post as I felt relatively inexperienced, but I was very keen to be placed on the interview panel. As it turned out, no candidates were shortlisted, and the University decided to advertise externally, including a professorship in the package. By now I became aware of some encouragement at various levels for me to apply for the post, but once again I felt a reluctance. In retrospect I cannot understand why I had such a resistance to putting myself forward. Perhaps the job appeared lofty, too senior, outside of my aspirations. Needless to say, there were no female deans in the University. I waited. Once again no candidates were shortlisted. By now the academic year was passing. The previous Dean had gone, and, as a group of Heads of Department we were operating in a vacuum and beginning to be anxious. There were three Heads of Department, and we discussed our concerns for the future of the Faculty. The University advertised again, and two of us decided to apply. This time, five candidates, ourselves included, were shortlisted. Once I chose to put myself forward, my competitive nature came to the fore, and I was far from reluctant. I was successful in gaining the post and became professor and Dean of the Faculty of Art and Design in July 1990.

I have felt it necessary to describe this process in some detail in order to convey the recurring tendency to resist opportunities for career development rather than to seize them, to adopt a reactive position rather than a proactive one and to maintain low levels of expectation and self-esteem. Hidden within this apparently negative approach there may be some positive factors. For example, there is satisfaction to be gained from the acknowledgment and encouragement of colleagues who perceive one's strengths and potential more than oneself. Once I became Dean of Faculty, I truly moved into a male world. My seven fellow deans were male, and all senior posts in the university were occupied by men, other than that of the Academic Registrar. So, a new kind of loneliness and alienation immediately became evident. My work in the Faculty brought many new challenges but regardless of the undoubted pressures, there remained a warmth and collegiality which sustained me, and support was constant. This presented a strong contrast to the University world which seemed to consist of large meetings in rooms full of men in suits. Perhaps my art and design background exacerbated the problem and I was experiencing pure culture shock. Fortunately, I came across some information about a networking organization called *Through the Glass Ceiling* which had just been formed by a small group of senior women in higher education. I was still searching for some training and development appropriate to senior women, as well as needing some female allies in a male world. Joining this group provided me with both. The first session I attended was an after-dinner discussion entitled 'What to wear for work'. It is hard to imagine men discussing such a topic, or understanding its relevance. As an understatement for a sense of difference this topic introduced me to other women with similar feelings of isolation and similar needs to gain confidence in *their* way of doing things. There followed, year by year, workshops and conferences about presentation skills, career development, assertiveness and, in particular, a session entitled 'Masculinity, power and culture', which involved memorable role play sessions where many of us pretended to be men. These workshops were complemented by inputs on research, financial management, management for change, and other current issues in higher education. Where possible, these were led by senior women, who acted as exemplars for the group, and demonstrated new styles and approaches encouraging transparency, frank questioning, lack of posturing, and lack of threat.

In six years, this organization has increased its membership substantially, as more women have gained senior positions. It has been for me an invaluable source of both inspiration and support necessary to alleviate feelings of discomfort and awkwardness. A yearning to be different, which I identified in my schooldays, and associated with my inclination towards art, has remained with me. However, when one has no choice about this, because, as a woman in a male world you are already visibly different, it loses its appeal. I have tried to use visibility in a male context to my advantage, by exerting a strong presence, but I perceive that there are far more advantages in being part of a group and having allies, as means of influencing the decisions and behaviour of others. While women can obviously cultivate male allies, the male networking which takes place outside of meetings is very dominant and often impenetrable. Predominantly male clubs, societies and organizations sustain the network, underpinned by the old school tie which knots and binds together. Male bonding is also effected through spectator sports such as football and rugby, participative sports such as golf, and overtly aggressive and competitive activities such as squash. Socially-based male networking can also exclude women as it is often bound up in a 'couples' framework, wherein 'wives' provide food and entertainment for senior male colleagues, and reciprocity is understood. It is difficult for a single female senior colleague to fit comfortably into these arrangements, and alternative strategies are looked for but not easily found. Once the particular male bonds are identified and recognized, one can make much more sense out of a meeting. A Chairman's favouritism is clear, the confidence of a particular male professor and the indulgence he receives is understood, and one no longer wastes time trying to get a word in. These kinds of bonds and networks are all-powerful and cannot be challenged by female means. Alternative networks and allegiances are required, and energy should be channelled into work outside of the meeting.

Despite the cynicism experienced here, I have found senior university meetings an enormous source of inspiration in relation to male behaviour, which can be irritating but very funny. In my first University senior meetings I encountered several male professors whose behaviour was predictable and easily classified into two types. Firstly, Professor 'Huff'n Puff' would swell up his chest, become red in the face, and visibly expand in size as he inflated himself with his own indignation. Usually another Professor 'Huff'n Puff' is required in the same meeting for this to be most effective, as each provokes the other, and their expansion to the point of possible explosion accelerates. The other predictable and familiar role is the Professor 'Bluff'n Guff'. He is an apparently cooler character altogether. He hasn't prepared at all for the meeting, and didn't even hear the question asked. But he is comfortable because he drinks regularly with the Vice-Chancellor, and he can ramble, say nothing really, but make it sound impressive by throwing in a few acronyms and statistics. These, combined with his underlying confidence, allow him to get away with murder.

The characters I describe are, I am sure, familiar ones to women in similar positions to myself. There are others also. My reference to them as 'Huff'n Puff' and 'Bluff'n Guff' represents my own private way of coping with my own impatience and frustration in senior meetings. Sharing a joke of this kind helps to diffuse these feelings. It continues to surprise women, when they join senior ranks, that the men they meet are often quite mediocre. The illusion that high status and power are automatically co-terminous with brilliance or even intelligence is soon shattered. Two factors play significant parts in establishing men in high positions. I have already identified both factors. The first is the sense of expectation and God-given right to achieve status. The second is the male networking and bonding which promotes and sustains success. Ability has little to do with it. Unfortunately, women score badly on both factors. Understanding of these factors provides little comfort but, once we have arrived in the board room, realization that we are brighter than many of our male colleagues can provide a spur to further achievement. I can actually remember my own belief in my twenties and early thirties, that men were more able to achieve power and success, that this was proven by their occupying positions of status and that therefore, they must be more capable.

Returning to my own career pathway, my years as Dean of Art and Design at the University of Ulster were both fulfilling and stimulating. My emphasis upon the culture shock encountered entering the male university world gives an indication of the strength of frustration and sense of difference felt. Much of my time in the Faculty was spent working with men and women with common aspirations and beliefs. Championing their concerns was straightforward and satisfying. My role as leader felt relatively comfortable and my management style seemed to be effective. I felt no yearning for change as higher education was and is changing all the time, and continued to present fresh challenges almost daily. Ironically, the *Through the Glass Ceiling* network created a new tension for me. As the organization grew in numbers and strength, more women achieved success as, for example, Pro-

Vice-Chancellors, and, ultimately as Vice-Chancellors. Regular reports were received at meetings of another woman taking up a senior post, and I began to feel the pressure of the Glass Ceiling. I had become aware, through many discussions with women colleagues, of my own low level of expectation, and that this was typical of many women. Colleagues told stories similar to my own, where they had been asked or encouraged to apply for senior posts at times of crises, and were surprised when they found that they could undertake senior jobs with real success. I thought I should try to make a change to the pattern of my life. I should take hold of my own career development and start to plan. This was, after all, one of 'Glass Ceiling's' messages, and we had received many training sessions about career development planning. This was during my fifth year as Dean and it seemed the appropriate time to consider a more senior post. A Pro-Vice-Chancellor's position became vacant in the University and, advertised internally, it acknowledged a lack of senior women at that level and particularly welcomed applications from women. I applied for the post, was shortlisted and interviewed, and expected to be successful. I was not. The post went to another woman and I had to cope with a new set of emotions. Having provided detailed descriptions of previous occasions where I was adopting a 'who, me?' approach to senior posts, in retrospect it all seems disingenuous. To adjust from a series of low-expectation scenarios which achieved success to a high expectation scenario which failed was difficult for me. The effect was unsettling, and the outcome significant.

With wounded pride, I settled back to my position as Dean, and reminded myself of the strengths, advantages and opportunities the job afforded. But, I had been bitten by the bug. My need for change remained, despite my contentment with my life in Northern Ireland. I had been based at the same institution since 1973, and had never envisaged leaving. A post came up at Sheffield Hallam University, which brought a larger portfolio of responsibilities. I knew the institution as a visitor and external adviser. I received encouragement from friends and colleagues there, and found myself once again tempted by encouragement, which was particularly welcome at that time. This was the first time I had ever applied for a post outside of the University of Ulster. In common with several other women I have met, building up a career in one place had been a preferred option. I had never been attracted to the globe-trotting career pathways many men took, and I had thought that commitment and loyalty to one employer was a strength rather than a weakness. I was successful in getting the job of Director of the School of Cultural Studies and I took up the post in September 1996.

For me personally, the change has been splendid. I find that, by moving to a completely new institution, I have substantial experience to bring, matched by a fast learning curve regarding local knowledge. Having worked in an institution where I knew everyone and they knew me had advantages and disadvantages. Being a new girl has its attractions and I will be quick to exploit current advantages. While it is clearly too early to provide a reflective or comprehensive report on my development as a woman manager at Sheffield, some first impressions are worth recording. I am already experiencing a vast difference in management style at senior level. The large meetings include more women and the men do not often wear suits. I find that I can contribute to senior meetings; indeed, I am invited to do so, in a context which feels supportive and by colleagues who seem interested in what I have to say. There is an informality present in the management style, which leads to a participative culture. This informality is predominantly male in manner, but it is not exclusive to women. Regarding networks, while I can sense the existence of some established male bonds, the University is experiencing some radical changes, senior posts have recently been established, reviewed and adjusted, and future shifts are likely. This state of uncertainty regarding allegiances and favouritism may not last, but, given the current context of higher education, it is likely that constant change will remain on our agendas. In these times of crisis management, budget cuts and extreme pressures, established hierarchies and comfortable networks are threatened and women may find that their voices will now be heard.

While senior management continues to provide the public arena for performance and fulfilment, reflection upon self as artist provides clues to the private person, her beliefs and her aspirations. I was never comfortable with the stereotypical image of the artist as a lone figure, usually male and bearded, starving in a loft for the sake of his art. Nor was I comfortable with the more contemporary model of the successful high profile individual artist who 'made it' in *his* lifetime. The latter model I saw and see as perpetuating the notion of the artist as a selfish individual, a hero or superstar, a cowboy or hustler, an elite and distant figure, admired by peers and misunderstood by the general public. The commodity value of such artists often requires that they have an agent to help promote them and to capitalize upon the wealth generated. The majority of artists I know do not fit in with either model, and they care strongly about the society in which they operate. However, many of them are satisfied to work relatively independently, struggling to produce work of quality and to make a modest income sufficient to sustain their creative output. I admire them enormously. The commitment and motivation required to sustain creative energy in a generally unsympathetic world is outstanding. For myself, I recognized a need to work more directly with people, and sought ways to combine a creative drive to produce work with a need for employment. Employment has always provided justification for my place in the world. Teaching offered a perfect combination, whereby I was able to inspire and serve others, while developing my own practice.

My own work began to take real form once I began teaching as I learnt much more than I ever did as a student. I gradually built up the confidence, as a woman, to remove the censorship that had been imposed during my days at college, and to allow personal narrative and images to emerge in my drawing and painting. My own self-censorship as an artist is linked to the seeking for approval which has been dominant in my life. Fashions and tastes predominate the fine art world, and, relatively unconsciously, many artists, particularly students, adopt the trends that are prevalent, and gain respect and praise from tutors and peers. Having the confidence to expose private, more personal, and more vulnerable areas of work takes time, and can be charted in retrospect more easily through a review of work, painting by painting, drawing by drawing.

My subject matter has always been people; their behaviour, their mannerisms. This includes myself as several people, my relationships and the many layers of meaning and understanding that exist between people. Public performance and private behaviour, the rituals and casualties of courtship, male and female body language, continue to provide sources of inspiration. I seek to convey much which cannot be expressed by words, and observe an obsessive quality to my work. Images are repeated and adjusted, identities are hidden and revealed, and visual metaphors provide clues rather than describe the obvious. The arena in which I now operate holds much for me as an artist. In recent years, I have not been able to give direct form to all images. Many are still waiting to emerge, but, meanwhile, they are in storage.

It is unusual for a female artist to find herself in the sort of world I now inhabit. The restraints imposed serve to contain the imagination rather than con-strain it. Creative drive is, in a real sense, directed towards management activities, and these provide some fulfilment and sense of achievement. But, at times, I feel like a voyeur, gaining insights and glimpses of behaviour and performances truly indicative of human nature. A sense of humour has always pervaded my work and it will hold me in good stead during the next few years.

# 13    From Rags to Riches to Rags Again

*Date of Birth: 24 March 1942*
**Professor Dorothy Severin**
Gilmour Professor of Spanish, University of Liverpool

There aren't many real Losangelinos of my generation, but I'm one of them, born during World War II. My infancy was spent travelling with mom and dad from one heavy bomber base to another (San Antonio, Texas; Ardmore, Oklahoma; Boise, Idaho; Sioux City, Iowa; Salt Lake City, Utah) until dad was finally sent to the Philippines in 1945. He really shouldn't have been in uniform at all, as a petroleum geologist in oil exploration, but he had been in the Reserve Officers' Training Corps in both high school and at UCLA, and he decided that the shortage of officers in 1942 was greater than the need for petroleum geologists. They made him a meteorologist, no doubt concluding that one -ologist was much like another. While mother and I awaited the arrival of my baby brother in Los Angeles, with his mother and a houseful of pregnant aunties, dad actually overflew Japan for weather reconnaissance on 5 August 1945. They thought that there was going to be another massive firebombing of Japan. But the next day the bomb was dropped.

Life back in Hollywood wasn't exactly uneventful. My very clear memories of toddlerhood kick in at this point. Shortly before VJ Day I managed to put my arm into an old-fashioned washing machine mangle, while 'helping' grandma with the wash. Grandma was an intelligent woman, but she never had a cool head, so I hung there and she screamed until heavily-pregnant aunt Maxie precipitated herself downstairs into the cellar and gave the mangle a god almighty whack. Maxie's stock rose in my estimation. (She had been an army nurse before marriage to my uncle Tod.) On VJ Day I was in plaster (sprained not broken), but gamely I set out with my single aunt Ruth and eldest cousin Lola to join in the celebrations. It was wild, and I actually recall a drunken sailor hanging from the top of a lamppost.

The next year brought big events straight away; first the birth of my brother and immediately after that, the return of my father. Our nomadic life continued. After demob and going back into the field (Bakersfield, California, in fact), dad decided to abandon the life of a geologist for a post with the Joint Chiefs of Staff in Washington, DC. His military career had been nothing short of spectacular: from Second Lieutenant to Lieutenant Colonel in three years, finally in charge of mop-up operations for the Army Air Corps (later the Air Force) in Japan at the end of the war. So off we went to Alexandria, Virginia, and the Pentagon for another two years. Our nomadic life and the fact that I was the first-born (and one of the eldest of the many cousins on the coast) had meant that my brightness had so far gone undetected. I was obviously a quick study for songs and nursery rhymes, and it can't be all that common for 4-year olds to twig to the non-existence of Santa Claus and to demand to help the parents set out presents for baby brother, but everything was done by the book (Dr Spock) in those days and any attempt to teach me anything was resisted. At five years I had nearly driven my parents to distraction with demands that they read to me, so they found a private kindergarten which would start pre-schoolers on the ABCs. The first day of class proved to be my undoing. The teacher explained the alphabet and how you put letters together to make words. This seemed simple enough to me, so I answered all her questions and started to read the little texts on the flip-chart. The teacher later taxed my mother with having started me reading 'too early' and broken what was then the golden rule, but mother pleaded not guilty. The teacher apparently wrote the parents a letter claiming that I was the brightest child she had encountered in many years of teaching. This probably wasn't much of a claim, if I recall the motley assemblage of war brats of every social background imaginable who were my classmates. However, golden rule number two was then invoked; never let the child know that s/he is intelligent. This party line was assiduously followed throughout my youth, leaving me constantly surprised by my academic achievements, which I put down to a combination of hard work and good luck, and to my father's expectations that I would always be the outstanding student in any class. It also explains everyone else's strange attitude towards me when young, as though they were dealing with an unexploded package bomb. Once an outsider, always one, so I determined finally to fashion a life as the archetypal outsider, a line that I have pursued successfully throughout my career.

After two years at the Pentagon, dad did another *volte-face* and went back into the oil business, so on my seventh birthday we boarded a plane (a DC7, I think) for the twenty-four-hour flight to Rio de Janeiro, where he would work on a secondment from a Dallas firm of petroleum consultants as a consultant to the Brazilian National Petroleum Council. Dad has a trick memory for figures (he remembers them all) and was effectively a human computer when it came to oil logs (stated on graph paper as charts). If he saw one unusual log that reminded him of another successful well log, he knew that he was on to something. Which is why he found the biggest oilfield in Brazil while he was there. He was constantly in the field, away for periods of six weeks or more, up the Tocantines, down the Amazon, all over the many states of Brazil, while we lived in a luxury apartment (the entire fifth floor) with the picture postcard view of Sugarloaf mountain on the other side of Guanabara Bay. We had a cook and a maid, but mother hated the cockroaches. Brother Dick (now 4) and I learned Brazilian Portuguese immediately from the cook and couldn't understand why mom and dad seemed to have so much trouble learning the language. I had good school luck and was sent to the American School, a forty-five minute school-bus journey from home. Rio in the late forties and early fifties was heaven on earth, with five beautiful beaches, most of which seemed virtually empty when we visited them. I was taught to swim (very well — my only decent sport) by an ex-Olympic swimmer of Scandinavian (or possibly German) background at the Copacabana Palace Hotel swimming pool. Peron and Evita were in charge next door in Argentina, and for a short time South America was the place to be. We even lived in the next-door block from the daughter of ex-dictator Getulio Vargas, who would stay with her during the election campaign which brought him to power as President of Brazil. We weren't especially amused to be awakened in the middle of the night by enthusiastic voters who unfurled the Brazilian flag and sang the National Anthem.

On the other hand, poverty was rife and we lived cheek-by-jowl with the dispossessed, who occupied shanties on wasteland near our flats and lived on the hill behind the flats, the aptly-named Mouro da Viuva (Widow's Mountain). We witnessed one suicide of a desperate man who jumped off the sheer face to his death. So I immediately became aware at an early age that I was privileged, an awareness denied to many of my more sheltered suburban contemporaries in North America and Europe. My first shock occurred at school. I was placed back a form in school, as they correctly asserted that they were far ahead of American schools, which had just entered the child-centred era. I was also teased, for which my stop-and-go early childhood had ill-prepared me. My hysterics were greeted with fear from my teachers and a lecture from mother (incidentally the world's nicest woman) on controlling my emotions and not letting people get me down. Lesson learned — I adopted my mother's sphinx-like exterior, which in both our cases conceals a sensitive soul. However, hysterical nagging obviously did get results at home, and I was bored stiff in class. My father insisted that I be tested at school and placed in the appropriate form. I never learned the result of these tests until dad finally came clean about two years ago. I was more than a bit miffed to hear this news, forty-odd years too late; I have always had a Walter Mittyesque interest in astrophysics. Still, I'm unlikely to have the requisite talents. However, it gave me a new perspective on my brilliant career; not hard graft but an easy option. The school tried to move me two forms ahead but mother insisted on my 'skipping' one year not two, so I went straight from 'first grade' to 'third grade', and was always one or two years younger than the other members of my class. This was never physically noticeable as I gained my height early, and it only noticed socially in the sense that I always related better to adults than to the other children. I did what I could to remedy this; I was mistress of the revels in my apartment block (the other kids were younger); I wrote and produced plays for them, and made the costumes as well. I had inherited mother's seamstressing talents. On the school bus I entertained the younger children with ghost stories. What can I tell you? I won the spelling bees and even the maths quizzes (no doubt we don't do this sort of competition any longer — not good for the self-esteem of the losers). The nasty German maths master never threw the blackboard rubber at me, just at the others. I was the Head of the Scout Troop (Brazilian division, the Bandeirantes). I swam; I took tap and ballet (although clumsy and slightly chubby); I ignored the children who called me the brain or snobby Dobby (the latter my nickname); I read dad's copy of *Time* magazine the moment it got to the house; I scoured the local English language lending library; I nagged the folks into many trips to the local museum; I buried myself in schoolwork; wrote poems and little novels, and generally was a miserable pre-adolescent, probably because my psychological adolescence was occurring between the ages of 9 and 11 years.

I actually managed to complete my primary school years (through grade 6) by the time we left Rio, a rare treat to live in the same place for four-and-a-half years and attend the same school. We returned to Dallas, Texas, in 1953, where again I had good school luck (a rich ghetto school called Highland Park) and where I would spend six uninterrupted years and complete my schooling, first at the Junior High School and then at the High School. We even managed to live in the same house for the last five years, although suburban Dallas in the fifties was a comedown after Rio and the servants. Dad, of course, was all over the map again — the Caribbean, Indonesia, Nigeria, Turkey. He ended up the President of a small oil company, which enabled me to go to an Ivy League college — but I get ahead of my story.

By this time my academic achievement was a fact of life. But what happened to me physically between the ages of 11 and 13 was totally unexpected. I haven't mentioned the fact that my parents have always looked like movie stars (fitting for Losangelinos, even Losangelinos by adoption, since they were born Midwesterners and had moved there as children). In fact, they looked rather like Cary Grant and Vivien Leigh. At 11 I really began to grow and shed the puppy fat. *Voila.* By 13 I looked like mother, but with rather bigger eyes, and more pronounced cheekbones and jaw. Thick black hair, blue-green eyes, very fair skin — Snow White, please stand up! Everyone was terrified. They stopped teasing me. I began to be the object of envy, an emotion which it took me years to identify and understand. It is to my credit that I fought against this, even trading in one set of girl friends for another when the first lot turned nasty. I also never experienced any shortage of suitors (those were the olden days, before efficient contraception and sex on demand). The birth of my little sister when I was 13 at least ensured that the middle-class princess treatment wasn't overdone at home. In high school I was a prom queen, wore hundreds of yards of net frills, traded in poodle skirts for The Sack, saw Elvis in person at the Cotton Bowl, rooted for the football team, edited the yearbook, and ended up class valedictorian (the top student). I also had two perfect scores on my Scholastic Aptitude Tests (for university entrance), which seemed to amaze even my peers. I had offers from Vassar and Radcliffe. Radcliffe won hands down on two counts: first, it was really Harvard and men outnumbered women 10:1, secondly they offered me the year's only Honorary Scholarship (the family by now was too well off to need real money).

Bliss was it to be at Harvard in the sixties with Kennedy in the White House and a group of hyper-bright undergraduates to relate to. Alas, I was the odd woman out again. The fancy Dallas duds and crimped hair went down like a lead balloon with the girls in the dorm, who were already into the long straight hair and peasant-skirted look of the late sixties (not to mention a few who were roped into Timothy Leary's LSD experiments). I also seemed to be a good student, despite dancing the night away with a succession of beaux. After two uneasy years in the dorms I took the only escape route available at that time, an early marriage and my own home, where I could study in peace and relate to a coterie of postgraduates. In class it was sink or swim, since a small subject like Spanish depended on its postgrads and they crowded out even the undergraduate classes. I turned out to have a special talent for literary criticism and was singled out by two professors for attention. I completed the course *summa cum laude* (first class honours), and thanks to the wonderful Woodrow Wilson Foundation, was given a full scholarship for my first year of postgrad study.

When I graduated from Radcliffe College in 1963, I was one of six women with a first class degree from a class of about 300 women. The men's college had about four or five times as many students, as was common in those days when women's numbers were artificially limited by college entry, as in England at Oxbridge. Harvard was the most enlightened of the men's Ivy League colleges, and the only one to accept women at the time. I did have one or two letters from other universities inviting me to consider studying with them, and I thought myself extremely lucky to have any offers at all. Even the armed forces wouldn't deign to extend an invitation to a woman in those days. Teaching was effectively the only career open to women, and most of us trained as school teachers, a career considered suitable for unmarried women and a few women past childbearing age who were widowed or had otherwise fallen on hard times. In businesses women were only secretaries; in retail businesses they could not progress past the shop room floor. A few pioneers had gone into medicine and law but placements were difficult or impossible to get. Harvard Business School had just graduated its first class of MBAs with a handful of women; one of these women with a unisex first name managed to get an interview but when they saw that they had made a mistake, they told her that they did not hire women. In all truth I cannot say that we took all of this with good grace. In fact, a lot of us were becoming very angry at the idea that we were being highly trained with nowhere to go except into the home. Even women postgraduates in the arts were not exactly welcome, and we discovered that our Head of Department, the former Dean of Graduate Studies, had a discriminatory policy which meant that he would favour male students over female for all scholarships and teaching fellowships, especially married women. There was a fair amount of turmoil because of this, and I felt the effect of the policy in my third year because I lost my departmental tutorial work and had to enlist the help of my professors Steve Gillman and Paco Márquez to scrounge up some work for me in related departments. Presumably I had been OK in my second year because they were obliged to match the Wilson Foundation's contribution. Oddly enough it never occurred to any of us, including the kindly professors, to try to complain about this to anyone, to the Wilson Foundation nor to anyone else in authority. It would have cut absolutely no ice. Nothing being done was illegal, and the world was an unfair place. It was simply the way that things were. Anyone who made a fuss would be considered a troublemaker.

Tragically, my husband Jack Vivian would be called up from inactive reserve status (ex Marine Corps) for Vietnam duty, and would eventually go missing in action. I completed another year of teaching and dissertation preparation, met and married a young Englishman called Tim Severin, and headed to England and Spain with another year's funding from the wonderful Wilson Foundation to complete my dissertation. Looking back on this turbulent early period of my life I am amazed at the resilience of my youth. I had already packed in enough incident for any one lifetime by the tender age of 24 years. But the fun was only about to begin. The dissertation year in Europe was a hoot. Tim is, of course, a writer and explorer, although he considerably confined his writing to histories of exploration for the first few blissful years of our marriage, until he got itchy feet to recreate some of these voyages. Before I met him he had already memorably tracked Marco Polo on motorbike during a summer vac from Oxford, and written a book about it. He had also explored the Mississippi by tiny launch to research a history book on the topic, the latter with assistance from a Commonwealth (Harkness) Fellowship, which explains how he fetched up at Harvard and married me. So although our first year was library dominated (British Museum and Biblioteca Nacional Madrid), we had many adventures, not least a trip from England, through France and across the Pyrenees in a tiny 1932 Austin 7. Tim wrote for the *Geographical Magazine* and worked on his history books while I completed the dissertation. I had expected to return to Harvard after two years, and on completion of the PhD took a one-year temporary lectureship at the University of the West Indies in Jamaica (Mona, near Kingston). My teaching replaced that of a colleague who had just taken the chair at Exeter, Keith Whinnom, who would become an important mentor until his early death in 1986.

The year in Jamaica was interesting, but I did wonder what the Jamaicans were making of medieval Spanish literature and whether it was particularly relevant to their experience or needs. Presumably those were still the days when the British-founded universities of the Commonwealth were heavily influenced by the British syllabus and staff. The Harvard job failed to materialize, so after a summer spent on assignment in El Salvador and Mexico for *Geographical Magazine*, I went to another women's Ivy League college for a semester. There was a baffling contretemps with my English husband's visa, perhaps because of hostility towards American campuses during the Vietnam war, and we finally departed for London, he with a job offer and me without one. Providence came to the rescue within three months with an offer from Westfield College, London, where I started teaching in the summer of 1969, and the rest, as they say, is history. If I had to recreate an academic milieu which was a close as possible to heaven on earth, it would be that college experience. I stayed there for thirteen years and finally left to become the first woman Chair of Spanish in the British Isles. In the meantime the academic cuts had introduced their worm into the apple of Eden, and the Westfield campus would eventually be closed and the surviving staff moved to Queen Mary College in the East End of London, a somewhat far cry from Hampstead. What Westfield provided were supportive colleagues and an atmosphere leisurely enough for me to have a daughter and manage to do a fair amount of research and publication. We also had a thriving community of postgraduates working in Medieval Spanish, thanks to my close friend and senior colleague in the area of specialization, Alan Deyermond. There were also many young lecturers my own age and overall a good attitude towards women because of the history of the College as originally a women's foundation. However, there was a severe promotions block and some hostility on high towards promoting women to senior posts and professorships, so as the decade wore on I began to look around. It was then that I discovered that there was considerable hostility towards hiring women professors in Spanish, an attitude which did not seem to prevail in other languages. Why this was so is a great mystery, since there seemed to be good opportunities for women in Spain and Latin America.

Meanwhile back at the ranch, home life was never dull. We spent our daughter's first summers (even the one before her birth) in a very small sailing yacht, traversing France by canal, and then sailed the Mediterranean, including the Tyrennian, Adriatic, Ionian and Aegean seas. Tim finally decided that he had had enough of armchair exploration and that the only way to sell a lot of books was to follow his original course and replicate early historical voyages. Hence the Brendan, the leather (yes, I said leather) Irish curragh which sailed the North Atlantic over two summers from Western Ireland to Scotland, the Faeroes, Iceland, around Greenland, and finally to Labrador and Newfoundland, in the wake of the Irish monk St Brendan and his more-or-less historical voyages. The expedition and the book were a sensation, and Tim became one of Britain's best-known travellers. However, the strains on the marriage were too great, and at the age of 36, with a 7-year-old daughter, I found myself alone again. This time I listened to the advice of the old adage 'lucky in life and unlucky in love', and determined to concentrate on my career and my daughter, a course which I have pursued for the past eighteen years, although I hasten to add that I 'never say never again' when it comes to matrimony. Ida herself is now married and I wish her much better luck than mine. Perhaps juggling marriage, career and children will at last become easier; at least women's opinions on this subject are beginning to be heard.

At any rate my career aspirations finally bore fruit, and after a semester guest-lecturing at Harvard, I suddenly found myself the incumbent Gilmour Professor of Spanish at the University of Liverpool, the oldest Chair of Spanish in the country. Alas, I was to remain the only woman Chair of that language in the UK for thirteen years, until 1995 when three other women joined me at Birkbeck, Glasgow and Manchester. Liverpool in 1982 was a curious place. They prided themselves on being enlightened enough to have just appointed three women professors (the one in English had recently left), myself and two sociologists. The sociologists lasted one-and-a-half and two years, if my memory is correct. Perhaps my conditioning in Latin America, Harvard and Spain stood me in good stead, for I determined to hang in there. After all it was the oldest Chair of Spanish in the country, and included the editorship of a prestigious learned journal. The headship of department was fun and not too stressful, and I held on to the London house for research purposes (my obscure field is best served by the London libraries, although for other purposes the Liverpool Spanish holdings are first-rate). This also avoided the problem of extreme isolation which the other new women professors found most difficult. Since everyone took the rather old-fashioned view of professors as a breed apart (not part of my London experience), women professors simply had no natural constituency. Other women were in awe, and the men had their own closed social circle. For a number of years the other women professors were chiefly nurses (with their own female world) and in education (again a primarily female constituency). Although there were a number of women lecturers in languages, promotion to senior level was rare. In Spanish we even had quite a number of young men as undergraduates, which I found an improvement over the Westfield situation. But it was ten years before a concerted effort was made to increase the number of female professors, and I found myself suddenly confronted with the dizzying prospect of ten female colleagues. What to do? I immediately organized a women's professors' lunch before meetings of the Senate, and discovered that even the married women felt isolated and were delighted to find some friends with the same problems.

Since I have been at Liverpool, I held the headship of the department for several years, finally becoming Pro-Vice-Chancellor for three years in the early nineties (another first). I have also been editor of the *Bulletin of Hispanic Studies* throughout that period. At the moment I am working for the Funding Council in Northern Ireland and have just finished stints for the British Academy Humanities Research Board and the Higher Education Quality Council. I have also just returned from a visiting professorship at Berkeley, which recharged my batteries and enabled me to do more medieval teaching than is now the norm (I mostly concentrate on Renaissance and Golden Age teaching here in Britain). Since a period in the States seems always to presage a major change in my life, I eagerly await what the future holds in store.

# 14    Always a Catholic? Guilt, Rebellion and 'Trying A Little Harder For God'

*Date of Birth: 24 March 1947*
**Professor Eileen Green**
Director of the Centre for Social Policy Research, University of Teesside

Catholicism, with its emphasis upon guilt and the need to 'try a little harder for God', still exerts its influence from my sub-conscious despite the fact that I have been a 'lapsed' Catholic for years now. I was born during the memorably snow-bound winter of 1947 in rented rooms in a Berkshire village noted for its stables and riding fraternity. My dad was an apprentice metallurgist at Harwell, a UK atomic energy establishment. After the war he and my mother had sought a cleaner environment than the East End of London, where he was from, in which to raise their family. This was a geographical move that my mum was never to come to terms with, as she missed her native Liverpool. City life for all its pollutions spelt excitement and company, qualities in short supply in the rural shires.

Both my parents came from large extended working class families, with which we maintained close contact. My dad was thought to have 'bettered himself' by gaining professional qualifications, although several uncles had their own businesses and were successful in other spheres. The complexities of social class differences were a strong feature of my childhood, most of which was spent on a greenfields works estate owned by the Atomic Energy Authority. In a similar fashion to military barracks, the housing was rigidly stratified. Workers or 'the industrials' as they were called, lived in the steel houses (a mixture of timber and metal cladding) and the staff lived in brick houses. Streets contained a mixture of both, but never on the same side of the road. I clearly remember thinking of the three little pigs nursery rhyme and the wise one who built his house of bricks, when the deficiencies of the steel houses were under discussion. Harwell provided transport to the work site at 7.30 am for the workers and thirty minutes later for staff. Observable class differences between the staff in the brick houses were more subtle since the houses themselves were of uniform proportions and painted regulation colours. Although on the staff, my dad was actually a skilled manual worker, with technical qualifications which he never improved to degree level. Status, income and personality were revealed in the form of conspicuous consumption on furnishings, domestic appliances and, of course, cars. My siblings and I absorbed tense adult conversations about neighbouring graduate EOs (Experimental Officers) who could afford new three-piece suites and the public shame, felt particularly by my mother, of not being able to carpet all floors of our three-bedroomed house. Money, or the lack of it, was a constant source of friction between my parents, and I learned the feminist lesson of the power of your own money early on, from my mum and Liverpudlian gran, who scrubbed office steps as a single parent and was to outlive three husbands.

Victorian ideologies of the husband as provider conspired to keep my mum at home as a frustrated housewife, but she escaped into the local labour market as often as possible to jobs which varied from waitressing to glass-blowing. As kids we breathed a sigh of relief when she was in work. Then she exuded confidence and fulfilment and gran came to stay to childmind and to act as a buffer between my parents, when, in common with many other husbands in the 1950s, and despite their obvious need for her income, my dad raged about his wife having no need to work. As the eldest daughter of five children, I was aware of gendered power from early on. My elder brother was put in charge of us on numerous occasions, but care of the little ones and domestic chores fell to me. We had the freedom to play in the woods and nearby fields after school and at weekends, excepting Sundays, when Mass was a priority. My elder brother was also the recipient of parental ambitions in education. Disappointment was constantly expressed when he failed to fulfil them, whereas mild suprise greeted my news that I had passed the 11+ examination. At this point, religion took hold, despite my mum not being a practising Catholic. She honoured her marriage vows to bring up her children as Catholics. My dad insisted that I sit the entrance exam to the Catholic girls' boarding school in a neighbouring town. It was run by nuns and none of my peers in the street were going, but my reluctance went unheard and I duly became a scholarship day pupil at an independent girls' grammar school.

This was to set me apart from my two brothers who were nearest in age, and my occasional playmates, and from my friends in the street. I had previously enjoyed a reputation as a tomboy due to being able to outclimb all the boys of my age in the local woods. Suddenly I was painfully visible in a different uniform, 'stuck up' and above all 'a girl'. Reflecting upon it now, I realize that having to wear a formal uniform with skirts, dresses and, above all, gendered hats, marked the transition to adolescence and effectively ended any attempt to participate as an equal in games with the boys on my street. Life at the convent was bewildering. At first

I showed great promise and being a Catholic endeared me to the nuns. They only tolerated fee-paying Protestants in search of an English convent education because the school needed the income, but they failed to accept them as God's chosen ones.

My lack of status was, however, visible to the well-heeled daughters of the middle classes who went home for 'hols' in exotic places, and I worked hard as a clown to amuse them and to gain entry to the edges of their world. Despite this, the relentless religious rituals, the petty tyrannies of the nuns who made up most of the staff, and the traditional nature of the curriculum conspired to make school a most unattractive place. I still marvel at the status-related jealousies and spitefulness between the nuns, who were part of the Sisters of Mercy Order. Status differences were detected in the tone of voice with which the Oxbridge-educated headmistress addressed the nuns who worked in the school kitchens, as we trooped behind her down the stairs, which always smelled of cabbage, to the basement dining room ajoining the nuns' quarters. A reading of Antonia White's brilliant evocation of a Catholic girlhood in *Frost in May* (1933) gave voice to my previously confused emotions about that period, and convinced me of the power of religious ideologies.

My most powerful memories of what I now know to be an excellent school in academic terms involve knowledge of myself as an outsider and an under-achiever who took refuge in humour and rebellious behaviour. The role models provided both by the nuns and the few female staff who supplemented the nuns as teachers were equally unattractive to me. They conformed to the stereotypes of admirable career women with a passion for their subject but little observable sex appeal. The exception to this came in the form of Miss Drew, a history graduate filling in the time between university and marriage. In the early sixties she was the epitome of glamour with her sloppy mohair sweaters, grey pearl stillettos and sleek beehive hairdo. Unfortunately, all she did for me was to remind me of the impos-sibility of coaxing my naturally curly hair into such a shape, or achieving the height and body shape necessary for such sophistication and the gaining of the diamond engagement ring which she flashed at us while chalking up line after line of historically (un)memorable dates for us to copy down. Only Miss Drew came close to the stereotyped pre-Barbie doll images of the 'girls' spread across the pages of *Jackie*, a teen magazine which I read under the desk during daily lessons on the gospels. I was regularly ticked off for my 'defaced' uniform, 'bold' attitude and lack of interest in the curriculum. It was a relief for all parties concerned when final speech day came. Saved from the private chat about a possible religious vocation by my surly attitude, I waited with sinking heart while my parents took their turn for a chat about my future with the headmistress. Their set expressions as they emerged said it all: a course in shorthand and typing and/or marriage were recom-mended, in that order. With four Ordinary Level examination passes and a deter-mination to avoid both the above, I scoured the evening paper for jobs.

### Only Fit for 'Women's Work'

This search led to a four-year stint as a dental nurse in local practices and then eventually in North London. Along the way I acquired a boyfriend who introduced me to sociology, marriage and a lifelong friendship. Amid the excitement of the sixties, I attempted to alleviate my boredom by handmaiding dentists, by temping (doing temporary jobs) in exciting areas of London, sharing flats with young women who always seeemed to be preparing for or recovering from wild parties, and desperately trying to understand the sociological jargon of my boyfriend and his student friends. By the age of 20, I realized that my salvation lay in higher education, but without Advanced Levels, I was fortunate to scrape a place on a teacher training course. The enlightened woman Head of a College of Education in Roehampton Lane, South London, bent the rules, luckily for me, and admitted me as a mature student in 1966.

## Discovering Higher Education and the Pull of Ideas

When I successfully gained my certificate in education with sociology as a special subject, I finally understood the jargon at student parties and had a job ticket into the bargain. Specializing in sociology as a primary teacher was unusual and a testimony to the radical nature of teacher education at that particular college. In February 1996 it was with an overwhelming sense of nostalgia that I walked the corridors of my old College, now part of Roehampton Institute, as a sociology assessor inspecting the quality of degree courses as part of the national quality assessment process imposed upon universities by the Higher Education Funding Council for England (HEFCE). During that week I learned that Roehampton is famous for its long line of women heads and professors, among them my benefactress.

Hippy culture and the reemergence of the women's movement passed me by. In 1971 I became a married woman and started my first teaching job in a primary school in north London. However, the confines of a staff room populated by married women teachers who shopped for dinner during the lunch break, and a Head near retirement and unimpressed by child-centred education and sociology, dampened my interest in teaching. Yet again I felt like an outsider. I yearned for the excitement of ideas. Against advice, I tried out the new teaching methods I had brought with me from College. I also boosted my confidence by becoming a part-time evening student at the local polytechnic. There I found the buzz of intellectual conversation, student culture and encouragement to develop my ideas that I had been missing. I was hooked on being a student. On graduating in 1974, I was ecstatic when I gained an award from the Economic and Social Research Council to do postgraduate study. At the stage when my contemporaries were beginning to have babies, I was commuting to university, and spending longer periods of time away from home. In retrospect, the final ingredient in becoming an academic in my own right was to separate from a husband by then well-established in the same field. I was entranced by student culture in the heady days when rent strikes and student occupations of Academic Board meetings made news. Heavily involved in a student culture dominated by class politics and exploring my new-found autonomy, I failed to notice the maleness of that culture and viewed the emergent women's groups with a mixture of puzzlement and scorn.

## And so back to Teaching

The detour into teacher education stood me in good stead for my first lecturing job. Being a trained teacher gave me an advantage, at a time when lecturing posts were becoming more difficult to achieve. My first post was a temporary one-year job at a religious College of Education in South Yorkshire, teaching sociology to trainee teachers. I thoroughly enjoyed the job, having been one myself. I happily taught a sociology heavily informed by Marxism and feminism which I had discovered as a postgraduate. However, the real world soon reemerged. My new Head of Department confided that my uncertain status as an impending divorcee and my unconventional ideas about sociology had almost cost me the job. I would do well to avoid socializing with and dressing like the students. Most of my salary for the first six months was spent on trips 'home' since I missed London desperately. I also avoided the well-meaning College matchmakers who attempted to adjust my uncertain status by inviting me to events populated by 'suitable' men. Before too long I was hauled over the coals by the College Principal for failing to listen to my Head of Department's advice on the unsuitability of teaching such 'radical' perspectives to fledgling home economics teachers. He duly warned me that my contract would not be renewed if I persisted. I refused to teach 'Noddy sociology' and the job was offered to someone else. Fortunately for me, the end of my temporary contract coincided with the major national reorganization of higher education which amalgamated colleges of education with local polytechnics. My small Department became part of the Sociology Department at the expanding Polytechnic nearby, where my theoretical interests were recognized as legitimate and I was offered a permanent job.

## From Teacher Education to Industrial Sociology and Women's Studies

Although relieved to be joining a 'proper' Sociology Department and to be given the opportunity to teach degree courses, I soon noticed the robust male culture of the place. The Head and senior staff from principal lecturer upwards were male, as were course leaders and the chairs of key committees. I spent my time travelling between two sites, one of them a former College of Education, where I again taught sociological perspectives to prospective teachers. In addition, I began to develop an interest in feminism, which had been embryonic and confined to my dissertation work as a postgraduate. Together with a newly-appointed female colleague, I began to offer 'women and . . .' options on the sociology programme and discovered the delights of teaching feminist perspectives to mature women students. By this time I had consolidated a new relationship and given birth to a baby son. At around the same time I was introduced to the pleasures of empirical research by a woman colleague. I gained my first external research funding contract in 1980, which financed a study of working mothers in the steel industry. The majority of my male colleagues sneered at such pursuits as they sped past me in the promotion stakes, becoming course leaders with reponsibility for large undergraduate teaching programmes. 'Polytechnics are not the place for research' they chortled, 'we're about applied, innovative courses; it won't get you promotion.' How right they were, but for different reasons. Motherhood and a joint directorship of a major research grant (with Diana Woodward, co-editor of this volume) to study gender and leisure kept me too busy between 1983 and 1987 to notice how many men were promoted over me, or how long I had then been at the same institution. In common with many women, I didn't have a career plan. I was content in that I enjoyed the job and found time for a life outside.

The project on leisure changed my working life. Suddenly the work was high profile and I belatedly realized how small was the proportion of Polytechnic staff who were successfully gaining research council funds. Trips to international conferences and invitations to address public bodies built my confidence and enlarged my ambitions within the institution. Despite living with a partner who took equal shares of parenting and domestic chores, this kind of research work, combined with a teaching load and expanding departmental administrative duties characteristic of the time, took its toll on my emotional life and I became a lone parent. In 1987 I directed a project on gender and information technology funded jointly by the Economic and Social Research Council and the Science and Engineering Research Council, which developed my skills in action research and interdisciplinarity, not to mention those of research management. We were a sizeable team by then, with the usual associated tensions and conflicts. This high profile in research gained me recognition within the Polytechnic, which was beginning to establish a reputation for its research, and I was eventually invited to join key committees, albeit as the token woman. Whilst serving on such committees, which have become an enduring part of my working life, I have developed a sociological interest in the multiplicity of agendas which are attended to before, during and after key meetings. It is here that the patriarchal cultures characteristic of university life are at their most complex.

As Kerman (1995) notes, I became accustomed to being made to feel out of place by the use of sporting metaphors, cricket scores as an entrée to the main agenda, and social isolation at the end of the table. As I gained confidence, I tried different strategies to make myself heard and visible, but I failed to join the inner circle who were offered lifts home by the Chair, or gained invitations to join sub-groups. I did not fully realize that it was my actual 'bodily presence' as a woman and token that barred me. Only since I have been researching in the area and exploring how gender processes 'work' in large organizations, can I empathize with Angela Coyle's observation that 'the more effective women are, the more they are experienced as a threat and the more men try to block their initiatives' (1989, p. 22). I learned to lobby potential allies before meetings and hope that they wouldn't be nobbled by 'the boys' in pursuit of their bigger goals.

The late 1980s marked a pivotal point in my career. Opportunities opened up on a number of mostly external fronts, and I learned the lesson echoed by many an academic, that your work and skills are often more appreciated by external audiences than those in your own institution, let alone your own department. On returning to the office after a trip to deliver an international conference paper, I was greeted with: 'Enjoy your break, then?' as if work doesn't constantly lurk in your mail in-tray. I am aware that male academics suffer from the same syndrome, but I am still of the opinion that women suffer more jealousy in this context, firstly, because there are fewer of us and we are more visible as 'strangers' in academia; and second, because we have smaller, less influential support networks to protect us (Heward, 1996). However, the late 1980s was also the time of a new relationship and another child for me, bestowing both pleasures and also the pressures of time. I took the minimum maternity leave and carted my baby daughter to numerous conferences, since I was still heavily involved in research. At the same time I also developed and ran an MA in Women's Studies, one of the first of its kind in the UK. This gave me a platform from which to develop a specialist Centre for Women's Studies (CWS) and an international profile in the area. One of the numerous reorganizations characteristic of large organizations resulted in the appointment of a woman Dean for my Faculty. Under her direction, women's studies flourished, taking its rightful place in the curriculum and providing the backdrop for the establishment of CWS, of which I became Director. During the four years of its life it provided me with a base from which to develop an innovative, feminist inspired series of courses for women managers (mentioned, incidentally, in Elaine Thomas' chapter); to be the contractor for an ERASMUS contract which established a European Women's Studies Network (WISE); and to host one of the conferences which launched the UK women's studies network (WSN(UK)A). This time was a major growth period for women's studies within universities (Davies and Holloway, 1995), an exciting time, the achievements of which are in danger of being dissipated by the way that recent research assessment exercises have been conducted.

### Addressing the Glass Ceiling

Aware of women moving into management positions by choice or default, I also noted women's isolation and eagerness to find support networks to sustain them. This knowledge provided the impetus for a series of highly successful courses for women managers in higher education. The CWS courses for women managers, with their unique blend of feminist support and organizational agendas, attracted a mixed group of participants, including a number of now famous women academics seeking a supportive environment within which to explore the institutional blocks which constitute the 'glass ceiling'. The topics we covered ranged from assertiveness training to securing external research funds, but the most important ingredient came in the form of the women's shared experiences of isolation and invisibility. The broad range of women, from lecturers to Assistant Principals, who came on them pooled experiences and coping strategies, although the mix of expectations and levels of seniority did cause tension at times, expertly dealt with by a very experienced team of trainers from a voluntary organization named Research and Training Initiatives (RTI), which sadly no longer exists. Regular participants included two former chairs of the *Through the Glass Ceiling Network* and other current members. Indeed, it was during one of the CWS courses that the idea of forming the Association was proposed. In retrospect, I realize that it was the mixture of feminist perspectives and management issues which made the courses so attractive, but it also set up political tensions which prevented them from becoming mainstream in the management training area. Yet it is precisely that cutting edge which is crucial. Management training for women which does not include a gender analysis of organizational structures and cultures limits itself to encouraging women to fit in with male values and trying to beat men at their own games.

## Management or Research?

In 1992 a major reorganization of higher education institutions brought a sharpening of competition between academics, especially in research. CWS found itself marginalized, with no place in the new structure, despite its profit-making activities. I accepted the invitation to become Head of section, since I was deeply involved in defending the profile of sociology in the new regime. I immersed myself in an ever-expanding set of managerial responsibilities. Flattened management hierarchies and a devolved budget ate up my time for research and presented me with a steep learning curve as I became one of 'them'. Effective time-management skills were sabotaged by the shadow of my ex-headmistress, Sister Gabriel. Her disembodied voice unhelpfully reminds me still that 'good enough' is not a substitute for 'excellence in all things', including routine paper work, which gobbles up quality time. Reentering the mainstream of sociology, I began to be perceived as a threat, whereas previously I had been sidelined in the women's studies ghetto. Male colleagues who had scoffed at my research activities now rushed past me to head up specialist research centres. Taking on a management role at a time which, as Davies and Holloway (1995) comment, was characterized by increased pressure on universities to bring in external funds and to gear their objectives to meet the requirements of industry and commerce, presented me with an increasingly demoralized staff group. My sympathies lay more often with them than with the newly entrepreneurial face of a senior management under pressure to conform to new funding arrangements. But I developed new leadership skills as I negotiated the tensions of a dramatically altered working environment, intent upon maintaining a viable subject group.

During the same period I sought recognition for my research achievements in the form of a readership application, only to find myself blocked. Learning from previous 'mistakes', I insisted on a written statement detailing my 'deficiencies' and embarked on a series of regular review meetings with a third party present as I systematically addressed them. Over a year later, I reapplied and was to learn that, once I had the vital letter of support from my male managers, my face fitted.

## Moving On

I became acutely aware of the impossible tensions between maintaining a research active profile and being a good manager. Searching for a post which would allow me more research time, I came up against the prejudice against academics from 'new' universities whose CVs display a mixture of management and research experience but lack continuity in single-subject publications. The Glass Ceiling Group and my network of female friends and colleagues were a strong source of support and identification, as I worked on my interview technique and reflected upon my priorities in a new job. Meanwhile all sociology departments became immersed in the rigours of preparing for the national quality assessment exercise imposed by HEFCE. Comfortable by now in my leadership role, I saw this as a chance to consolidate the reputation of sociology within the institution. Good teamwork from a strong staff group, whose members were convinced by the argument and enjoyed the necessary close exchange of curriculum ideas and teaching method, alleviated the inevitable stresses associated with preparation for a major public inspection. I also enjoyed being needed; I had absorbed my womanly, caring messages well. An excellent result consolidated our position and provided me with a high note on which to leave the institution.

I was successful at gaining a Chair in Sociology at a smaller university in the North in June 1996. Attracted by a reduced teaching load, negligible management responsibilities and time to develop my own research, I have reduced the tension between management and research and refocussed my priorities where I get the most satisfaction, namely developing research. However, restructuring — the plague of those of us who work in large organizations — has overtaken me yet again, and my honeymoon period in the new post was slightly marred by the moving on of the Dean who had appointed me and who had agreed my range of responsibilities. A university in the throes of major change and a new manager have both created inevitable tensions, as I struggle to maintain clarity around a carefully negotiated contract.

Six months into the job, I am becoming established, enjoying the autonomy provided by a senior academic role and reasonably comfortable with the challenges ahead, as the pressure to generate income and maintain quality with declining resources continues. More visible than before in an institution struggling to come to terms with its heavily male-dominated culture, the senior women are few but growing in number. At present my voice is heard on key committees; indeed I am invited to express my views. Taking on and restructuring a social science research centre is a rewarding task, especially when it is done in collaboration with colleagues who value my skills and experience. My sense of humour carries me through the surprise expressed when I comment on the 'white, maleness' of the institution: 'It is the North, after all.' Having time for my own research compensates to some extent for the commuting involved and the time away from my family. My Catholic legacy ensures that the guilt involved in the careful juggling of time between my personal and professional life is as strong as ever, particularly in relation to my children's needs. I am now constantly reminded of the permanent state of crisis in which higher education finds itself, and make a mental note to nurture and expand my support networks.

### Concluding Remarks

My experience of higher education, heavily influenced as it has been by class and gender, is not that unusual, but having the opportunity to write about it is. Another thread running through the narrative is perhaps not as visible as it should be. Personal support networks, both within and outside of academia, have been and continue to be paramount. Such networks are vital as a source of identification, creativity and renewal for me. My membership of the *Through The Glass Ceiling Network* gave me the courage as a working class feminist to aspire to promotion; hopefully my long experience as an 'outsider' will provide me with the strength of character needed to survive in a culture increasingly marked by rapid change, underresourcing and an intensification of work.

## References

COYLE, A. (1989) 'Women and management: Fit work for women?', in COLE, S. and COYLE, A. (eds) *Women Educating Women: Exploring the Potential of Open Learning*, London: Open University and City University.

DAVIES, C. and HOLLOWAY, P. (1995) 'Troubling transformations: Gender regimes and organisational culture in the academy', in MORLEY, L. and WALSH, V. (eds) *Feminist Academics: Creative Agents for Change*, London: Taylor and Francis.

HEWARD, C. (1996) 'Women and careers in higher education: What is the problem?', in MORLEY, L. and WALSH, V. (eds) *Breaking the Boundaries: Women in Higher Education*, London: Taylor and Francis.

KERMAN, L. (1995) 'The good witch: Advice to women in management', in MORLEY, L. and WALSH, V. (eds), *Feminist Academics: Creative Agents for Change*, London: Taylor and Francis.

WHITE, A. (1933) *Frost In May*, London: Virago.

# 15    The Accidental Manager

*Date of Birth: 5 May 1945*
**Professor Dianne Willcocks**
Assistant Principal, Sheffield Hallam University

I begin with a self-portrait. Typically referred to as a 'manager' in higher education, my job title is Assistant Principal, a label which defies simple interpretation. I am a member of my University's senior management executive; and I am seen by others to have traversed an interesting route through the groves of academe to a position of some significant managerial authority. So why does this set of descriptors seem inappropriate or inadequate? Somehow it fails to convey the tone and texture of my scenic journey through personal and professional commitments to an exciting place, where I am astonished to find myself apparently peering through my own personal glass ceiling but still struggling, enthusiastically, after all these years, and conscious of the many happy 'accidents' that helped me to construct my career as a manager. Strangely, I have often been ill-equipped for this challenging journey. There is little evidence of skill in forward planning, yet my social obligations and a sense of political connectedness have given me a clear direction, together with a passionate desire to make things happen for the better in the world around me. So I choose as my title the 'accidental manager' . . . for it is my thesis that woman-as-manager is the maker of her own history (and maybe that of others) — but in a rich melée of circumstances, not necessarily of her own choosing. Inevitably, the accidents of a particular historical moment can have a major effect. So, too, the inheritance from forbears and from community.

And so to my formative years . . . I was a first child; a working class girl, born in the dying moments of World War Two. As such, it was predictable that I would enter the world with a very particular inheritance: I was the daughter of a war-time bride and working mum; raised in those first few months in a household where the men were still conspicuous by their absence on war duty; and nurtured by a capable and coping mother who would soon be defying tradition and voting in the first Labour government, as an act of faith and commitment to a better world. So, I entered a society newly-fired with ambition and promise. And I grew up supported by a set of social structures which had been designed to ensure that my life chances and those of my generation were predicated on ability and endeavour — not on social position. How different from the experiences of my mother, a bright but frustrated grammar-school girl, who was obliged to enter the workplace at age 14 as the main family breadwinner. Accordingly, my brilliant mum made sure that we seized every opportunity created within the post-war welfare state (and my dad helped a bit too!). I lived in a newly-built council house in rural Herefordshire. As an accident-prone youngster I enjoyed access to this new creature, the general practitioner. And as a child who was passionate about learning, I graduated to grammar school, albeit undergoing a sad social dislocation, since in my village only a handful of working class children outshone the myriad prep-school products of the surrounding market towns; and none of my class friends made it to grammar school. Perhaps this was an early example of my latent skills in 'self-managing' the learning process!

Described by some as a bossy child, I 'managed' my way through the village school; at the same period, I was 'managing' my Brownie career as the proud sixer of the fairies; and, simultaneously, my school gang, as leader of the Fearsome Five. I then set about succeeding in grammar school. A failure at every physical sport designed to torment the adolescent girl, it was necessary for me to excel academic-ally in order to justify parental investment. Fortunately, I had masses of ambition but not much by way of a sense-of-direction. So when, at the age of 15, I fell in love with the drummer of a local rock band it wasn't too difficult to balance my yearnings for emotional gratification with the recognition that a clutch of decent Ordinary Level passes would be useful! In 1961, I won both the lower school prize and my soon-to-be husband — with my mother attempting to maintain a steer towards higher things from the wings!

My sixth form years allowed me to align Baudelaire, Virgil and Chaucer alongside my awakening to womanhood and it became an urgent matter to persuade others that I was entering into a serious intellectual contract that would develop in appropriate ways when the time came . . . But, at age 18, independence, leaving home, first job and marriage plans represented, for me, an imperative that could not be ignored. My school leaver's report contained the acid remark that it seemed a pity my ambition had failed to keep pace with my intellectual ability.

So, I embarked upon the next part of my life story, equipped with little more than youthful confidence and optimism; some good traditional Advanced Levels, and not a single, work-related skill that could be formally articulated. But I was still in love, as I abandoned my rural idyll for the challenges of the capital city, landing in suburbia as an accounts clerk in Bentalls, a traditional department store, where we were expected to address the senior 'Bentall' person as 'Mr Jonathan'. Good fortune smiled in the form of a chief accountant who just happened to be on the Board of (what is now) the University of Kingston (formerly Kingston Poly and, in 1963, Kingston College of Advanced Technology). (See Chapter 9 by Dulcie Groves.) An early advocate of positive action, this senior executive singled me out and directed me to a new part-time Higher National Certificate in Business Studies, where I found myself a lone female in a man's world. Indeed, in 1966 when my early flirtation with business management culminated in a mass examination for the Institute of Marketing finals in central London, I was the only woman in an examination hall laid out for 500 candidates — not necessarily a conducive setting in which to give of one's best!

Meanwhile, the 'personal' moved on apace — and just weeks before my HNC finals, in 1965, I was married in white to my childhood sweetheart — still a rock musician but now also an aspiring sound engineer in the world of television. By this stage, I had entered the world of market research. And during the latter half of the sixties, whilst my student contemporaries were erecting and defending barricades in pursuit of higher ideals, I became a home-owner, an active member of the Market Research Society, a researcher/promoter of marketing efficacy in the pharmaceutical industry — and, ultimately, a dissatisfied person! However, I did keep faith with my working-class roots and represented a lone voice in my Surrey village cheering in a Labour government. And I did enjoy my exploration of markets for pain killers and/or a new range of super antibiotics. But in my work I was prevented from exploring the social context of health needs and drug use. What I learned from relatively successful ventures in commercialism confirmed the preaching of my sixth-form Shakespeare: 'all that glisters is not gold; oft-times have I heard that told . . .'. Hence, my decision in 1969 to become a mature student, with a place offered warmly by the University of Surrey. Initially, an unplanned pregnancy caused me to defer take-up (planning never was one of my claims to fame!) but the University persisted in their offer, and, in 1970, whilst I was still coming to terms with the wonder of engaging with my beautiful daughter Eleanor, a prompt came from Guildford to encourage me to take up my unfilled place in the following session. 'Just one more year,' I said . . . and so I was deferred to 1971. When the call came that year, daughter number two was on the way! There followed a golden period where I crocheted the best blankets; baked the best cookies; and smocked the best baby clothes in my Surrey circle . . . but it was not enough. And, so, finally I entered university, at age 28, in 1973.

My experiences as a mature student are typically those of the seventies. This was a time when the return-to-learn concept was ill-defined and the rules of engagement non-existent. Consider the Chair*man* of Surrey County Council's Education Committee who denied my application for a student grant; she commented: 'but you've had your chance at higher study, my dear, (this being my part-time HNC!) and, anyway, why would you want to abandon your beautiful little daughters?' Then there were the engineering students (male, of course) who struggled 'manfully' with the notion of why I was promoting a petition for a campus crèche (they wouldn't sign). And, of course, there was the sociology professor who publicly denounced me in a mass lecture theatre as I left ten minutes early to pick up my children.

Not surprisingly, my domestic arrangements were obliged to move on apace. A member of my baby sitting circle registered as a childminder for Ellie and Jenny; my husband, Pete, became a real partner in the childcare enterprise; and, of course, grandma took her turn. Somehow I survived the trauma and triumph of managing the morning departures; I enjoyed my early evening/weekend parenting; and I juggled heroically the responsibilities of managing birthday parties, first-day-at-school; and assessment deadlines. And, I still ran the local Shelter Group (a housing charity) and grappled with the contradictions of active Labour Party membership in Surrey! Against this backcloth, my earlier intellectual passion for literature and the romantics was displaced by a Marxist awakening, tempered with a liberal flavour of Tawney and Titmuss. A first class honours degree in sociology with philosophy was my reward.

Postgraduate study followed hot-on-the-heels of my first degree, as I launched myself enthusiastically into the world of housing research. A frenetic three years of personal and professional development followed, where I supplemented my grant income with a combined teaching/research assistant portfolio, adding substantially more to my CV then to my bank balance. But at the end of three years my research productivity slumped as familial and financial pressures took me into the market place before the completion of my doctoral work. And, so my first 'proper' research job at the then Polytechnic of North London (PNL) commenced, albeit in the absence of a fully written-up thesis. Nevertheless, the excitement of crossing the threshold of higher education as 'one of them' was profound.

I began my thirteen-year career at PNL as a 'jobbing researcher'. My early experiences in market research, my intellectual journey at the University of Surrey, and a willingness to engage with processes of social change and to take risks were the source of my claim to competence . . . possibly a fragile claim. However, my first efforts at resource bidding were unusually successful and I began a major study funded by the (then) government Department of Health and Social Security (DHSS) to investigate old people's homes. A grant of £180,000 (in 1980 monies) was a generous sum indeed, all the more so from a newly-elected radical right administration with an avowed commitment to dramatic reductions in the public purse and to what was soon to be known as 'the rolling back of the welfare state'.

It was at this strange historical moment that my accidental career hit a break point. I became seduced by old-age as a research topic and by working with my two excellent and continuing collaborators, Sheila Peace and Leonie Kellaher, who shared this obsession. Together we established the Centre for Environmental and Social Studies in Ageing which took on an ambitious programme of research and development work on issues of design, management, advocacy, citizenship, welfare pluralism — all concerning elder care. Our work attracted attention and acclaim with policy makers, providers of care services, and the burgeoning private care sector. And we lived on our wits, shifting from short-term contract to short-term contract. A major imperative was to make our research findings useful, so we developed an active programme of dissemination, which took us to venues as disparate as the Fourth International Congress of Gerontology in Hamburg; the Transport and General Workers' Union annual pensioners' forum in Eastbourne; the Barnum

Broome Country Club for the Norfolk Private Home Owners Association; and Westminster Centre Halls for the DHSS. And, of course, it also incorporated a range of student groups in my Polytechnic! My doctoral thesis receded into the background as my research reputation gained momentum.

At the same time, a different career track began to secure my interest. The 'brothers' in my workplace branch of the National Association of Teachers in Further and Higher Education (NATFHE) had taken the view that a new, politically engaged yet uncontaminated 'broad left' person like myself could be useful! Cognisant of the claim that 'a woman's place is in her union', I succumbed to their encouragement and got involved. And I thereby took the first step on a steep learning curve, where in just four years I achieved accelerated progression from Trades Council Rep, to Branch Secretary, to Coordinating Committee Secretary, to Regional Council Rep, to Polytechnics Secretary for Inner London. This represented a whirlwind of activity around the major questions of the day for higher education and brought me into dialogue with impressive Inner London Education Authority officers and politicians, senior managers and academic leaders from a wide range of backgrounds. This was a challenge, indeed, for a relative newcomer, and one where I was brilliantly supported by my union colleagues (the brothers) and my research group (the sisters).

Not surprisingly, stresses and strains were starting to occur between the professional, the political and the personal domains in my life. All my good efforts to meet the demands imposed upon the 1980s super woman were doomed to crash! Reluctantly, I recognized that the intellectual argument and negotiating skills that secured my success at work were insufficient to protect my marriage, no matter the commitment and care that we shared. We parted company in 1982 with a sad exchange of words. He to she: 'the problem with you, Dianne, is you've changed . . .'; she to he: 'the problem with you, Pete, is you've *not* changed . . .'. And so I partially left my comfortable suburban Surrey habitat for the precarious life of a contract researcher in Hackney, Ellie and Jenny sharing our two homes and surviving with some difficulty a parental mismatch of expectation and ambition which love alone could not surmount. But, at weekends, for two more years, I went back to Surrey to do the washing and fill the freezer . . . yes, I really did!

Then, in the mid 1980s, a new Director arrived at PNL — at a time of deep institutional trouble and turmoil — and he set about designing a survival strategy. Determined to move academic excellence higher up the Polytechnic's agenda, he took soundings on the qualifications and characteristics one might expect from a poly-wide leader of research. The rationale behind this proposal for an internal promotion opportunity was to strengthen the senior management skills base; enhance productive links with external agencies; and refocus Polytechnic ambition. As a reputed research leader *and* the Coordinating Committee Secretary for NATFHE, mine was clearly a voice to be heard. And I took seriously the task of gathering views and representing them faithfully to my leader. I performed this task diligently and then sat back for a moment of brief reflection. I looked at the challenges that my colleagues and I had built into the new post; and in a rare moment of immodesty I took the view that only one person was equipped to perform appropriately and to deliver the Polytechnic research ambition — me! So I then threw my energies into a multi-stage application and interview process, where I aimed to seize the higher ground. For my assessors I posed a 'compare and contrast' scenario between two hypothetical candidates: one with an acknowledged and established international research record of excellence as a lone (male) scholar in a traditional subject area with a personal reputation at research council level; and, the other, a newcomer who had proved herself by carving out a new multidisciplinary area of expertise — with colleagues; who had demonstrable skills as a team player and team leader; who was now recognized by a range of national and international agencies and was active and well-networked in the local public and voluntary care sectors; and who was achieving fluency as a political leader operating with Polytechnic management. I convinced them that I represented a positive choice for future change; and in 1985, I joined PNL's senior management team as Director of Research and Consultancy. It was a brilliant opportunity with some interesting in-built facilitators and inhibitors. The urgent requirement was to bring about a cultural reawakening among the wider academic community to the possibilities of a real corporate role for research. And whilst there were many isolated individuals and groups who had maintained a relatively covert research presence at PNL during its dark days, it did not necessarily occupy an elevated ranking in the priorities established by the Polytechnic's first generation of elected deans. So I needed to set about the task of winning friends and influencing key people; gently testing out my new-found authority; using the tried and tested collegiate structures to promulgate my message; designing new, light-touch mission-oriented structures to engineer policy reformulation and support operational change. These were heady days, where in an institution that had effectively constructed and delivered a distinctive access mission amongst local communities, I was able to reinforce that mission by insist-ing on access to 'the best' — a high quality and flexible curriculum, underpinned by a research profile that combined excellence with relevance. Significant and visible products from this period were a user-friendly research manual for staff; a high quality published research report; a research database; a resources and informa-tion library for researchers; a redesign/repackaging of research publications; and an improving track record in winning research contracts.

A further change in leadership at PNL brought new opportunities. Encouraged to look outwards, I began an effective personal staff development programme which included membership of the Committee of Directors of Polytechnic's (all male) Research Advisory Group; and I joined the Institutions Committee of the Council for National Academic Awards (CNAA) — an early introduction to the embryonic quality industry. Then came a dramatic shift in internal management structures: deans of faculty at PNL were to be appointed, not elected. Another accident, another breakpoint — in 1988 I applied, successfully, to become Dean of the Faculty of Social Studies. And this really did start to feel like a risk too far! I was obliged to move from the management heart (or head?) of the Polytechnic in Holloway, back to a mid-distant remote site in Highbury — back to colleagues who had previously known me in my developing (but junior) research fellow role and a supportive (but for some oppositional) trade union role (the Trots were not well pleased!). So there was a whole series of important bridges to the future that needed to be constructed.

Importantly, there were good allies and, as ever, team-building was the key to future victories. The Faculty was emerging from a period in which the fortunes and reputation of social sciences had become tarnished. The good news was that a radical and robust modular curriculum was about to be launched, notwithstanding the in-built conservatism of some few dinosaurs; and there were pockets of willingness to develop a corporate responsibility, a major subset of which was to balance the books! But it was never going to be easy. What it did represent was the classic management challenge in higher education: the alignment of a widely diverse student group with an appropriate and flexible curriculum delivered in accessible ways. Linked to this, was the requirement to manage human resources and the learning environment within a resource formula which stubbornly refused to accommodate a historical legacy of profligacy! So, once again, I embarked upon an urgent learning curve. I restructured, through a consultative process, and developed a new resource allocation process. Importantly, I acknowledged my interdependency on the skills of fellow and sister academic leaders within my senior team. And, of course, my associated roles continued. I protected my research reputation as an active member of my research group with a major programme of Department of Health development work; I was a member of the Polytechnic Deans' Group within the senior management team; and externally I was invited to join the research policy team of the Polytecnics and Colleges Funding Council.

All seemed to be going well, until suddenly the Director determined that five faculties was at least one faculty too many! A Poly-wide debate on appropriate alternatives was generated against a tentative model from above that linked the Business School with Social Studies; and the Faculty of Science with Environment. From virtually every corner of the institution the cry went up that civilization as we knew it had died, with mourning and mayhem being most pronounced in the Business School. But I encouraged Social Studies to adopt an alternative strategy. Naturally, we welcomed the opportunity to enrich our disciplinary balance and to share our own successes with others; and, naturally, we described the possibility of a business link as a 'promising opportunity'. However, we pointed out that a more creative option might be to combine Social Studies and Environment. We fought a sustained campaign — we wooed, cajoled, lobbied and negotiated and, finally, achieved our objective. And, of course, I was then required to compete, yet again, with my fellow Dean for the leadership job. The struggle to succeed was becoming tougher but, on this occasion, I made it! During this latter period of my 'deanship', at the start of the 1990s, I continued to cultivate my external profile as an academic leader, not in any calculated sense but delighting in the opportunity to stand at the heart of policy debate in uncertain and changing times; being witness to some significant territorial disputes between governmental and the higher education sector giants; and, in some cases, having the chance to make a difference. A personal triumph during this period came with the realization that I had reached the threshold of academic respectability: I applied to the University professoriate, and was accepted.

Meanwhile, in the glorious dying moments of the Council for National Academic Awards, I undertook a substantial number of accreditation visits to aspiring institutions nationwide; I then shifted track and joined, simultaneously, the first cohort of quality auditors and the Open University Validating Committee, a mechanism whereby much that is new, specialist, future-facing and deviant from the traditional norm for higher education has found support and quality enhancement. And on the research front, I was invited to join the Economic and Social Research Council's Postgraduate Training Board, taking up the standard-bearing role for polytechnic research. And, finally, the Polytechnics and Colleges Funding Council's Policy Group on Research, having convinced their sceptical masters (using the term advisedly) to invest in research, I became part of the key positioning exercise where a substantial sum of public money was allocated to support relevant research programmes in the polytechnics and colleges.

Around this time, a rather different kind of collegiality captured my imagination. I met this rather dramatic and impressive Assistant Principal from Staffordshire Polytechnic who was determined to mobilize the intellectual and political resources of a senior sisterhood. The aim was to address a number of key agenda issues for higher education. This included the whole equal opportunities debate around career progression and contribution for 'under-performing' groups, alongside the enskilling and empowerment of those groups — to the benefit of themselves and the sector. The *Through the Glass Ceiling Network* started to define its terms and its territory. Initially, I experienced some doubts: after all, I was part of a senior management team of eight in which four members were women; my Polytechnic had achieved a 70 per cent participation rate for mature students and 29 per cent participation for black students. Did I need *Through the Glass Ceiling*, and did it need me? The answers came swiftly: 'yes' and 'yes'. Indeed, I became quite evangelical after my initial meeting; a bit like one of the zanier Smirnoff ads: 'I was a tranquil and non-critical under-achiever until I discovered Glass Ceiling!' It was just an astonishing experience, encountering so many powerful women contributing to a joint endeavour, with none of the noise, jostling and posturing of the male combat mode.

And it was through such encounters that my ambitious antennae were attuned to the possibility of higher office. In 1991 I applied and was shortlisted for the post of Deputy Principal at Sheffield City Polytechnic. This was the start of a strange love affair with a new and exciting city; with its people; and with a new institution, but sadly, it was not at this stage the start of a new career! I was rejected, and I began to appreciate the maxim that it gets tough at the top, and even on the approach routes to the top. Undaunted, I next threw my energies into an application for the same deputy position which became vacant in my own Polytechnic. Here I received warm support and encouragement from colleagues at all levels; yet I was to experience disappointment once again, the post being won by my sister Dean. This time it felt a lot more personal and painful, and this time it was important to accept gratefully and graciously the warmth and support that came to me from many caring sources, including my Glass Ceiling Network.

Clearly, more opportunities for change would arise; and I told myself that the persuasive CV which had taken me thus far must have some merit and could, therefore, be reflected upon, dusted down and repackaged for a future occasion. But I was equally clear that I was not just in a 'buyer's market'. I wanted to go somewhere that would espouse my values; enable me to develop my professional practice in a different kind of higher education environment; and one which would throw in a few odd challenges as well! My attention was soon drawn to yet another opportunity at what had now become Sheffield Hallam University. And, on this occasion, I was able to map out a close match with my own criteria for career change. Certainly, SHU scores high on the 'challenge' side! My sisters in Glass Ceiling did, however, warn me of troubled waters ahead. In a thinly veiled reference to the leadership style, I was advised that the management culture at Sheffield Hallam was akin to 'death by squash racquet'! Apprehensive, but determined, I proceeded with my repeat bid, and was successful, arriving in Sheffield as Assistant Principal in 1993.

This is the point at which words become difficult. How best can I describe the confused feelings of elation and dismay that characterize my sense of culture shock in those early days? It was a huge change in so many, many ways: I moved from my rambling Victorian London abode (a female home, shared with grown-up daughters and a woman friend) to a flat in halls of residence; my sometime lover remained in the south; and SHU seemed, and is, a really massive, male and complex University when compared with PNL. Yet I accumulated a wealth of advice and warm support to accompany me on my journey Northwards and a spontaneous welcome on my arrival; literally, my first in-tray was overflowing with cards and greetings from women I had mostly never met! There was a mood of optimism abroad; but here, I was the one woman academic member of the senior executive; there were two women professors including me out of fifty-five; and just two out of twelve School Directors were women. Sinister shades of command-and-control management appeared to lurk in every corridor. Yet, it was a powerful and successful University, with a leader who had helped to define the future contours of higher education and whose commitment to create new opportunities for new students, particularly those from disadvantaged parts of the region, was to have a profound influence on social and economic regeneration. My big question was how much more might be achieved through an approach which was experienced as empowering and participative for all sections of the wider university community? Equal opportunities had been effectively forged by active groups on the ground and powerful sentiments were encapsulated in the formal policy statement. The next stage would be to address implementation at all levels.

Part of the challenge for me was learning to love the city context. Raised in rural Herefordshire; spending my middle years in suburban Surrey, followed by multicultural Hackney and Islington, nothing had prepared me for the proud historical legacy of a white male, industrial aristocracy in Sheffield, whose contribution to industrial and economic change though steel and coal had literally helped to construct twentieth century Britain. And yet, that tradition alone would not ensure survival and success in a changing world. So, Hallam was part of an urgent agenda for change, serving as a key partner in multiple city groupings, and in particular, moving social and cultural dimensions of city life centre stage as a balance for the economic and technological imperatives to succeed. It was in this redefined context that I started to relocate my own personal and professional commitments in ways that might start to have an effect.

As I struggled in those early days, it became important for me to place on record a degree of achievement and contribution in areas such as curriculum change; in student support; in staffing strategy; and in equal opportunities, as my male counterparts exercised position and power in a more florid and flamboyant mode! But the position of Assistant Principal is an odd one, all the more so, in an institution which chooses to balance (or blur) the differential contribution of a managerial and a collegiate modus operandi; and, at the same time, espouses the devolution of major responsibilities for development and delivery within explicit institutional frameworks.

So, the Vice-Chancellor's decision to create a Deputy Principal role to strengthen the team provided yet one more avenue for me to test out the limits of my ambition and the realism of my expectations. This was a strange process where my application did progress to the final three, but it culminated in the time-worn phrase: 'thank you for your excellent presentation, but on this occasion, we regret . . .'. However, it was not a wholly negative experience, and I did emerge calmer and wiser; all the more so, since I was confident that the successful candidate, a comparative outsider, would bring new experiences and a commitment to team building that I could complement with my own set of competences. This proved to be so, and an early exercise in appraising and restructuring the senior team resulted in more coherent allocation of portfolios, the consequences of which are presently being exploited.

So what sense can I make of all this? Reflection on my progress through workplace hierarchies on my accident-prone route to senior management reveals a number of interesting features. First, I must confess that the journey was wholly unplanned: there was no apocryphal moment in my early childhood when I announced to the world that when I grew up I would be a university professor! It was more a mid-life discovery that I had somehow stumbled into this amazing place. Second, there have been no maps, no signposts and no obvious guides for women of my generation — indeed, the troughs of despondency or rocky inclines may loom up at any moment to beset the unwary voyager! Third, it is difficult territory to occupy even when you *have* arrived! What helped me on my way was the ability to learn from and work with some significant others and to be (mostly) honest with myself about where my capabilities might best be directed. In this respect, I received masses of support and encouragement from unsung heroes and particularly heroines, who helped me through the good and the bad times. What got in the way is a structure and a set of traditions in higher education whose mediaeval trappings have yet to be fully reconstructed in line with changing public expectation of a modern university experience — for both educational and employment ends.

One further and important reflection is that the journey has been fun! A happy moment to register came in 1995 when Sheffield Hallam was the venue for my fiftieth birthday celebration. Half-a century of my personal, professional and political history gathered together in a splendid marquee on our verdant Collegiate

Campus. My father won hearts and minds with an affectionate and wholly indiscreet account of my life and times; my mother commended the Vice-Chancellor on his excellent judgment and good fortune in bringing me to Sheffield; my daughters Ellie and Jenny (and about-to-be granddaughter, Zoe) were eloquent testimony to a real life achievement; NATFHE colleagues, research collaborators and a whole host of the sisterhood affirmed our joint successes over the years; and ex-husband, Pete, provided an echo and a continuity from our earlier happy times. This was a meeting of worlds that was not wholly coincidental . . . since for me, as for many women managers, there is a necessity and a joy in the juxtaposition of like with unlike; and the translation of values, skills and orientation between different dimensions of a single lived experience.

As to the future, there are new challenges to be faced. We know that the next generation of women will enter a world of employment that is characterized by structural change and uncertainty. Inevitably, career management skills will be the next developmental priority not the development of careers, as such. The key to unlocking success will be a person's ability to learn, to work with others, to solve problems, and to manage themselves. In this context, women are well-placed to translate their skills and experience, acquired in diverse domains, to meet new requirements. A *sine qua non* will be continuing support from networks such as *Through the Glass Ceiling*!

# 16 'You Know Where You Are With Numbers'

*Date of Birth: 29 March 1949*
**Maggie Deacon**
Director of Finance, University of Brighton

My father worked for British Gas for forty years as an engineer, having obtained an external degree from the University of London, the first person on either side of our family to get a degree. Being in a reserved occupation, he was not enlisted in the armed forces during the war. His father had spent his entire working life in the City of Birmingham Corporation Gas Department, and I still have the framed certificate and clock he was given in 1939 on his retirement, also after forty years' service. I suppose that it is this inheritance that has given me my commitment to public service. My mother's father was at one time a racing car driver but later worked in a car factory. My grandfather was fun. He smoked and drank beer, taught me to play cards and had a one-eyed dog. I think it was from him that I got my independent/entrepreneurial streak. My mother worked as a comptometer operator, and she was also a very clever and creative seamstress. She gave up her paid employment to get married. I like to think that I recognize this combination of mathematical expertise and creativity in myself. None of my women relatives undertook paid work except a 'spinster' great aunt who worked as a dressmaker.

I was born in 1949, in our front room in Birmingham, the youngest of four children, two boys and two girls. I started school when I was four and remember very well walking to school with my friend Marion on our own and being seen across the road by the garage man. It was a journey that I cannot imagine letting a 4-year-old do today. My parents were teetotal and committed Christians so when

I was small, most of their and our social life revolved around the church. When I was 7 we moved from Birmingham to Wolverhampton. There was no room in the local primary school and so from the age of 8 I had to go on a bus journey of several miles to school on my own. I thought nothing of it, but again I would not have let my children do the same journey at that age. My primary school served a large council estate and was very informal and jolly, although I do not remember any discipline problems. The headteacher was a woman and we all knew she was the boss! I passed the 11+ exam and went to Wolverhampton Girls' High School. My background was working class and my early schooling was working class, so having to do elocution and deportment lessons was quite alien and I felt 'different'. I found it very difficult to settle. In fact, it is true to say that I always felt alienated to a greater or lesser extent. I find this sad now as it was really a privilege to be at such an excellent school. My feelings were partly to do with the rules. For example, we had indoor and outdoor shoes and had to stand in a line in the classroom and lift up our feet behind us for our shoes to be inspected for any signs of dirt! Our skirts had to be regulation length and we had to kneel down to prove that they just touched the floor, and were neither too long nor too short. We were not allowed to talk to each other within the main school buildings and had to walk in single file on the left. I hated this sort of illogical discipline. I always thought of myself as the naughtiest girl in the school, but reading my school reports again now, I suspect that this was not so, although there was a lot of exasperation that I would not work harder.

It seems to me to be entirely right to give access to the widest possible range of opportunities to all social and ethnic groups. However, it is also important to understand the effect of the received language and culture of any organization or profession on those who perceive themselves to be different. This strikes me as important, whether we think merely in terms of good customer care, or go further and consider avoiding alienation and enabling all members of society truly to embrace opportunities, and not just to present individuals with possibilities which they feel too insecure to turn into opportunities. In the end, however, it seems to me to be a matter for all of us to be sensitive to this issue and to treat others as we would wish to be treated ourselves if we were the 'different' one.

When it came to Ordinary and Advanced Level examinations, I did well. I made a deliberate decision that when it mattered, I would work, so I guess that although I was something of a rebel, I knew when to give it up! Of course, the education I was given by the school enabled me to perform when I needed to, and I suspect that the absence of boys removed a powerful distraction and enabled me to do well in mathematics, further mathematics and physics in my Advanced and Scholarship Level examinations. A final memory of school: Enoch Powell, our local Conservative Member of Parliament, visited the school and we were allowed to ask him questions. I asked him how long he thought it would be before we had a woman Prime Minister. He gave me a look and said 'Not in my lifetime, I hope'. We sat there like good little girls and laughed. Why did we not rise up and tell him where to get off? Still, I guess we had the last laugh on that one — well, maybe.

I could not decide what I wanted to do next. I loved the pattern and problem-solving of maths but I also felt a burning need to save the world by becoming a social worker. The choice was too difficult, so I applied to three universities to study maths and physics, and three for the social sciences. I accepted a place at the University of York to do social sciences as they asked for the highest grades, and that was a spur to working hard at my revision. Being asked for a D and an E grade (the lowest pass grade) to study maths and physics did not seem to me to give a good message about the university offering it or about me. The degree at York was designed so that we took all subjects in the first four terms — sociology, psychology, economic and social history, economics, statistics, politics and logic. We took examinations at that point and were given an opportunity to review our initial choice of degree subject. Thank goodness we did. I had originally chosen sociology as I thought that was what I needed to be a social worker. Imagine my horror at the first lecture when the lecturer said 'All of you who think you are here to learn how to be social workers can leave now!' As it happened, I was looking for the answers to life's mysteries, but what I got from sociology was more questions. At 18 I was obviously too immature to cope with life's mysteries so I opted for economics and statistics. You know where you are with numbers!

I duly obtained my Upper Second Class degree and set about interviewing all the employers who were lining up to employ me! How times have changed. When I left university in 1970 I had no consciousness that women were disadvantaged, no idea of sexism, racism or homophobia. I guess this was because I did not feel disadvantaged at home, at school or at university. This did not necessarily mean that discrimination did not exist, but that in part I had not experienced it and in part, where I had, I just accepted it as the norm. For example, none of us helped my mother in the house. It was her role to look after us and we accepted this as right and normal. My personal ambitions as far as work was concerned were originally limited to the period until I followed her example and became a housewife and mother.

I decided to accept an offer from the engineering company GKN to enter their management training scheme. I also got married and had to ask GKN for permission to continue on the scheme as a married woman. They agreed, but made it clear that they still expected my commitment for twenty-five hours a day! Interestingly, I was more concerned that the twenty-five hours was unreasonable than that I could have lost my job because of getting married. I have since met women not much older than me whose employers required women staff to resign when they got married, and this was just accepted as the way things were. It is so important that we do not forget that this sort of discrimination was normal within living memory. My increasing consciousness and anger at the unfairness of sexism came from experience, although the door was opened by a friend who told me about a women's support group that had been established at York, and how angry they had become at how they were being treated both at work and at home.

When I was a trainee at GKN we were flown around the country to visit different plants. At one plant in Wales I asked the manager what he thought of the idea of women working in industry, meaning me as a potential plant manager. He said 'Well, they're very dextrous with their hands. I'd rather employ them than men.' I guess that this was one of the first times that I began to see the implication of the accepted mind set, that I shared, about the role of women in society. After a year with GKN I decided that I was never going to be motivated by the generation of profit for shareholders and looked for alternative employment. My husband and I moved to Brighton, and I went to buy a refrigerator. I was not allowed to sign the hire purchase order, even though I earned considerably more than my husband. I had to take it home for him to sign. A little bit more consciousness-raising!

I had been appointed economist to Brighton County Borough Council, based in the Treasurer's Department. The Council was a unitary authority with responsibility for housing, social services, education, public health, water, highways, planning, leisure, tourism, environmental health, trading standards, and many more services. I loved it. This was in the early 1970s when society still believed in the value of public services run by locally elected and accountable authorities, and people felt very proud to work for the local council. The last fifteen years have correctly made local authorities more efficient, but it seems to me to be a terrible shame that they were vilified at the same time as being required to be more efficient. Something has been lost — pride in public service, respect for civic leaders, a coherence of structure that provided a kind of civic security for an urban area like Brighton.

Brighton Council offered me the opportunity to train as a public finance accountant. I had never thought of this as a career option. I had the normal stereotypical views about accountants being boring grey-suited men who like rules and regulations so that they can say 'no'. Sadly, these 'Abominable No Men' still exist in many private and public sector organizations. At Brighton I had been privileged to see the contribution that creative financial managers could make to the achievement of social outcomes, and the pleasure and satisfaction that flowed from this. So I jumped at the chance of becoming one of them. I remain committed to the high quality financial management education and the culture of public service for which my professional body, the Chartered Institute of Public Finance and Accountancy (CIPFA), stands. While working at the Council, I think I gained most satisfaction working on housing and social services issues. It was great to be part of the team that masterminded the regeneration of the Whitehawk council estate to provide decent homes for rent. I could actually walk round the estate and know that I had played a small part in it.

Although all of the senior managers at the Council were men, I actually had no sense of being discriminated against and felt very encouraged by the support of the Treasurer and his Deputy. In 1974 the incoming government rejected proposals by the Redcliffe Maud Commission for unitary local authorities and instead opted for the two-tier system which saw social services and education at county level while housing stayed at district level. This was a disaster from my perspective. I felt that my greatest commitment was to social services and because there were no suitable posts in the East Sussex County Council Treasurer's Department, I applied for and was appointed to the post of Planning Officer in the Council's Social Services Department. Luckily I was able to complete my accountancy training in this post. I spent two years investigating resource allocation in relation to services for elderly people and the impact of basing a social worker in a local medical practice. This experience was invaluable in teaching me the value of rigour in relation to research activity and the importance of basing strategy and policy on sound information, including in particular the customer's perspective. In addition, it also gave me insight into how it feels to be a customer of the finance function, a lesson that I have tried to keep in mind ever since as a provider of this function.

In 1976 I gave up work to have children, still intending to make homemaking my career. I had two daughters and feel that the time at home with them balancing priorities, coping with competing demands, meeting deadlines, handling crises and planning effectively within an ever-changing context was invaluable management training! It is sad that the benefits of this type of career break in terms of personal development and ability to handle complex management tasks is rarely recognized. In 1979 my husband and I decided to role swap. I applied for the post of Chief Accountant of Brighton Health Authority for interview experience, and got the job! I had not worked in the finance function for over five years, and never in the National Health Service, so it was a challenge. For three months I was breastfeeding my daughter at 6am and 6pm, before and after work. Shortly afterwards the Assistant Treasurer left and the Treasurer flew to the USA for a five-week holiday, leaving me in charge. We were preparing the budget and I had to work extraordinarily hard, but I learned a great deal. Colleagues in the Area Health Authority were very supportive and have remained friends ever since. It was a really good lesson in teaching me not to be afraid of the unknown or of asking for help when I need it.

During this period, when I was responsible for preparing and managing a £50 million budget, my tax return was still sent to my husband and he had to sign to say it was correct. I recently listened to Professor Christine Grant of the University of Iowa talk on gender equality in university sport in the USA. She made a very telling point when she suggested that a true test of whether a process offered gender equality was to offer men the deal offered to women and vice versa, and see who accepted! Can you imagine the furore if men's tax returns had been sent to their non-working wives? I did include a protest letter with each tax return and, as we all know, eventually it changed but it is as well to remember how recent this was, when some people protest that the pendulum has swung too far.

In 1983 I was promoted to Assistant Treasurer and later that year my next-door-neighbour suggested that I should apply for the post of Assistant Treasurer of Brighton Borough Council. I was successful despite the fact that it was a Conservative Council and I was a Labour councillor at the time. I did not regard this as a problem because all of my professional training has taught me that my duty at work is to implement the policy of the governing body of the organization and not to promote my personal political views. This is not always easy, as sometimes there can be a grey area between personal and professional views, for example in regard to housing or personnel policy. Before long I found that being a councillor was inconsistent with my senior post, as my professional responsibilities made it impossible for me to speak as powerfully as I wished as a councillor on matters relating to East Sussex County Council. Subsequent legislation would have made it illegal, anyway.

In 1985 I attended my first senior management course. I was one woman with twenty-nine men. The chairs were set in a wide circle. I was one of the first to go in, and sat near the door. Gradually the other seats filled up except those on either side of me. I felt very exposed. Eventually one man sat next to me but the final person who walked in went to get another chair to put into the circle. Later I talked to some of the men about why this had happened. The reply was 'We didn't want people to think we fancied you.' So the only role these very intelligent senior managers could put me in was potential sexual partner. I found this depressing, but it was also interesting that when some of them found the going tough, they used me as literally a shoulder to cry on. Would they have done this if it had been all men? It felt natural for me to offer the shoulder but should I have done, or was I just reinforcing the stereotype?

In 1986 after Labour gained control of Brighton Council for the first time in 150 years the Council wished to implement an equal opportunities policy, and its Chief Officers were to go away for the weekend to explore the issues. Unfortunately there was only one woman Chief Officer so a colleague and I who were Deputy Chief Officers were also asked to attend. Two incidents I will never forget. In one exercise we were asked to split into gender groups and to write on flip charts 'The disadvantages of stereotyping women'. The women's group wrote fast and furiously for the fifteen minutes allowed, filling seven sheets. The men came in with a blank sheet of paper, saying that they could not think of any disadvantages. I was so angry I said 'Have you no daughters, wives or sisters?' Of course they had, but sadly maybe these men's aspirations for them were not that they should be rounded human beings, achieving their full potential, whose ability to do so might be limited by stereotyping. My second recollection of the weekend was the final session, sitting in a big circle, when the Chief Executive solemnly gave each of the Chief Officers a big brown envelope, leaving out me and the other woman deputy. I asked 'What is in the envelope?' The Chief Executive replied very seriously 'It's the draft equal opportunities policy, and I'm afraid it's confidential'! So we were good enough to give up our weekend so that they could have women there, but not good enough to have the confidential policy. I now wonder why I was not more angry.

In general my recollections of the six years spent at Brighton Council are happy ones. I was offered all sorts of opportunities for personal development, for example a senior management development programme at Ashridge Management College. I received a great deal of support from the Treasurer, who was absolutely adamant that there would be no unfair discrimination in his Department. When I was appointed I was the one woman in a department management team of eleven. By the time I left there were six women in the team. Both the Treasurer and I were influential in creating an environment in which women could flourish and were not seen as a risk or indeed in any way 'different' but simply as equal professional colleagues. When I began to think about moving on I applied for the post of Treasurer to a neighbouring authority. At the interview I was asked questions like 'What does your husband think of you applying for such an important job? and 'Do you realize that this is more than a 9-to-5 post?' Having been at Brighton, where such behaviour would have been impossible, I had not thought through how I would react so I was thrown by it and have no doubt that my performance in the interview was affected by it. Afterwards the Chief Personnel Officer rang me and asked me not to make a complaint about them to the Equal Opportunities Commission. I did not. It was around the time of the Alison Halford case (which is also mentioned in the Introduction to this book), and I felt that I had more to lose than they did. Getting a reputation for being a troublemaker, as well as being a woman in public sector accountancy, could be regarded as the kiss of death! However, a part of me still feels that I should have done something, that I let myself and other women down by not doing so. I am full of admiration for those who have the guts to make a stand even if it is at considerable personal cost.

It was a shock when I was appointed Director of Finance to the newly independent Brighton Polytechnic (now the University of Brighton) Higher Education Charitable Corporation in 1989, to find that no-one in the Finance Department could remember anyone in the Department ever going on a training course. There were no staff undertaking professional or accountancy technician training. The budget for staff development was £1000 and this had always been spent by the Head of Department. It was as if, in this seat of learning which had a large Business School, no-one thought administrative staff could develop as a result of educational opportunities. Before the first awards ceremony I was even asked by the Registrar whether I had any qualifications. There was no equal opportunities policy or related recruitment and promotion policy in 1989. There is one now. Women represent 50 per cent of the students and staff but under 20 per cent of senior management. Three out of the six faculties have no women in their management teams. Three of the nine central departments are led by women. There are very few black or ethnic minority staff or students, with none in senior management. The University's recruitment policies are rigorous, equal opportunities training has been provided for all managers, and audits of academic course content and departmental procedures have been undertaken. Action has been taken if we have not measured up to our policy. However, we have not taken positive steps to understand why more progress is not being made, nor to give women and minority groups opportunities to develop the skills necessary to achieve promotion. There does appear to be some ambivalence in that while the Chair of the Academic Board and its committees have voted to have a Chair, the Board of Governors and its committees have Chairmen — and they are all men, whether Chairs or Chairmen!

In 1989 my husband and I separated, which has had a profound effect on my life and that of my daughters. I dreaded waking up on a Monday morning to find a daughter obviously too ill to go to school when I had a meeting at 9am. Trying to find someone to look after her was very stressful, as were the feelings of guilt that I was putting the job first, as in my experience women usually do. Once I was on my own with my daughters I often felt torn between my responsibility to my job and to them, as for example when the Board of Governors insisted on having its meetings at 8am, which cut right across my arrangements for getting them to school, and meant either that they stayed at a friend's overnight or I had to get them up at 6am to be dropped off at 7am. The achievement of equality does not in my view mean women having to adapt their lives to function effectively in a world designed by men. Ideally it should mean everyone adapting, in order to create a way of living that enables all parents to play a full part in their children's upbringing as well as to undertake satisfying paid work if they wish. We are a long way from this Utopia and need significant investment in child care, including after school and holiday services, and acceptance throughout society of a new and respected role for fathers before we can achieve it.

One of the best aspects of working at the University of Brighton for me has been that I have been offered opportunities to take on further responsibilities, either on a project or a permanent basis. This has meant me taking over responsibility for all new accommodation developments, for residences management for three years, for developing a system of administrative department review, and for sports development in the university and recently for the university's business development activity including its Alumni Association. Naturally I have to be careful that my main role as Director of Finance remains my priority, but in a local authority the Director of Finance would be most unlikely to be able to spread their wings in this way, and I am very grateful for these opportunities.

If I look back over my career I feel that all of the incidents I have described are trivial in themselves, but lay one on top of the other, add hundreds more over several years, and you need a lot of positive reinforcement if you are to continue believing in yourself. Luckily I have had many colleagues who have given me encouragement, but I can readily imagine women who decide that the prize is not worth the effort, and turn their energy and imagination into other areas of their lives. When I look at my younger colleagues in accountancy I do think that things have improved. There are now numbers of young women at meetings and on courses, so that they do not need to feel different. I also see opportunities being seized: young women achieving equality in examination results (at the 1996 CIPFA conference all the prizewinners were women); women becoming chief executives in the National Health Service as a result of positive action by Virginia Bottomley (former Secretary of State for Health) and the NHS Women's Unit; women pilots on package holiday planes; women signing their own forms; six women Vice-Chancellors; women taking out loans and doing their own tax returns! But the battle for equality is not won and there are vested interests who would try to put the clock back, and there is certainly great anger at positive action such as all-women shortlists in the Labour Party's procedures for selecting candidates for Parliament and yet look at the difference that has made to Parliament.

A recent tale from close to home illustrates the need for vigilance. I was concerned that my daughter was not doing very well at physics and that this could pull down her overall science mark in the General Certificate of Secondary Examination. Her male teacher said 'Well, of course girls don't like physics. What can we do?' My amazement was not just that he felt like that, but that he felt safe to say it quite openly.

While my career has been fascinating, satisfying and full of interest, I have felt disadvantaged and humiliated and angry and defeated at times. With hindsight I feel that at the heart of many of these incidents is the inability of some men to see women in other than traditional roles and the insecurity that they feel in the face of a strong assertive woman presenting as an equal. On the other hand, I have worked with men who have treated me as just a colleague — what a delight!

In summary, I would say that my gender may have inhibited my career progress. Although some of this has been about my continuing need to defeat my original conditioning, much of it has been the extra burden of fighting a system that saw me as a risk or a threat. On the other hand, once I have been appointed my gender has often been an asset because people remember me, and I do find it easy to be open and talk and listen to a wide range of colleagues with no regard to my or their status. So within a relatively short period of time I am well known in any organization in which I work, and in the network of organizations to which it needs to relate. Obviously the denial of opportunity is not just an issue of gender. Throughout my career I have come across people whose progress has been limited because other people have taken their self-confidence by bullying or generally undermining them. These people have become apathetic, almost dead souls at work, because they feel written off by the organization. This seems to me to be merely another aspect of societal and organizational culture that denies opportunity to some of its members, the sadness of which is not only that individuals achieve less than they might, but that we all lose the contribution that they could make in terms of energy, creativity, intellect and a, different, perspective.

# 17 Women's Careers in Education: Theoretical and Practical Considerations of How the Glass Ceiling Might be Cracked

*Date of Birth: 19 April 1949*
*Died: 9 September 1997*
**Dr Myra McCulloch**
Pro-Vice-Chancellor, University of Reading

This chapter represents an attempt, first presented at a conference of *Through the Glass Ceiling*, to make sense of what relationships might be found between theorizing about women's careers in education and participating in one. The evidence for the underrepresentation of women in the higher levels of educational management, both in schools and universities, is discussed, forms of opposition to this inequality are considered, and the likelihood of change reflected upon. This theoretical framework is used as background to discussion of my own experience working in education. Most of the studies to which I refer are from the discipline of sociology; as an undergraduate I was introduced to the recognition that the world is a social world and therefore is both made by and making us. In other words, our world doesn't have to be like this; we can change things; a powerful and empowering concept on which to hang a career. However, as Miriam David argues (in Acker, 1994) '. . . all these solutions and strategies require enormous reserves of strength and energy to keep up the political fight, which may detract from the more serious pursuit of knowledge' (p. 6).

Another important insight was that life is not neat; not just my life, but social life itself. Planning is a very problematical activity and the notion of a rational career plan may seem sensible, but one is right to suspect that it limits the imagination. The best image I can create for this is that of colouring in maps at school. I always sat next to someone who had felt tipped pens in all the colours of the universe and she never went over the lines. I was deeply envious of this material and aesthetic wealth, until realizing one day that style and substance can be different and that of the two, substance is more important. It is, therefore, important to recognize the substantive contribution to equality of opportunities to be found from the most unlikely sources. For example, although universities are male-dominated political institutions, they are also subject, through Charter, Statutes and Ordinances, to a bureaucratic core of rules guarded by a strictly hierarchical administrative system. In Weber's (1947) bureaucratic system individuals are free and subject to authority only with respect to their impersonal official obligations within a clear hierarchical framework; their obligations in a defined sphere of competence are explicit and the relationship between employer and employee is a freely entered contractual one. This leads to a 'social levelling' (p. 340); everyone is subject to formal equality of treatment. Thus bureaucracy provides protection from 'invidious discriminations on such grounds as birth, individual favouritisms, ethnic or class status' (Parsons, in his introduction to this volume of Weber's work). In contrast with fear of the lack of human agency, Parsons' fears were of the effects of human agency in subverting the system. I would wish to argue that such advantages of bureaucratic organization have been insufficiently weighted in the debate about equal opportunities. The 'value neutrality' of bureaucracy has been wrongly interpreted as an absence of values; a value laden ethos can be better protected through bureaucratic administrative structures than otherwise. This interpretation of equality promotes a high degree of social mobility, the recognition of individual potential and respect for personal wishes rather than traditional obligations.

I shall try to make my points with reference to my own career by referring to some of the sociological debates on the concept and nature of career and by putting forward what might be called the garbage can thesis of career planning; problems and solutions do not exist in direct relation to one another. Every career decision I have made has turned out to be more or less wrong, but it's turned out right(ish). The roles of chance or contingency are central to this thesis (not luck, I hasten to add, which is one of the traditional ways in which women explain success, but not opportunity).

Giddens (1971) in describing the quality of the writings of Marx, Durkheim and Weber, wrote 'I have attempted to convey the partial and incomplete character which each stressed as qualifying the perspectives which he established and the conclusions which he reached' (*Preface*, p. xvi). He also described Weber's methodology as 'the trained relentlessness in viewing the realities of life, and the ability to face such realities and to measure up to them inwardly' (ibid., p. 242). This is probably the best advice one could give to any academic, but particularly to women academics; the world won't change simply because we want it to, or even because we may be right. Our control of life is tentative and the relentless acceptance of what *is* must be necessary for the promotion of what might be. Furthermore we must object to the simplistic male/female dichotomy. Social class, age, ethnicity, religion will all have an impact as will different kinds of masculinity and femininity. The problem remains in the asymmetry in the different qualities ascribed to the masculine and the feminine (Billing, 1994). Giddens (1982) argues that sociology '. . . necessarily has a subversive quality' (p. 2). '. . . the study of sociology, appropriately understood, unavoidably demonstrates how fundamental are the social questions that have to be faced . . .' (ibid., p. 3). 'We cannot approach society, or "social facts" as we do objects or events in the natural world, because societies only exist in so far as they are created and recreated in our own actions as human beings' (ibid., p. 13). This necessitates a '. . . double involvement of individuals and institutions: we create society at the same time as we are created by it' (ibid., p. 14). Sociology is, therefore, seen as critique and a form of study which involves the historical and anthropological understanding and critical sensitivity of what C. Wright Mills called 'the sociological imagination' (Wright Mills, 1959). For the achievement of equal opportunities in higher education this seems to me to be a formidable basis.

To illustrate this point I shall refer to a number of studies on the concept of 'career', all of which attempt to locate the nature of the theoretical perspective they use. I talk of 'career' in quotation marks to indicate that the very use of that term implies a particular theoretical framework, for example the positivist writings referred to by Evetts (1992). But it serves as a useful generic term to cover the writings I discuss. Different frames of reference (which propose different issues for discussion) require explicit articulation to be properly understood and criticized. Evetts makes this point clear. She describes the ways in which essentially positivist writings on careers in the 1950s and 1960s reified the concept and gave it an apparent structural reality. Individuals therefore see themselves as operating in '. . . a structure that has an objective existence, not as constituting that structure by their actions and/or inactivity. In that way, career structures are reproduced in the minds, actions and interpretations of career builders themselves' (ibid., p. 1). Structures take on the 'phantom objectivity' she quotes from Lukacs (ibid., p. 2) and careers become 'a structure of opportunities and a manifestation of objectively assessed achievements, rather than a collection of actions by certain people some of whom have connections, networks and sponsors, then they bolster the power, authority and legitimacy of those who have used, benefited from and achieved promotion in a career' (ibid., p. 2). Of perhaps of even more importance is the location of knowledge, both as a feature of power and as a tactical stratagem. In the university, the particular distribution of knowledge which may, or may not, in differing circumstances be seen to constitute power is one of the characteristics of the organization. Expertise may be located in the most junior member of a department, whose authority is legitimated by the simple test of its being the best authority.

Thus, different perspectives in theory define the same concept in distinctive and competing ways which imply varying and conflicting implications. Evetts identifies the organizational level of analysis which tends towards reification and preservation of the status quo; individual levels of analysis which suggest subjective careers, and career strategies implying a relativistic notion of the term career structure; a form of explanation she finds most compelling which links individual action with the system. Following Giddens (1981), she adopts the notion of structuration where 'action and structure stand in a relation of logical entailment: the concept of action presumes that of structure and vice versa' (p. 171). In other words there are interrelationships between career actions and career structures; what we do can actually affect the structure and linkages between positions (see also Kanter, 1977). Evetts (1992) argues that this suggests moving from the concept of a normative order with structure and system determination, to a cognitive order based on how things are understood (p. 13). Thus, it is argued, the notion of structuration permits recognition of the duality of structure where society, through its rules and resources which 'structure' actions is reproduced through those actions. The intended and unintended consequences of these actions are that career patterns emerge but that they are changeable. Evetts, following Giddens (1984), writes 'By analysing processes of change we can have such interrelations between structure and action constantly in mind. Thereby we might be able to prevent both the reification of structure and the "oversocialized concept of man" (Wrong, 1961) as well as avoiding the denial of the existence of reality — defining structures and systems of power' (cited in Evetts, 1992, p. 18). The study of an issue is located firmly in the nature of the theory to be used to understand it.

Acker (1989) makes a similar point. Understanding teachers' careers involves recognition of a power structure within which individuals are striving to achieve change and development in tune with their own values. 'Some time ago Peter Berger (1966) observed that a humanistic sociology might still depict individuals as puppets controlled by social forces, but that they would retain the capacity to look up and see who pulls the strings' (Acker, 1989, p. 19). However, Fullan's conviction that '. . . focusing on the individual is not a substitute for system change, it is the most effective strategy for accomplishing it' (1993, p. 125) suggests that even the isolated woman academic can make a difference once the possibility of change is accepted. Evetts (1989) identifies, between the interactionist concepts of subjective careers and the macro contexts within which teachers work, the concept of the internal labour market for primary teachers. The macro context (of recession or expansion, for example) determines which of the subjective characteristics (individual striving, continuous service, post-entry qualifications, and so on) are given priority in awarding promotion. Both Acker and Evetts are concerned to see how their understandings of career relate to the experience of women in education. Grant (1989) makes this explicit. When studying careers in teaching, despite variations in methodology applied to studies and methodological inadequacies in some cases, three major findings consistently emerge: women are consistently underrepresented in management levels in all schools in which men form a significant group; men are more active in seeking promotion; and women perceive themselves to be disadvantaged because of their gender. Indeed, 'as competition from men for scarce promotional awards strengthens, women fare increasingly badly' (p. 36). Grant's conclusions suggest that in order to achieve more equal opportunities, an alternative way of approaching the question needs to be adopted. Career patterns need to be legitimated not simply *reified* on the basis of a male dominated model. After all, '. . . most people with the power to promote are men' (ibid., p. 47).

Riseborough (1985) reminds us that success in school is not straightforwardly a competition between teachers, male and female; 'the social construction of "good" and "bad" teachers in schools and the social distribution of their competencies is related to the ideological and cultural hegemony exercised by their superiors and *counter hegemony exercised by their inferiors*' (p. 262). The context of the teacher's career is the pupils' world and, indeed, the school organization itself where, for example, qualifications and status can arbitrarily be undermined through mergers between schools or the appointment of a new headteacher (Ball and Goodson, 1985, p. 19). It is certainly clear that the views of students may be sought and used in the context of the university's appraisal system and, indeed, that student opinion is sought and taken very seriously in the teaching quality assessment process.

Bennet (1985) reminds us that teachers are not a homogeneous occupational group and that, for example, art teachers have a very distinctive response to the notion of career. The status of art in schools, the nature of art teacher training and the art teachers' own subjective career orientations and attitudes mean that their challenge to the system (individual versus structure) is not to compete. Bennet quotes a teacher in her research sample: 'I have a delightful sense of freedom in *not* being career oriented, and *not* having to resort to strategies' (p. 130). Of course, you will never win the lottery if you don't buy a ticket. Ozga (1988) reinforces this point by showing how individual choices deny certain opportunities. She quotes a woman National Union of Teachers representative for her school as saying 'In this authority you have to make a straightforward choice between pursuing a career and working for the union. If you choose to work for the union, you know you'll never be a headteacher. It's as simple as that' (p. 141). Lawn (1988) continues this theme of power relations within systems and structures, noting 'the influence of the employer in defining "the good teacher" not just by adding or subtracting "technical" skills but by defining personal qualities in such a way that they become necessary jobs skills, blurring the boundary between "technical" and "non-technical" skills' (p. 175). Nevertheless, he too notes the effectiveness of individual and collaborative action in making or resisting change. 'The women primary teachers ... found a number of ways to contest the patriarchal management of their schools and in so doing ... have tried to protect their definition of "the good teacher" and so of their skills' (ibid.). The management of change literature certainly supports the view that what is intended from the top can rarely be found to be fully implemented at the bottom.

Where do studies lead us in terms of applying theory and understanding equal opportunities? Kanter (1977) suggests that 'equality for women cannot be solved without structures that potentially benefit all organization members more broadly' (p. 606). This involves structural changes within which individuals can act. The male-dominated criteria for promotion need to be replaced not simply by affirmative action but by enabling strategies such as developing new jobs; developing eligibility for promotion; encouraging job rotation; decentralizing to create more leadership opportunities and, perhaps most importantly rewarding managers for subordinate mobility (ibid., p. 615). 'To empower those women and others who currently operate at a disadvantage requires attention to both sides of power' (ibid., p. 616). However, whatever success may be gained at organization level, there are still the constraints imposed by the socioeconomic structure as a whole. The current recession, for example, does not help innovative, employee-centred projects to be established. Bartol (1978) made the same point. If the personal characteristics, skills, knowledge and qualifications of men and women are considered to be equivalent, and perceived to be so by subordinates and superiors, why are women excluded from some parts of the organization rather than others and from some levels of leadership altogether? She identifies a process of organizational filtering that occurs at all stages of the system: pre-entry; at entry; at basic training; initiation; development and promotion. Women can and do respond differently at these various stages in order to proceed but Bartol and Kanter suggest that some responses (mother, seductress, pet) 'tend to preclude outstanding performance' (ibid., p. 810), Bartol reminds us that women are not the only groups to be filtered out of success in this way, but their visible and systematic failure makes it obvious.

Thus is emphasized again the impact on organization of structural patterns in society. Acker (1983) suggests that when looking at teachers' careers we need to look for correspondence between the sexual division of labour in teaching and in the family and the economy:

> ... the sexual division of labour among teachers contributes to the reproduction of patriarchal and/or capitalist social order, especially by providing models to students of male-female power relations and sex differentiated subject specialities and responsibilities that reinforce the connection of 'femininity' with caring, serving, conforming, mothering. (ibid., p.134)

On the other hand, 'The academy, like any other major organisation, is riven with paradox and contradiction as both a source of oppression and location for exploring liberation and empowerment' (Morley, 1994, p. 202). So, what does this mean in relation to my own career and my thesis that promotion is not just affected by the asymmetrical relationships within society but also by the contingency effect of seeking to make a difference and achieving an unpredictable and different result altogether?

If I may summarize briefly, I started as a teacher in an inner London secondary modern school which was called a comprehensive. I hadn't got a job, didn't know what I wanted to do, and the school was down the road wanting someone to teach Advanced Level sociology. I loved every minute. It was the early 1970s. If you had an idea, the Inner London Education Authority could fund it, and here were the children I had been reading about; bright, street-wise children, failed by the system and compounding that failure by their own rejection of what was on offer. Here was the change to see whether I could make a difference. I don't know whether I did. I certainly learned enough not to patronize school failures. One of my fellow probationers was Kate Meyers of Genderwatch fame and we still work together on trying to make a difference. They certainly made a difference to me.

I resigned from school to accompany my husband to the Sudan, where I hoped to work in teacher education in the College in Khartoum, a decision which combined gender and academic factors. A brief outbreak of gunfire at the airport which happened to catch the relevant finance minister and cancelled my husband's project left me unemployed and determined never to take a gender-related career decision again. A brief spell filling in for a maternity leave appointment at the then City of London Polytechnic was followed by a two-year stint at the CNAA (Council for National Academic Awards) looking into the relationship between theory and practice in Bachelor of Education degrees. The prime candidate turned out to have got another job the day before the interviews. This time, at the centre of what was then the bright light of curriculum development in teacher education, provided me with friends for life, skills and knowledge for a solid career move, and a love of the peer review system which I still hold today. CNAA was shabbily treated in my view and the rhetoric on quality which we hear today insufficiently recognizes the contribution made by the processes and policies CNAA promoted. From CNAA I moved (from two one-year fixed term contracts) to a permanent post as a Senior Lecturer in Sociology at Bath College of Higher Education, back to my first love of sociology, but drafted, before long, to the redesign of the BEd degree, which was moving from University to CNAA validation. The work at CNAA had fitted me for the one thing I didn't really want to do: the management of a degree programme, and from there to management of a Faculty of Education. I considered this experience carefully. I had always wanted to be a sociologist but it appeared that the thing I was good at was management. If a decision was made on rational grounds, it had to be to go for management jobs. Bulmershe College of Higher Education: a star in the teacher education firmament. I applied for the Principal's job. No chance; not necessarily because I was a woman, but I was too young. (When does too young become too old?) OK. I'll go for the Deputy's job. I started on 1 February 1987. In April the White Paper was published which changed the face of higher education permanently. It seemed to us then that the future of the small colleges was limited; large institutions which could accommodate all the changes required by incorporation would be needed. Within two months my rational decision had been totally undermined. What would happen if a merger with the University of Reading took place, working within a University which had little value for all the things by then I was good at, and held in highest esteem all the things I'd stopped doing? Head of Department, starting to write and research and present and publish all in the wrong career order. Then Dean of a Faculty born of two traditions and essentially trying to transform its profile from 'teaching only' to 'teaching and research'. And we did it, by the way, getting a four for virtually the whole Faculty in the 1992 research assessment exercise.

But here the butterfly effect so wonderfully described by Gleick in his book *Chaos* came into effect. Academic Audit came to town, and the report showed that all those bureaucratic processes the former College had thought important enough to work into its systems actually did have a legitimacy and a purpose in the bigger world of the traditional university. So what happens? The University decides it needs a senior position dedicated to improving teaching quality throughout the University. The most effective (and the cheapest) way of showing it is serious is to create a new post of second Pro-Vice-Chancellor with responsibility for teaching: me.

So, all the things I'm good at but don't want to be; all the things that aren't supposed to be valued in universities but increasingly are; all the wrong decisions that turned out to be right and all the right decisions that turned out to be wrong combine to support my thesis. Career is an unhelpful concept. It implies a linear progression. It implies rationality. What is needed is commitment to chaos, to contingency, to accommodation, flexibility and resilience. The best compliment I ever had was from a pupil who had been caught by ROSLA (Raising of the School Leaving Age) and had to stay until he was 16. I got him into the class for the Certificate in Secondary Education Social Studies because he wasn't to be trusted in woodwork. 'Miss, why do you keep on trying?' But he did pass his CSE, so you *can* beat the system but only if you keep on trying and if you never put your trust in rationality.

## References

ACKER, S. (1983) 'Women and teaching: A semi-detached sociology of a semi-profession', in WALKER, S. and BARTON, L. (eds) (1983) *Gender, Class and Education*, Lewes: Falmer Press.

ACKER, S. (ed.) (1989) *Teachers, Gender and Career*, Lewes: Falmer Press.

ACKER, S. (1994) *Gendered Education*, Buckingham: Open University Press.

BALL, S.J. and GOODSON, I.F. (eds) (1985) *Teachers' Lives and Careers*, Lewes: Falmer Press.

BARTOL, K.M. (1978) 'The sex structuring of organisations: A search for possible causes', *Academy of Management Review*, October, pp. 805–15.

BENNET, C. (1985) 'Paints, pots or promotion? Art teachers' attitudes towards their careers', in BALL, S.J. and GOODSON, I.F. (eds) *Teachers' Lives and Careers*, Lewes: Falmer Press, pp. 120–37.

BERGER, P. (1966) *Invitation to Sociology: A Humanistic Perspective*, Harmondsworth: Pelican.

BILLING, Y.D. (1994) 'Gender and bureaucracies: A critique of Ferguson's "The Feminist Case Against Bureaucracy"', *Gender, Work and Organization*, **1**, 4, October, pp. 179–93.

DAVID, M. (1994) 'Critical Introduction', in ACKER, S. (1994) *Gendered Education*, Buckingham: Open University Press, pp. 1–11.

DENNISON, W.F. (1985) 'Education and the economy: Changing circumstances', in McNAY, I. and OZGA, J. (eds) (1985) *Policy Making in Education: The Breakdown of Consensus*, Oxford: Pergamon Press.

EVETTS, J. (1989) 'The internal labour market for primary teachers', in ACKER, S. (ed.) (1989) *Teachers, Gender and Career*, Lewes: Falmer Press, pp. 187–202.

EVETTS, J. (1992) 'Dimensions of career: Avoiding reification in the analysis of change', *Sociology*, **26**, 1, February, pp. 1–21.

FREEDMAN, S. (1987) 'Burntout or beached: Weeding women out of woman's true profession', in WALKER, S. and BARTON, L. (eds) (1987) *Changing Policies, Changing Teachers: New Directions for Schooling?*, Milton Keynes: Open University Press.

FULLAN, M.G. (1993) *Change Forces: Probing the Depths of Educational Change*, London: Falmer Press.

GIDDENS, A. (1971) *Capitalism and Modern Social Theory*, London: Cambridge University Press.

GIDDENS, A. (1981) 'Agency, institution and time-space analysis', in KNORR-CETINA, K. and CICOUREL, A.V. (eds) (1981) *Advances in Social Theory and Methodology*, Boston, MA: Routledge and Kegan Paul.

GIDDENS, A. (1982) *Sociology: A Brief But Critical Introduction*, London: Macmillan.

GIDDENS, A. (1984) *The Constitution of Society*, Cambridge: Polity Press.

GLEICK, J. (1987) *Chaos*, London: Cardinal.

GRANT, R. (1989) 'Women teachers' career pathways: towards an alternative model of '"career"', in ACKER, S. (ed.) (1989) *Teachers, Gender and Career*, Lewes: Falmer Press, pp. 35–50.

GRANT, J. and TANCRED, P. (1992) 'A feminist perspective on state bureaucracy', in MILLS, A.J. and TANCRED, P. (eds) *Gendering Organizational Analysis*, London: Sage Publications, pp. 112–28.

KANTER, R.M. (1977) *Men and Women of the Corporation*, New York: Basic Books.

KNORR-CETINA, K. and CICOUREL, A.V. (eds) (1981) *Advances in Social Theory and Methodology*, Boston, MA: Routledge and Kegan Paul.

LAWN, M. (1988) 'Skill in schoolwork: Work relations in the primary school', in OZGA, J. (ed.) (1988) *Schoolwork: Approaches to the Labour Process of Teaching*, Milton Keynes: Open University Press.

McNAY, I. and OZGA, J. (eds) (1985) *Policy Making in Education: The Breakdown of Consensus*, Oxford: Pergamon Press.

MORLEY, L. (1994) 'Glass ceiling or iron cage: Women in UK academia', *Gender, Work and Organisation*, **1**, 4, October, pp. 194–204.

NIAS, J. (1985) 'Reference groups in primary teaching: talking, listening and identity', in BALL, S.J. and GOODSON, I.F. (eds) (1985) *Teachers' Lives and Career*, Lewes: Falmer Press, pp. 105–19.

OZGA, J. (ed.) (1988) *Schoolwork: Approaches to the Labour Process of Teaching*, Milton Keynes: Open University Press.

RISEBOROUGH, G. (1985) 'Pupils, teachers' careers and schooling: An empirical study', in BALL, S.J. and GOODSON, I.F. (eds) (1985) *Teachers' Lives and Career*, Lewes: Falmer Press, pp. 202–65.

SILVERMAN, D. (1970) *The Theory of Organisations*, London: Heinemann.

WALKER, S. and BARTON, L. (eds) (1983) *Gender, Class and Education*, New York: Falmer Press

WALKER, S. and BARTON, L. (eds) (1987) *Changing Policies, Changing Teachers: New Directions for Schooling?*, Milton Keynes: Open University Press.

WEBER, M. (1947) *The Theory of Social and Economic Organisation*, New York: Free Press (translated by A.M. HENDERSON and TALCOTT PARSONS, edited with an introduction by Talcott Parsons).

WRIGHT MILLS, C. (1959) *The Sociological Imagination*, Harmondsworth: Penguin.

WRONG, G. (1961) 'The oversocialized conception of man in modern sociology', *American Sociological Review*, **26**, 2, pp. 183–93.

# Postscript

# 18  Postscript

*Date of Birth: 9 August 1945*
**Professor Miriam David**
Dean of Research, The London Institute; formerly, Director,
Social Sciences Research Centre, South Bank University

*Date of Birth: 22 October 1948*
**Professor Diana Woodward**
Dean of Graduate School, Chelthenham and Gloucester College of
Higher Education

## The Themes of the Book: Opportunities and Obstacles

The book has presented sixteen autobiographical accounts of women's careers in
higher education. What has been fascinating and intriguing are both the similarities
and differences in their lives. In this final section we want to consider some of these
issues, to argue that although women's lives in academia may each be seen as a
unique blend of the personal and professional, from childhood, family and education matters through to subject, institutional and organizational questions, there are
some critical opportunities and obstacles or constraints which warrant particular
attention. Our aim is to draw out these threads and themes from the essays, by
focusing first on childhood, education and family issues and second, professional
and organizational matters, indicating how they may both provide opportunities and
present obstacles to personal and professional development.

## Higher Education as a 'Negative Dowry' for Women?

Serendipity was a major theme in all the accounts. It is crucial to note that none
of the women saw their lives as having been planned or as a direct consequence

of their experiences as children. Indeed, several women of both 'generations' referred to their careers in academia as having developed 'accidentally' or by chance, whether it was a matter of the position in higher education in which they now found themselves, or how totally unplanned their career had been. Although the women came from a range of social class and family backgrounds, all had the benefits of educational opportunities in relatively elite secondary schools. Most of the British women had attended selective and single sex secondary schools and, for the older generation, fee-paying secondary education whether day or boarding schools (Dorothy Wedderburn, Meg Stacey, Hilary Rose, Dulcie Groves and Angela Crum Ewing). Even the British women who saw themselves as from relatively working class family backgrounds had attended selective grammar schools (Mavis Ainsworth, Eileen Green, Elaine Thomas and Dianne Willcocks), as had Myra McCulloch and Maggie Deacon. The four women from abroad also told of their unusual educational experiences, with Gertrude Pfister's remarkable account of herself as a lone girl attending a boys' single sex high school and its formative influence. The two American women — Karen Doyle Walton and Dorothy Severin — both had remarkable educational histories in elite women's education, as did Chryssi Inglessi in Greece and Berit Ås in Norway.

Despite these modern and progressive educational backgrounds, all the women told of how they had been brought up with relatively traditional notions of family life, so that most of them had assumed that the accepted paths of marriage and motherhood would follow on smoothly from childhood and young womanhood. This traditional notion was, in any event, a structural element within the British education system through streaming and curricular options until the late 1960s, and clearly influenced at least the 'older' generation, where only the daughters of middle class families effectively had opportunities for higher education and, even for them, family views of the impact of higher education on their marriage prospects might still hold sway. The Committee on Higher Education which met between 1961 and 1963, under the chairmanship of Lord Robbins, considered the question of a graduate tax or student loans:

> In particular, where women are concerned, the effect might well be either that British parents would be strengthened in their age-long disinclination to consider their daughters to be as deserving of higher education as their sons, or that the eligibility for marriage of the more educated would be diminished by the addition to their charms of what would be in effect a negative dowry. (Robbins Report, 1964, para 645)

Indeed, for most of the women, marriage and bearing children constituted a significant part of their accounts. Moreover the vast majority of these women — fifteen out of sixteen — had married (or cohabited) at some point in their lives. Many of them, however, had also divorced and/or were no longer living with their initial partner and/or husband (two as a result of very early widowhood); but some had remarried. Two-thirds of the women (eleven) had also borne and brought up children, and indeed having children often preceded developing an academic career. All of the women of the older generation who had children (Berit Ås, Meg Stacey, Hilary Rose, Angela Crum Ewing and Mavis Ainsworth) reflected the fact that their raising of children preceded their major career developments, whereas the picture was more mixed for the younger generation (Karen Doyle Walton, Chryssi Inglessi, Dorothy Severin, Eileen Green, Dianne Willcocks and Maggie Deacon). Interestingly, it was the women of the older generation, and perhaps the rather more upper middle class ones, who had tended to have the larger families — Berit Ås, Meg Stacey and Angela Crum-Ewing have had thirteen children between them — whereas the median number for the others is two children. Several of the women described how they married and had children before embarking upon a career, including rather dramatic accounts of what Janet Finch has called 'being married to the job' and travelling to follow a husband's career. The most moving account of this can be found in Chryssi Inglessi's very traditional patriarchal middle class Greek family, but there are echoes of this across the social classes for several of the British women, in particular Hilary Rose, Eileen Green and Dianne Willcocks. They also all married before going to university; but the former two — Hilary Rose and Eileen Green — had pursued a traditional women's occupational career in teacher training after school and Dianne Willcocks had become involved in further education and training. Patterns of family care also took their toll, with Hilary Rose's moving account of her very early widowhood which left her with a small child to care for. Dorothy Severin also lost her husband whilst in her early twenties. Hilary Rose, like Chryssi Inglessi, Eileen Green and Dianne Willcocks, then studied for a degree as a mature student, with only Eileen Green *not* following the now typical path of being a *mature mother student*. Eileen Green deferred motherhood until she became an established academic and, in this respect, here appears relatively unusual.

Meg Stacey, Angela Crum Ewing, Berit Ås, Mavis Ainsworth and Maggie Deacon all graduated before marriage, but then pursued motherhood as a prelude to embarking on a career in academia, with the women from the 'older' generation typically spending a considerable period in what might be seen as enforced full-time motherhood, largely as a result of discrimination or the lack of viable alternatives. Dulcie Groves' story of the need to care for her elderly mother is another instance of the importance of family care as a component of women's lives. In other words, nearly all the stories illustrate the fact that women, whatever their circumstances, have a period of their lives involved exclusively with family matters, mainly but not invariably with children. Indeed, it could be argued that involvement in the family is a significant trigger for professional involvements, particularly for those women who had achieved well at school and then eschewed higher education in favour of marriage and, usually also, motherhood — Chryssi Inglessi, Hilary Rose, Eileen Green and Dianne Willcocks.

It has been remarked before, for other groups of women, that education is not only an important factor in social change but also in family change; in fact some have gone so far as to argue that education can lead to family 'break up'. This may not be far from the truth for several of our women, where family bonds have been seen as confining and constricting. Higher education is seen as the challenge and the salvation. When the break comes, it can be experienced as sharp and deeply transformative. Even those women who travelled straight through the education system to graduation found themselves considering and contemplating marriage and motherhood, influenced to a great extent by parental expectations, albeit with little sense here of higher education being in effect a 'negative dowry'. This is clear particularly from Gertrude Pfister's account of life growing up in Germany, and there are parallels with her life in the stories of Dorothy Wedderburn, Meg Stacey, Angela Crum Ewing, and Mavis Ainsworth, as well as the 'younger' generation, with Karen Doyle Walton, Dorothy Severin, Elaine Thomas, Maggie Deacon, Myra McCulloch and Eileen Green.

The notion of 'travel', or the career as a journey, is common for our women and has been used as a metaphor without our prompting. Berit Ås' chapter gave fullest voice to this idea. Many have travelled in the conventional sense, with movements between and across continents, particularly for our overseas contributors — Chryssi Inglessi, Karen Doyle Walton, Gertrude Pfister and Dorothy Severin — but also as part of normal academic career development, such as by Berit Ås, Mavis Ainsworth, Dulcie Groves and Dorothy Severin. Local travel, and commuting as part of life in academia, was also a not uncommon feature of these stories, often as a consequence of marital relations, whether of harmony or disharmony; here referred to frequently by Gertrude Pfister, Eileen Green, Dianne Willcocks and Hilary Rose. Movements within and between academic institutions to accommodate differential career developments within partnerships also feature in these stories, especially those of Berit Ås, Gertrude Pfister, Chryssi Inglessi, Karen Doyle Walton, Dorothy Wedderburn, Meg Stacey, Hilary Rose, and Eileen Green. Home was rarely the secure base it is often said to be, with many of our women experiencing life as 'refugees' seeking comfort in a haven of education away from family or other educational and organizational institutions. Indeed, many of the stories evoke Virginia Woolf's notion, in *A Room of One's Own*, that personal autonomy requires psychological and physical space for growth and development.

## Higher Education as 'A Room of One's Own'?

The vividness of these accounts may have to do with the fact that virtually all are drawn from contributors in the social sciences, arts and humanities, for whom the skilful use of words is a way of life. The orientation away from the sciences is probably an inevitable consequence of this kind of reflexive approach to such women's careers in higher education. However, the inclusion of seven women (Berit Ås, Gertrude Pfister, Karen Doyle Walton, Angela Crum Ewing, Mavis Ainsworth, Dorothy Severin, Elaine Thomas) whose careers have not been based on the social sciences may have as much to do with the constituency of the *Through The Glass Ceiling* network as from the ease of locating such women colleagues elsewhere. Four of the six 'current' accounts, all from members of TTGC (Maggie Deacon, Eileen Green, Myra McCulloch and Dianne Willcocks) are from women who originally studied some aspect of the social sciences but whose routes through their careers have had amazing contrasts. Three of them included sociology in their undergraduate courses — Maggie Deacon, Eileen Green and Dianne Willcocks — but their academic careers took very different turns, with Eileen Green and Dianne Willcocks taking up research and then moving variously into management, and in the case of Eileen Green, out again and back into research. Maggie Deacon never considered a career as an academic and only 'returned' to the academy as a senior manager in finance (an interesting turn for someone who started out as a sociologist!). Two started off their careers as school teachers — Eileen Green and Myra McCulloch — but Myra McCulloch moved into academe as a 'manager' before taking up a belated route into 'research' whilst a very senior manager, that is a Pro Vice-Chancellor (PVC). Two of these women entered higher education as mature students, as we noted above, with Dianne Willcocks having the edge on Eileen Green in terms of 'maturity' as an undergraduate. Finally, four of these six accounts present stories of very senior management, but with the two from the 'old' universities as PVCs, only formally having a transitional attachment to their post (Dorothy Severin and Myra McCulloch) whereas Maggie Deacon and Dianne Willcocks have 'permanent' posts in new universities as Director of Finance and Assistant Principal respectively.

Our other eight contributors offer equally intriguing comparisons and contrasts, despite superficial similarities in their origins in the arts and social sciences as undergraduates. Four of these are women whose careers have flourished largely within the 'old' universities in the British social sciences (Dorothy Wedderburn, Meg Stacey, Hilary Rose and Dulcie Groves) mixing sociology, policy and theory in differing ways. Dorothy Wedderburn provides us with a most fascinating account of how she, in our terms, broke through the glass ceiling very early on, through her eminent academic career, to become a Principal of a College of the University of London, originally only for women. Yet she still encountered the enduring problems of patriarchal forms of organization. Meg Stacey, who also does not recognize the concept of a glass ceiling, nevertheless also sees her life and career in hierarchical male-dominated institutions as a path strewn with obstacles. Some of these are visible but others only came to light when inadvertently challenged. Hilary Rose's unique mixture of left politics, feminism and passion has brought her up against persistent forms of patriarchy, and she, too, does not acknowledge the concept of the glass ceiling. Dulcie Groves was one of the first women to succeed at a very young age in climbing the administrative and managerial ladder in what was then a polytechnic (now a new university — South Bank), only to leave for a more 'comfortable' research career in an 'old' university. The other four provide us equally fascinating similarities and contrasts. Berit Ås may well be compared to Dorothy Wedderburn in having become the head of an institution. However, Berit Ås' University is an explicitly feminist institution, created for the explicit purpose of educating women in Norway in the present day, whereas Dorothy Wedderburn's College was the first in the University of London to be established specifically for women, in the nineteenth century, and seemingly progressive developments signalled its move to a co-educational institution in the 1980s. Karen Doyle Walton's senior managerial position in a relatively new university in the USA compares well with those of first, Dianne Willcocks in a new university in England, and second, Myra McCulloch's move from a new to an old university, into a very senior post, providing us with optimism for women's career prospects and opportunities in new developments in academia in the late twentieth century.

In the former West Germany married women's rates of participation in the labour force have been much lower than in Britain, with higher education no exception. Gertrude Pfister's account of the German university system makes British and American higher education look positively woman-friendly. The enforced migration from position to position in search of promotion or a permanent contract places an unendurable burden on personal relationships and does not augur well for women's prospects. Her story provides a salutary reminder of the continuing obstacles to women-friendly academia. Chryssi Inglessi provides a frank account of how she became a mature woman student, with a growing passion for education which led her into studying women like herself, to enable her to reflect upon her own position. It is indeed by reading this life-story of an admittedly privileged middle class Greek woman that we are able to see the persistency of patriarchy and oppressive forms of organization that both block our creativity and yet at the same time drive us on.

These varied paths through family and education to careers in higher education are becoming more usual, particularly in Britain, with many of the women undergraduates, who now make up half of all undergraduates, being mature women/ mother students. However, as these varied stories of both opportunities and obstacles illustrate, such paths will not necessarily be strewn with roses. It is only with constant vigilance and care that obstacles will be avoided and opportunities seized.

## Reference

Woolf, V. (1945) *A Room of One's Own*, Harmondsworth: Penguin Books.